THE HISTORY OF HUMAN SOCIETY

General Editor: J. H. Plumb, LITT.D.

Christ's College, Cambridge

THE ROMANS

THE HISTORY OF HUMAN SOCIETY

General Editor: J. H. Plumb

THE ROMANS

DONALD DUDLEY

Professor of Latin, University of Birmingham

Hutchinson of London

HUTCHINSON & CO *(Publishers)* LTD
178–202 Great Portland Street, London W1

London Melbourne Sydney
Auckland Johannesburg Cape Town
and agencies throughout the world

First published 1970

© Donald Dudley 1970
Introduction © J. H. Plumb 1970

*This book has been set in Garamond type, printed in Great Britain
on antique wove paper by Anchor Press, and
bound by Wm. Brendon, both of Tiptree, Essex*
ISBN 0 09 103640 2

Contents

ACKNOWLEDGEMENTS

A complete list of those whose help I have drawn upon in one way or another, while writing this book, would be a long one. To all of them I express my gratitude.

Certain names call for special mention. The text was read in manuscript by Dr J. J. Wilkes, Lecturer in Roman History at the University of Birmingham, and also by Dr J. H. Plumb, General Editor of the series. I have tried to profit from the specialist knowledge of the one and the synoptic outlook of the other: neither must be charged with any mistakes I have made. The illustrations have been planned as an integral part of the book, and here I am especially indebted to the help and advice of Dr Ernest Nash, Foteteca Unione, Rome. Other sources are acknowledged in the list of illustrations. Maps 4 and 5 are reproduced by kind permission of the author and publisher from *Marcus Aurelius,* by Anthony Birley, Eyre and Spottiswoode, 1966. Mrs Penelope Waller typed the manuscript, and Mrs Heather DuQuesnay helped with the proofs and index. Both are members of the Department of Latin at Birmingham and I am glad to record my thanks for their skill and patience.

Birmingham 1970   D.R.D.

List of illustrations and maps

(Photographs 1–6, 8, 9, 11, 14, 15, 20, 22, 23, 25, 26, 28–30, 32 are by Fototeca Unione, Rome; 7, 10, 13, 18, 27 by Alinari; 12 by Anderson; 17 by the Museum of Antiquities of the University and the Society of Antiquaries of Newcastle upon Tyne

MAPS

Introduction

BY J. H. PLUMB

I

OVER THE LAST fifty to a hundred years man's belief that the historical process proved that he was acquiring a greater mastery over nature has received a brutal buffeting. In his early youth H. G. Wells, a man of vast creative energy, of rich delight in the human spirit, and of all-pervading optimism, viewed the future with confidence; science, born of reason, was to be humanity's panacea. When, in the years of his maturity, he came to write his *Outline of History*, his vision was darker, although still sustained with hope. World War I, with its senseless and stupid slaughter of millions of men, brought the sickening realisation that man was capable of provoking human catastrophes on a global scale. The loss of human liberty, the degradations and brutalities imposed by fascism and communism during the 20s and 30s, followed in 1939 by the renewed world struggle, these events finally shattered Wells's eupeptic vision, and in sad and disillusioned old age he wrote *Mind at the End of its Tether*. His hope of mankind had almost vanished. Almost, but not quite: for Wells's lifetime witnessed what, as a young writer, he had prophesied—technical invention not only on a prodigious scale but in those realms of human activity that affected the very core of society. And this extraordinary capacity of man to probe the complexities of nature and to invent machinery capable of exploiting his knowledge remained for Wells the only basis for hope, no matter how slender that might be.

If the belief of a man of Wells's passionate and intelligent humanism could be so battered and undermined, it is not surprising that lesser men were unable to withstand the climate of despair that engulfed the Western World between the two world wars. The disillusion of these years is apparent in painting, in music, in literature—everywhere in the Western World we are brought up sharply by an expression of anguish, by the flight from social and historical reality into a frightened, self-absorbed world of personal feeling and expression. Intellectual life, outside science, has pursued much the same course as artistic life, although it has shown greater ingenuity and a tougher-minded quality. Theology, philosophy and sociology have tended to reduce themselves to technical problems of exceptional professional complexity, but of small social importance. Their practitioners have largely ceased to instruct and enliven, let alone sustain the confidence of ordinary men and women.

In this atmosphere of cultural decay and of professional retreat, history and its philosophy have suffered. As in so many intellectual disciplines its professional workers have resolutely narrowed the focus of their interests to even more specialised fields of inquiry. The majority of historians have withdrawn from general culture in order to maintain, at a high intellectual level, an academic discipline. They have left the meaning and purpose of history to trained philosophers and spent their leisure hours tearing to shreds the scholarship of anyone foolish enough to attempt to give the story of mankind a meaning and a purpose: writers as diverse as H. G. Wells and Arnold Toynbee have been butchered with consummate skill. The blunders of scholarship and the errors of interpretation have counted everything; intention nothing. Few academic historians, secure in the cultivation of their minute gardens, have felt any humility towards those who would tame the wilderness. In consequence, an atmosphere of anarchic confusion pervades the attitude of Western man to his past.

A hundred years ago, in the first flood of archaeological discovery, scholars possessed greater confidence: the history of mankind seemed to most to point to an obvious law of human progress. The past was but a stepping-stone to the future. First adumbrated by the philosophers of the late Renaissance—Bodin in France and Bacon in England—the idea of progress became an article of common faith during the Enlightenment. And progress came to mean not only the technical progress that had preoccupied Bacon but also moral progress. By the 19th century the history of man demonstrated for many an improvement in the very nature of man himself as well as in his tools and weapons. Such optimism, such faith in man's capacity for rational behaviour, was shaken both by discoveries in science and in history as well as by events. By the middle of the 20th century man's irrational drives appeared to be stronger than his intellectual capacities. Freud and Marx laid bare the hollow hypocrisy of so-called rational behaviour either in individuals or in society. Also, the rise and fall of civilisations, laid bare by the spade, seemed to point to a cyclical pattern in human destiny which made nonsense of any idea of continuous progress; and this naturally attracted the prophets of Western doom. Yet more persuasive still, and, perhaps, more destructive of confidence in human destiny, was the utter loss of all sense of human control brought about by global wars and violent revolutions. Only those men or societies who felt life was going their way, the revolutionaries and, above all, the Marxists, believed any longer in the laws of historical progress. For the rest, retrogression seemed as tenable a thesis as progress.

This disillusion in the West suited academic historians. It relieved them of their most difficult problems. If they happened to be religious they were content to leave the ultimate meaning of history to God; if they were rationalists they took refuge either in the need for more historical knowledge or in the philosophic difficulties of a subject that by its very nature was devoid of the same objective treatment that gave such authority to scientific enquiry. In the main they concentrated upon their professional work. And this was an exceptionally important and necessary task. What the common reader rarely recognises is the inadequacy of the factual material that was at the command of an historian one hundred years ago or even fifty years ago. Scarcely any archives were open to him; most repositories of records were unsorted and uncatalogued; almost every generalisation about a man or an event or an historical process was three-quarters guesswork, if not more. Laboriously, millions of facts have been brought to light, ordered and rendered coherent within their own context. Specialisation has proliferated like a cancer, making detail livid, but blurring the outlines of the story of mankind, and rendering it almost impossible for a professional historian to venture with confidence beyond his immediate province. And that can be very tiny—the Arkansas and Missouri Railway Strike of 1921; the place-names of Rutland; 17th-century Rouen; the oral history of the Barotse; the philosophy of Hincmar of Rheims. And so it becomes ever more difficult for the professional historian to reach across to ordinary intelligent men and women or make his subject a part of human culture. The historical landscape is blurred by the ceaseless activity of its millions of professional ants. Of course, attempts at synthesis have to be made. The need to train

young professional historians, or the need to impart some knowledge of history to students of other disciplines, has brought about
competent digests of lengthy periods that summarise both facts
and analysis. Occasionally such books have been written with
such skill and wisdom that they have become a part of the West's
cultural heritage. A few historians, driven by money or fame or
creative need, have tried to share their knowledge and understanding of the past with the public at large.

But the gap between professional knowledge and history for
the masses gets steadily wider: professional history becomes more
accurate, more profound, whilst public history remains tentative
and shallow.

This series is an attempt to reverse this process. Each volume
will be written by a professional historian of the highest technical
competence; but these books will not exist _in vacuo_, for the series
is designed to have a unity and a purpose. But, perhaps, first it is
best to say what it is not.

It is not a work of reference: there are no potted biographies of
the Pharaohs, the Emperors of China or the Popes; no date lists
of battles; no brief histories of painting, literature, music. Nor is
this series a Universal History. All events that were critical in the
history of mankind may not necessarily find a place. Some will;
some will not. Works of reference, more or less factually accurate,
exist in plenty and need not be repeated. It is not my intention to
add yet another large compilation to what exists. Nor is this a
'philosophic' history. It does not pretend to reveal a recurring
pattern in history that will unveil its purpose. Fundamentally
philosophy, except in the use of language, is as irrelevant to history as it is to science. And lastly this series will not cover all
human societies. There will be two volumes devoted to Russia,
none to Germany. There will be histories of China and Japan but
not of Indonesia. The Jews have a volume to themselves, the
Parsees do not. And so on. Yet the series is called _The History of
Human Society_ for very good reasons. This history has a theme and
a position in time.

The theme is the most obvious and the most neglected; obvious
because everyone is aware of it from the solitary villagers of
Easter Island to the teeming cities of the Western World; neglected because it has been fashionable for professional and Western
historians to concern themselves either with detailed professional
history that cannot have a broad theme or with the spiritual and

metaphysical aspects of man's destiny that are not his proper province. What, therefore, is the theme of *The History of Human Society*? It is this: that the condition of man now is superior to what it was. That two great revolutions—the neolithic and the industrial—have enabled men to establish vast societies of exceptional complexity in which the material well-being of generations of mankind has made remarkable advances; that the second, and most important, revolution has been achieved by the Western World; that we are witnessing its most intensive phase now, one in which ancient patterns of living are crumbling before the demands of industrial society; that life in the suburbs of London, Lagos, Jakarta, Rio de Janeiro and Vladivostok will soon have more in common than they have in difference: that this, therefore, is a moment to take stock, to unfold how this came about, to evoke the societies of the past whilst we are still close enough to many of them to feel intuitively the compulsion and needs of their pattern of living. I, however, hope, in these introductions, which it is my intention to write for each book, to provide a sense of unity. The authors themselves will not be so concerned with the overriding theme. Their aim will be to reconstruct the societies on which they are experts. They will lay bare the structure of their societies—their economic basis, their social organisations, their aspirations, their cultures, their religions and their conflicts. At the same time they will give a sense of what it was like to have lived in them. Each book will be an authoritative statement in its own right, and independent of the rest of the series. Yet each, set alongside the rest, will give a sense of how human society has changed and grown from the time man hunted and gathered his food to this nuclear and electronic age. This could only have been achieved by the most careful selection of authors. They needed, of course, to be established scholars of distinction, possessing the ability to write attractively for the general reader. They needed also to be wise, to possess steady, unflickering compassion for the strange necessities of men; to be quick in understanding, slow in judgment, and to have in them some of that relish for life, as fierce and as instinctive as an animal's, that has upheld ordinary men and women in the worst of times. The authors of these books are heart-wise historians with sensible, level heads.

The range and variety of human societies is almost as great as the range and variety of human temperaments, and the selection for this series is in some ways as personal as an anthology. A

Chinaman, a Russian, an Indian or an African would select a different series; but we are Western men writing for Western men. The westernisation of the world by industrial technology is one of the main themes of the series. Each society selected has been in the main stream of this development or belongs to that vast primitive ocean whence all history is derived. Some societies are neglected because they would only illustrate in a duller way societies which appear in the series; some because their history is not well enough known to a sufficient depth of scholarship to be synthesised in this way; some because they are too insignificant.

There are, of course, very important social forces—feudalism, technological change or religion, for example—which have moulded a variety of human societies at the same time. Much can be learnt from the comparative study of their influence. I have, however, rejected this approach, once recorded history is reached. My reason for rejecting this method is because human beings experience these forces in communities, and it is the experience of men in society with which this series is primarily concerned.

Lastly, it need hardly be said that society is not always synonymous with the State. At times, as with the Jews, it lacks even territorial stability; yet the Jews provide a fascinating study of symbiotic social groupings, and to have left them out would be unthinkable, for they represent, in its best-known form, a wide human experience—a social group embedded in an alien society.

As well as a theme, which is the growth of man's control over his environment, this series may also fulfil a need. That is to restore a little confidence in man's capacity not only to endure the frequent catastrophes of human existence but also in his intellectual abilities. That many of his habits, both of mind and heart, are bestial, needs scarcely to be said. His continuing capacity for evil need not be stressed. His greed remains almost as strong as it was when he first shuffled on the ground. And yet the miracles created by his cunning are so much a part of our daily lives that we take their wonder for granted. Man's ingenuity—based securely on his capacity to reason—has won astonishing victories over the physical world—and in an amazingly brief span of time. Such triumphs, so frequently overlooked and even more frequently belittled, should breed a cautious optimism. Sooner or later, painfully perhaps and slowly, the same intellectual skill may be directed to the more difficult and intransigent problems of human living—man's social and personal relations—not only directed, but perhaps accepted, as the proper way of ordering human life. The story of man's progress over the centuries, studded with pitfalls and streaked with disaster as it is, ought to strengthen both hope and will.

Yet a note of warning must be sounded. The history of human society, when viewed in detail, is far more often darkened with tragedy than it is lightened with hope. As these books will show, life for the nameless millions of mankind who have already lived and died has been wretched, short, hungry and brutal. Few societies have secured peace; none stability for more than a few centuries; prosperity, until very recent times, was the lucky chance of a small minority. Consolations of gratified desire, the soothing narcotic of ritual, and the hope of future blessedness have often eased but rarely obliterated the misery which has been the lot of all but a handful of men since the beginning of his history. At long last that handful is growing to a significant proportion in a few favoured societies. But throughout human history most men have derived pitifully little from their existence. A belief in human progress is not incompatible with a sharp realisation of the tragedy not only of the lives of individual men but also of epochs, cultures and societies. Loss and defeat, too, are themes of this series, as well as progress and hope.

2

STRIDING ACROSS THE VALLEY of the Gard in Provence is a vast three-tiered bridge: the huge blocks of masonry have easily withstood nearly two thousand years as well as the plunder of centuries. This great Roman aqueduct, a miracle of technology, as splendid for its age as the Rockefeller Centre, still looks capable of outlasting time. Across the narrow northern neck of England from Newcastle to Carlisle runs Hadrian's Wall: mile after mile of dressed stone, regularly broken by watch towers, that runs over hill and dale. In the desert at Palmyra, the ruins of Roman temples and theatres speak of a grandeur and a luxury that the Western World did not know again until the nineteenth century. Again, in the northern deserts of Africa, there are vast ruins of buildings of a magnificence that black Africa still lacks. No other empire which has collapsed into ruin has left so many visible signs of its greatness to haunt the imagination of man. By comparison the pyramids

of Egypt, the mounds of Babylonia and even the temples of
Greece are small and local: the remains of Rome, however, everywhere abound, from Persia to Caledonia, from the Libyan desert
to the Rhine. And these physical remains are a witness of one of
the greatest human achievements and, also, of one of the most
profound problems in human history. By the strange cunning of
Time, as much was achieved and created by the decline and fall
of Rome as by her imperial greatness.

We are all so familiar with the idea of Imperial Rome that we
often fail to realise the extravagant success, the almost incredible
achievement of those small embattled villages scattered on the
hills and promontories that overlooked the Tiber. There, and
there alone, were the embryos of Rome. Within eight hundred
years they were to become one of the most populous and wond-
rous cities in the world: and this city governed the whole Mediterranean basin from the Euphrates and beyond to the coast of
Portugal. The Rhine and the Clyde provided the north-western
frontier and the Danube basin the north-east. Never since Rome
fell has Europe achieved a similar unity of government; even the
startling achievements of Napoleon are a pale, fleeting and diminished shadow of Roman greatness. No empire, except that of
China, has rivalled the extent and integration of the Roman. The
T'ang dynasty, certainly, challenges comparison with Augustan
Rome: but no other. Both were essentially great iron-age empires
—the culmination of a series of thrusts by militant societies to
achieve Imperial greatness. The empires of Persia and of Assyria,
as indeed did that of the Han, presaged the final growth of vast
territorial empires in the West and East. Imperial China and
Imperial Rome reached the limit of size, bureaucratic and probably technological development available to societies without
large-scale industry. Both were capable of sophisticated mass
production, either of raw materials or consumer goods, but both
rested on peasant or slave cultivation and skilled craftsmen.*
Plentiful labour plus individual skill lay at the base of their
economies. Nevertheless their productivity, their capacity to feed
large urban populations—Rome probably possessed over a million
inhabitants at the time of Augustus—and the rich exploitive

---

*The Chinese government was always very conscious of its dependence
on the peasantry whom they knew were the life-blood of the State. The
situation was more complex in the Roman Empire because of the huge body
of slaves used in primary production.

nature of their commerce enabled them to support complex bureaucratic machines and very large professional armies. And another consequence of their wealth and power was the surplus wealth that could be poured into buildings and public works on a scale which had never been equalled before either by Egyptian Pharaohs or Babylonian Kings or Greek citizens. And again they could afford a comparatively large leisured class with all that means for the sophisticated of artistic and intellectual pursuits, although here Rome did far less than might have been expected—a few good poets, philosophers and playwrights, one or two outstanding historians, a brilliant novelist or so, but, except in architecture, Rome's achievement in the arts fell far short of Greece and lagged immeasurably behind China. Why this should be so is difficult, perhaps impossible, to answer. It may stem from the heart of Roman experience. From the very earliest days, even long before the Republic was established, Rome had pursued a colonising, almost an Imperial mission. The early Romans first attacked, then absorbed Sabines and Latins as they thrust out from their little hill forts over the Tiber. So very early the problems of absorption and government were to the fore. A higher degree, not only of social organisation for military service and taxation, but also of public commitment to the idea and ideals of Rome was needed to achieve their initial expansion, let alone their ultimate victories against Etruscans, Carthaginians and Gauls. The simple old Roman farmer, austere, patriotic, dedicated to republican virtues, came to represent the ideal man and citizen. No matter how sophisticated, decadent or rich the Roman patrician class became, they were always haunted by the spectre of Old Cato—the dedicated, frugal Roman who combined private and public virtue, who married integrity of the family with integrity in the State. Sophistication, intellectualism, artistic excellence were never social ideals in the same way that public duty, public service and an almost religious patriotism were. The Romans grew conscious very early of their divine mission to create the greatest Empire that the world had known! And yet, as the world became theirs, unlike the Chinese, whose sense of superiority and self-regard knew no bounds, they, or at least their intellectuals and publicists, began first to criticise, then almost to hate, the society to which they belonged—a situation not entirely dissimilar to America today. Not only Juvenal and Petronius, but also Livy and Tacitus, indeed all writers condemn the vulgar, sense-addicted, wasteful,

orgiastic Roman society of their day with its blood sports, cruel-
ties, barbarisms and slaves. They appeal, often with haunting
nostalgia, to the pure, noble, more Spartan days of Republican
greatness. Few societies have seemed so uneasy in the present or so
haunted by an illusory past as Imperial Rome. And yet by any
standards the achievements were quite remarkable—the great
roads hammered across the length and breadth of Europe, going
like arrows from city to city, the regularity of government, the
sensible application of general and local law, the acceptance of
diversity in religion and social practice, and, within the core of the
Empire, peace such as few societies have enjoyed. As a feat of
human organisation, considering the primitive nature of its essential tools, it borders on the miraculous, and one which Europe has
never since attained. Nor should one forget the astonishing
colonising and civilising role which Rome performed in the
north and west as well as the heartlands of Europe. In Spain, in
France, in Britain, in parts of Germany and certainly in Roumania,
Rome created embryonic nations bringing social organisations
and urban living to replace primitive tribal life. In this she completed what Greece had begun, the creation of a literate Europe,
capable of forming large social organisations.

Europe's debt to Rome is immense—not only in language or in
law or in the partial creation of large social entities which were,
some of them, to become the nations of Europe, but also in ways
less commonly understood. Rome's greatest influence on Europe,
and perhaps on the world, arose from her decline and fall; from
indeed her failure as an Imperial power. Rome failed, and China
succeeded for far, far longer. The consequences of both were
momentous for human history. China suffered batterings by barbarians; her Imperial throne was captured by the Mongols; often
Chinese emperors lost great tracts of territory; at other times the
country was savagely divided by civil war and rival emperors,
experiences which, of course, were very common to the Roman
Empire in the third and fourth centuries. But in China resurgence
followed temporary dislocation: with Rome the resurgences were
very temporary and in the fifth century came more or less to an
end. Not that the Roman Empire disappeared: much of the social
structure persisted, not only in Greek clothes in Byzantium, but
also in the West, partly in Christian guise, and partly through the
sheer inertia of social forms. In the West the decay was long and
slow, long enough and slow enough for the barbarian hordes to

absorb language, some customs, some modes of work and living, as well as the lingering concept of large social organisation, a concept which was fostered by New Rome—the Catholic Church.

After all, Rome gave Christianity, if not to the world, then certainly to Europe. It is idle to speculate on what might have happened. The conversion of Constantine, the adoption of Christianity as the religion of the State, the acquisition by the Roman Church of the relics of Imperial wealth in the West, as well as some of its powers, tied Europe to Christianity in a common fate. Furthermore, the attempt to destroy all vestiges of other religions, to subject all cultural life to the Church, the growth of monolithic intolerance to all other beliefs or even ideas not theologically sanctioned gave Christianity a rigidity, an absolutist authority, in intellectual life which it had never previously possessed and made it curiously appropriate as the handmaid of secular power, whether limited as in the Dark Ages, or extensive as in the rising nationalisms of a mature Europe. Had this welding of intolerant Christianity with state power not taken place before the final collapse of Imperial Rome, it is unlikely, perhaps improbable, that one monolithic religion would have embraced Western and Northern Europe. And there were further consequences of this marriage of Roman state power with Christianity which need to be explored, but the purely secular consequences, political and economic, of Rome's disintegration need to be grasped first of all, for fundamentally they are perhaps more important.

In this wise and perceptive book, Donald Dudley makes us realise both the extent of Rome's greatness and its limitations.In many ways it was two worlds linked through Rome, but worlds that were very distinct in economic enterprise, social development and culture. Greece, Asia Minor, Egypt, Palestine, Syria and those parts of Persia which the Roman legions came to dominate remained distinct. Their bureaucratic class tended to be Greek speaking, their culture hellenistic, their religion often mystical and esoteric; here and there were antique structures, ideological as well as social, such as Pharaonic Egypt, that were quite indigestible. These countries were also 'urbanised' to a degree that was unusual in the West, and their economies had long been influenced by, indeed were dependent on, a wide-flung trans-maritime commerce. The land to the west of Rome was, as in America, the moving frontier. There the Romans had created provinces and towns, pushed their primitive economies into the production of raw materials—minerals, wine, oil, timber, wool and slaves for use in Italy and beyond. And so the economy of the Mediterranean basin and the foreign lands beyond was like a gigantic seesaw pivoted on Rome which provided the security and the impetus that tilted the grade first this way and then that, but never broke down. For generations, even centuries, it held in balance even as it grew, and civil wars, violent invasions, social unrest, chronic inflation never upset it for long. As with China, here was a socio-economic entity which worked.

The collapse of Rome broke the seesaw in fragments and destroyed its fulcrum—true in a sad ghostly fashion it lingered on, there was still some trace even in the darkest days between the distant lands of the north-west—Britain, Frisia and the Near East—but it was feeble, a matter of a few score merchants, and in no way comparable to the international trade which the Roman Empire enjoyed.

As the nation-states and dynastic groupings slowly formed in the ruins of the West, they were never to be so economically self-sufficient as the great Roman Empire had been. They needed goods, they needed trade—ever increasingly, but they *all* did. Restless combative economies and societies, bent on expansion through war, replaced the economically self-sufficient Empire of Rome that had needed the rest of the world only for exotics. But the autonomous societies which replaced it could not be self-sufficient once they had begun to recover from the anarchy, devastation and depopulation of the dark ages. Hence this meant a Europe dedicated to internal war, not merely war on the frontiers, which apart from periodic civil commotion was to be the experience of the other great conglomerative land-based states of human history—China, America, Russia. And this situation—a geographically interlocked series of highly aggressive and combative societies—produced extraordinary effects as the centuries passed: not only a scene of unparalleled turbulence, but also of societies that were constantly reforged on the anvil of war. The failure of any power to succeed Rome and weld the Mediterranean basin and the rest of Europe into a self-sufficient Empire created a competitive, restless state system: a situation which was aggravated by the fact that so much of the rich, highly urbanised and economically sophisticated part of the former Empire fell under the dominion of a religious ideology, Islam, as aggressive and as unyielding as Christianity itself. In the long term, many of Europe's geo-political problems stem from Rome's collapse. And so do the world's, for in the end these aggressive societies were driven to exploit the world beyond Europe.

The collapse of Rome haunted thinking men century after century. The great buildings, not only in Rome or in the Italian cities, but also in distant London or Trier, slowly crumbled: the arrow-straight roads broke down into muddy lanes or weed-choked tracks. But the decay, though obvious, was slow, a constant reminder, therefore, of a greatness which had passed. The decay of the knowledge and learning of Rome was just as slow, if more haphazard. The acquisition of Latin as the language of ritual and government prevented total loss, indeed made survival certain, so that there were always the tools available to recover much of the culture of ancient Rome. Even in the most barbarous times there was sufficient knowledge amongst the literate to realise the enormity of the disaster and the loss. God's will it might be; nevertheless the severity of the punishment was undeniable. So this great fracture lay across Europe's past, creating what no other human society ever experienced—a duality of history. Beyond the fall of Rome lay the splendid pagan inheritance in science, in literature, in all that adorned the lives of men: after that fall there was the past of the Christian Church, a world of saints and wonders, encased in theological dogma. The most sensitive intellects of the medieval world were often conscious of its barbarity and backwardness in comparison with the ancient past. Time and time again men of learning plundered the ancient Roman treasure house of the mind; indeed reached through it to the even richer treasure hoard of Greece. Yet difficult as it might be, these piece-meal recoveries were made to fit into the ideological framework of medieval Europe. In the end that process failed, but the attempt to revive all that had been lost went on in an ever-broadening stream, made infinitely easier, infinitely more permanent and infinitely more widespread by the potent invention of printing. Yet the great question remained. Why? Why had Rome declined? Furthermore, to recover the past truly, scholars in the end had to make a conscious attempt to insert themselves into a totally different world of feeling—the pagan world. They were forced to treat the Roman, pagan world as a time almost totally different from their own, or at least from the Christian age that followed Rome; a situation which Gibbon immortalised in his

famous image of barefooted friars worshipping in the Temple of
Jupiter.

Therefore Rome and its collapse reverberated endlessly in the
intellectual life of Europe, moulding it in a hundred subtle ways,
some of which we still appreciate too little or only dimly per-
ceive. In a brief introduction such as this one can only hint at the
complexities of the inheritance from Rome, but one has only to
think of education or architecture, or urban planning, of social
engineering, of the Church of Rome, of our languages, even
English, to realise how we are still entangled in one of the greatest
achievements Europe has known. Just how great it was, and how
that greatness was both achieved and lost, is the theme of this
excellent book—one of the key volumes of the series, because the
subject is still so central to all our lives. The past of Rome has
been a living past, an inescapable part of our intellectual and
political heritage. Indeed, only now, nearly two thousand years
after Augustan Rome, is that past beginning to weaken its grip,
as power and cultural excellence shift from the core of Europe
to the great powers beyond.

CHAPTER I

Italy—geography and peoples

THE WRITERS OF THE AGE of Augustus cherished the belief that Italy was the most favoured of lands, presenting the optimum conditions for the life of plants, animals and men and so destined by Nature and the Gods for the seat of a world Empire. This belief informs the Georgics of Virgil and is expressed, in one of his noblest passages, in the Second Georgic. In his first book Dionysius of Halicarnassus writes in more prosaic terms. What he stresses is the range, variety and high quality of the produce of Italian soil. 'Italy has plenty of good arable land, but it is not treeless like a mere grain-bearing country: again, although it produces all kinds of trees, it does not give a poor corn yield, as does forest land: yet again, though productive in corn and trees, it is not unsuitable for ranching: finally, no one can say that, though rich in corn and cattle and timber, it is unpleasant for men to live in.' He goes on to justify Italy's claim to all-round excellence. 'What corn lands can compare with the plains of Campani, which yield three crops a year? What olives excel those of Messapia and many another district? What vines the Tuscan and Alban and Falernian? There are good pastures for sheep and goats, wonderful grazing for horses and cattle, in the water meadows and the mountain glens. The forest resources of Italy are the most wonderful of all—the Sila and the Monte Gargano and those of Alpine lands—giving first quality timber for ship-building, houses and all other purposes. Add to these hotsprings, minerals, wild game and abundance of fish and above all a temper-

I

ate climate, never by excessive cold or heat harmful to growing
crops or animals. In short Italy excels any other land in general
fertility and all-round usefulness.' I have quoted this passage at
length because it is the most explicit statement of the advantages
of living in Italy, but it could be supported by many a passage
from Strabo, Varro, Columella and Pliny.

Behind these Augustan and later writers lay a thousand years
and more of hard work on the land of Italy. The modern geographer is likely to provide a cooler appraisal. The long peninsula
of Italy juts out more than 700 miles to the south-east from the
main land mass of Europe. The great arc of the Alps seems to
provide a natural frontier on the north, with a wide barrier of
mountain land. This high mountain wall is most formidable in
its western sectors, where mountains of 12–15,000 feet and high
passes cut off Italy from Switzerland and France. Even the coast
provides no easy passage. The train between Genoa and Mar-
seilles keeps diving into tunnels; the motorist on the Corniche
road above finds it impossible to overtake heavy trucks on the
incessant bends. But on the north-east the Carnic and Julian Alps
provide a series of easier passes—the Brenner, the Plöcken and
the Pear Tree Pass—leading into the Danube Valley, the great
artery of communication in prehistoric Europe. These are the
routes by which the earliest land immigrants from continental
Europe came to the Po Valley and on into peninsular Italy. When
Virgil calls the Po the king of rivers we hear the voice of a man
who had spent his childhood in Cisalpine Gaul and who saw no
river so majestic when he moved south to Rome and Campania.
Swollen by the melting snows from the Alps, the Po and its
tributaries provided a primitive landscape of marsh, scrub, and
forest, with relatively few patches of drier ground.

Invading peoples who found their way to the crossings of the
Po would see before them to the south another mountain barrier.
The Apennines, beginning at the Gulf of Genoa, provide the
broad backbone of peninsular Italy and are protracted so far as
the toe of Italy, falling just short of a physical link with the high
mountains of eastern Sicily. The Apennine summits mostly run
between four and five thousand feet, though there is a patch of
high mountain country in the Abruzzi, where the Gran Sasso
d'Italia reaches 9,850 feet. The summits do not rise from a main
chain; there is instead a complex deeply dissected mountain
system, enclosing many deep glens and flanked by outlying ranges

on either side. The passes across these mountains are difficult but far from impossible, though the winters are surprisingly hard. They foster isolated pastoral communities, whose economy has lasted down to our own time. They make Italy a Janus-like land, facing in opposite directions. Its western coasts, washed by the Tyrrhenian Sea, look to communications with France, Spain and North Africa. The east and south-east coasts look across the stormy Adriatic to the treacherous, mountainous shores of Dalmatia and Epirus, to Greece and to the sea routes which lead into the Aegean. Neither coastline of Italy is blessed with good harbours. The Gulf of Otranto, the Bay of Naples and Genoa provide good harbours for modern liners; on the Adriatic side incessant labour is required to keep the port of Venice in operation and the city itself above the waves. Ancient ships could of course make use of much smaller ports, but only provided they could find sheltered anchorage.

On the western side of the Apennines—very much the more attractive—peninsular Italy has three notable areas of good soil—Tuscany, Latium and Campania. All three possess volcanic soils of exceptional fertility and in early times offered by far the most favourable prospects for settlement. They also posed a perpetual challenge to the pastoralists who looked down on them from their high grazing grounds in the Apennines. They needed these lowland pastures for their winter grazing and even when the drovers' ways and drovers' rights had been established by legislation, the passage of their flocks provided many disputes between them and the men of the plains. The Adriatic coast lacks such sharply differentiated lands as Latium and Campania. Instead, a long coastal strip extends from Ancona to Foggia, with the isolated peninsula of Monte Gargano as an outlier of the Apennines. This is the land known to the Romans as Picenum and its cultural history in early times is not very well understood. Beyond it the limestone grazing lands of Apulia and Calabria extend to the heel of Italy. This again is pastoral country, its low rainfall restricting the growth of agriculture.

In about 850 B.C., when our story begins, Italy was something of a cultural backwater. No ancient civilisation had appeared on her soil comparable to those of Crete or Mycenaean Greece, let alone the great civilisations of the Near East. Not that she altogether lacked contact with the higher cultures of the Aegean. Indeed a memory of such contacts is preserved in the legends of

the voyages of Odysseus and of the Argonauts, the coming of
Aeneas to Italy and even the flight of Daedalus. Archaeology can
point to evidence of a trade with the Aegean. There may have
been in Minoan times trading posts on Italian soil, the forerunners of the later Greek colonies. But this was trade, not
settlement—except perhaps at Cumae. There is no evidence that
any of the early cultures of Italy were able to produce anything
so complex, from a technological point of view, as Stonehenge
or Avebury in remote Britain. The culture of Bronze Age
Sardinia, with its *nuraghi* and its sculptures in stone and bronze,
represents the most advanced society known in Italian lands
during the second millennium B.C.

The Ligurians of the Maritime Alps were one of the earliest of
all Italian peoples. This ancient race, perhaps of Sicilian or North
African origin, also inhabited the islands of Sardinia and Elba.
They survived many centuries in their mountains before they
were overrun by the Romans. In the north-east another ancient
people, the Veneti, perhaps of Illyrian origin, occupied the lands
which still bear their name. We know little about the peoples who
in 850 B.C. inhabited what is now Lombardy and Piedmont—for
this is before the Etruscans or the Celts had penetrated those
lands. In the light of its later history, the most important peoples
in Italy were those kindred stocks who had already settled themselves in the highland pastures of the Apennines as far down as
the mountains that bound Campania and who were disputing
possession of the western plains with their earliest inhabitants.
These peoples—the Umbrians, the Sabines, the Marsi, the
Samnites, the Latins and a large number of smaller communities
into which they were divided, appear repeatedly in Roman
history. Their languages were closely related and two of them,
Oscan and Latin, would obtain wide currency. These were the
people who, from Latium northwards, had reached the level of
material culture best represented by the famous site of Villanova,
near Bologna. The exploitation of the mineral resources of
Etruria, and especially the use of iron, had produced in this
district the most advanced culture yet to be seen in Italy. Latium
was very much a backward area, compared with the north.

The land of Italy around 850 B.C. is thus one of little local
cultures, none of them very far advanced. Many languages are
spoken in it, and there is no kind of ethnic unity. The very name
is an anachronism. There is no common term as yet for the

peninsula as a whole. Complex as it is, the ethnic and linguistic map of Italy is still incomplete. Three important elements have yet to be added to it. During the eighth century B.C., the higher cultures of the Etruscans and the Greeks will be introduced. About two centuries later a new wave of invading peoples will bring the Celts from the Upper Danube into the valley of the Po.

The next chapter will have a narrower field of observation and will concentrate on Latium and on the progress of one of its early settlements—that of Rome.

CHAPTER 2

Rome and Latium

TWO PLACES ARE OF paramount importance for an under-standing of the origins of Rome. The first of these is the summit of Monte Cavo in the Alban Hills. The second is the broad plateau of the Palatine Hill in Rome.

Monte Cavo has a modest height of 3,115 feet—about that of Skiddaw in the English Lake District—but it commands one of the great historic landscapes of the world. The mountain itself was the Holy Mountain of the Latin peoples and on its summit was the shrine of Jupiter Latiaris, most important of their common cults. To the west the view extends over some fifty miles of coastline, from the great promontory of Mons Circeius in the land of the Volsci, past Ostia and the mouths of the Tiber and north-west as far as Civitavecchia in the land of the Etruscans. To the north the plain of Latium (the Roman Campagna) stretches out to the Tiber and Rome itself. Northward on the far horizon rise the broken hills of the Tolfa and of the Ciminian Forest—a wild country known as *claustra Etruriae*, the keys of Etruria, keys which it took Rome so long to possess. The deep trench of the Tiber Valley extends far to the north-east into the hills of the Sabine country and beyond to the passes through the main chain of the Apennines. Hills and mountains close the horizon to the east and south-east, the lands of wild mountain peoples, the Sabines, the Aequi and the Marsi. Closer at hand, the whole beautiful landscape of the volcanic Alban Hills with their crater lakes is open to view. A second famous Latin cult had its home in the grove by the Lake of Nemi (Diana's Mirror), the arcane cult of the Grove Goddess, whose rites are described in the classic work of anthropology, Frazer's *Golden Bough*. The Alban Lake is associated with Alba Longa, in Roman tradition the mother city of Rome.

6

Rome and Latium

The horizon thus toured was for many centuries the political horizon of Rome. The *prisci Latini* who worshipped on the Holy Mountain were traditionally thirty in number and of these the *populus Romanus* was one. It is generally agreed that the kindred peoples who made up the *nomen Latinum* had arrived in Italy about 1,000 B.C. Two centuries later they were well settled in their land, had established shrines and sacred places, discovered its best pastures and had made a start with farming. Their material culture was that now called Villanovan from the type site of Villanova near the modern Bologna, where excavation has discovered artifacts extending over the period from 900 to 600 B.C. These consisted of round hut-urns with conical roofs for the ashes of the dead and of a considerable range of instruments made of bronze and iron. Such goods are found at many sites in Latium. We must think of these early Latins as predominantly a pastoral people, keeping cattle, sheep, goats, pigs and living in scattered villages composed of round wattle-and-daub huts, speaking a language of Indo-European origin which might fairly be called

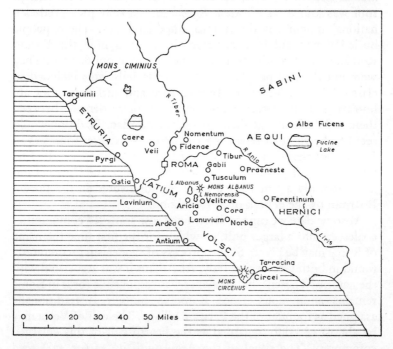

1. The horizon of early Rome

proto-Latin. (Archaic Latin is properly the language of the earliest inscriptions, which belong to the latter part of the sixth century B.C.) The whole culture was in a pre-urban phase, though some of the villages later developed into the famous cities of Latium—such as Tibur, Praeneste, Tusculum, Gabii and Lavinium. Rome is part of this context and it will be long before she gives any sign that she is destined to outstrip her peers.

Ancient legend and modern archaeology converge in the story of the Palatine Hill in Rome. On this hill, on the 21st April in a year later agreed upon to have been 753 B.C., tradition asserts that Romulus founded with due ritual the city of Rome. The year is uncertain, the day significant. The 21st of April, still kept as the Birthday of Rome, is the date of the Palilia, the sacred festival in honour of Pales, divine protector of shepherds and their flocks. Archaeology confirms the settlement of a pastoral community on the Palatine Hill sometime about 750 B.C. It has discovered the post-holes of their timber huts and a later but still archaic cistern. Tradition records that such a hut with its thatched roof was known as the *Casa Romuli* and piously preserved as a national monument down into Imperial times. These people buried their dead in a cemetery in what is now the Forum Romanum and continued to do so down to about 600 B.C. They were not the first people to settle on the hills later included in classical Rome. Traces of Bronze Age and earlier peoples are known, but there seems no continuity of settlement between them and the Iron Age shepherds of the Palatine. Tradition would seem to be right in regarding the latter as the first founders of Rome. But they were not the only Iron Age settlers on the site. Other such villages are known on the Esquiline and Quirinal and more recently a similar one has been discovered in the Forum Boarium by the church of St Omobono.

At some date we cannot determine these scattered communities coalesced into a larger unit, to which for the first time the name of Rome may be given. Such a process of synoecism is commonly found in both Greece and Italy. At Athens it was associated with the name of Theseus, but whoever was responsible for it in Rome remains anonymous, since Romulus himself is traditionally assigned as founder of the Palatine village. The cult of Vesta may be almost certainly regarded as the hearth cult of this enlarged community. The ritual of the Argei with its 24 (or 27?) reed puppets gathered from each of the *sacella* in the four ancient districts of Rome may also go back to this period. The Rome of the Four Regions may itself be only a later phase of synoecism; the festival of the Septimontium suggests a union of three communities, on the Palatine, Esquiline and Caelian hills. The rites of the Luperci may perhaps be more ancient still—a survival of the Bronze Age peoples. This, too, is the Rome of the early kings, though the three first kings of Livy's narrative with their suspiciously long reigns will hardly do. But one of them, Numa, the venerable figure who established the first calendar of Roman religious ritual, is indeed significant. He is the Priest-King, a very familiar figure in the early cultures of European peoples, whose powers continued, attenuated and fossilised, far into the Republic. Another of the early kings is said to have been of Sabine descent and tradition is emphatic and unanimous that there was a Sabine element in the population of early Rome. There is nothing improbable about this, though so far archaeology has failed positively to identify the Sabines.

We cannot give a political history for early Latin Rome. Its institutions must almost certainly have included a Council of Elders, prototype of the later Senate, and an Assembly, however constituted, where the voice of the people could make itself heard from time to time. (One of the matters which came before it was probably the choice of a king, for the monarchy seems to have been elective.) Nothing can be said about its relations with other communities in Latium. The traditional wars and conquests mentioned by Livy and Virgil, and officially recognised by the statues of early *triumphatores* in the Forum of Augustus, seem to be the fabrications of a later age, aimed at enhancing the glory of Rome. Great nations must be infant prodigies. But sometime towards the end of the seventh century B.C. this rather backward community like others in Latium was galvanised by contact with the higher civilisation of the Etruscans.

CHAPTER 3

The Etruscan civilisation

THE MODERN SCIENCE OF Etruscology has revealed the culture of the Etruscans both as a thing in its own right and as a major element in the culture of early Italy. Its material remains are displayed in many museums, notably on a magnificent scale in the Villa Giulia in Rome and the Archaeological Museum in Florence. The great necropoleis, such as those of Tarquinia and Caere, with their chambered tombs and painted frescoes bring thousands of people into direct contact with Etruscan civilisation. None the less problems remain. The language is not fully understood. It is not of Indo-European origin; its alphabet is familiar, and short inscriptions can be deciphered, but longer texts such as that in the museum at Zagreb are full of pitfalls. Nor has the debate on origins—autochthonous or immigrants from Asia?—yet been finally resolved. But increasingly it would seem that the arguments in favour of an Oriental origin as postulated by Herodotus are the stronger. If so, the Etruscans would fit very naturally into that phase of colonisation in which many bands of adventurers, Greek, Punic and Oriental, left the overcrowded world of the Aegean and its coasts for the wider and emptier lands around the Western Mediterranean. The first signs of Etruscan culture are to be found in the lands between the Arno and the Tiber about 800 B.C. If, as seems likely, these represent immigrants arriving by sea, they must be regarded as first-rate prospectors.

The Etruscans were called Tursenoi by the Greeks, Etrusci or Tusci by the Romans and their name for themselves was Rasenna. Tuscany, the land which now bears their name, is a rich and varied region which has shown itself at many periods suitable for an advanced civilisation. The Etruscans would seem to have

imposed themselves as a conquering aristocracy on an earlier
people of Villanovan culture. Parallels with the Norman Conquest of England are inescapable. The mineral resources of
Tuscany are perhaps what originally drew the immigrants there.
These are to be found in the Colline Metallifere, between Siena
and Livorno, in the peninsula around the ancient Populonia, and
on the island of Elba. They offered copper, lead, tin, and, above
all, iron. These the Etruscans exploited on a profitable and, by
ancient standards, prodigious scale. From the great slag heaps
around Populonia it has been estimated that an annual production
of between 10,000 and 12,000 tons of iron was maintained for
over four centuries. Although their land contained much marsh
and forest it also had good farming soils, especially in the north,
the *Campi Etrusci* of Roman history. By clearing and draining the
land and by building good roads and communications, the
Etruscans were able to obtain some of the highest crop yields
ever recorded in ancient times. They were also traders by sea, in
contact with Greece, the Levant and Egypt and maintaining
themselves on equal and usually friendly terms with the greatest
maritime power in the West Mediterranean, that of Carthage.
Like the English in the reign of Elizabeth I, they turned readily
from trade to piracy as and when it seemed profitable and they
may have practised it in the Adriatic as well as the Tyrrhenian
Sea. Above all the Etruscans were an urban people. Their cities
and those established by the Greeks in the south were the first
true cities in Italy. The twelve leading Etruscan cities were bound
together in a Confederation meeting at the Fanum Voltumnae near
Volsinii—a site yet to be discovered. This would seem to have
been primarily a religious and not a political union. It is possible
that political decisions were taken by the Confederacy as a whole,
but most unlikely that it had any means of enforcing them on
individual members.

The Etruscan cities were autonomous and their particularism
was as marked and as touchy as that of the Greek *polis*. We cannot
name at any one period the twelve cities comprising the Confederacy and it is best to think of them in geographical terms as a southern and a northern group. The first was established in suitable
places in the wild volcanic country south of a line drawn, roughly,
from the modern Orvieto to the sea. It included such famous
cities as Tarquinia, Caere, Vulci, Volsinii and Veii, Rome's
neighbour and rival in the lower Tiber Valley. Further north on

the low hills of what is now Umbria and in the Arno Valley were Cortona, Rusellae, Arezzo, Chiusi and Perusia: some of these survive as modern cities. On the coast were the mining cities of Populonia and Vetulonia. Each of these cities occupied its own territory of farm land and was as a rule the only major urban community within it. It has been estimated that Tarquinia ruled a territory of about 500 square miles, and that the population of Caere was about 25,000.

Most of the material objects of Etruscan culture reflect the life of its aristocracy, which was characterised by a love of luxury and the pleasures of the senses. The painted tombs of Tarquinia are full of scenes of banqueting and dancing, of hunting and gladiatorial shows. A love of display comes out strikingly in such objects as the gold pectorals and *fibulae* of the Regolini-Galassi tomb. Indeed, the entire contents of this tomb from Caere reveal Etruscan life at its most sumptuous. It contained three corpses, the most important being a princess called Larthia: the gold pectorals and the *fibulae* were for her adornment. The tomb also contains the remains of two chariots, a funeral bier and a bronze catafalque. This is the material background we should have in mind when we read Livy's account of Tanaquil at Rome. We are reminded irresistibly of another highly sophisticated aristocracy which lived in the land of Tuscany in Renaissance times.

Etruscan art may have borrowed the themes and conventions of Greek art, especially during the archaic period. But it had a characteristic note of fantasy, exemplified in such figures as the bronze Chimaera from Arezzo and the demon masks from Orvieto. We know the name of one Etruscan master, Vulca of Veii, to whom are attributed the splendid Apollo and other terracottas from the temples of that city. Etruscan music and dances were famous and the skill of their *tibicines* or flute players was said to be such that they were used to lure the wild game from the coverts into the nets. But there was another side to this brilliant culture. The Etruscans were famous for their occult knowledge (the *disciplina Etrusca*) which could reveal to them the workings of destiny. Destiny, or Necessity, was one of their cardinal beliefs, the deterministic *Fatum* which ruled and governed the lives of men and of cities. Through the *disciplina Etrusca* and through the correct interpretation of signs by the flight of birds or by the entrails of sacrificial victims, it was possible to understand the workings of this mysterious force. This knowledge was the speciality of the Etruscan diviners or *haruspices* and one of their working instruments has been discovered in the bronze liver from Piacenza in northern Italy.

Graves and their artifacts cannot of course tell us the whole story of a people, and so far very few Etruscan city sites have been scientifically explored. But there are two places where recent excavations have been able to reveal something of Etruscan city planning. The first of these is at Marzabotto, south of the modern Bologna, where an anonymous Etruscan city was overrun by invading Gauls about 400 B.C. and subsequently abandoned. It has been shown to have possessed a street plan of a grid-iron pattern, like those associated with Hippodamus in Greece and its buildings were of a standardised plan. At Spina, near the mouth of the Po, there have been disinterred from the mud the remains of a city of vast extent (more than 700 acres) which shows traces of both Greek and Etruscan culture. This would seem to have been an ambitious project for a great port at the head of the Adriatic, the first forerunner of Roman Aquileia and modern Venice.

Spina and Marzabotto are reminders that Etruscan culture in Italy was not confined to Tuscany. On the contrary, there were two ambitious projects for the expansion of Etruscan power which have rightly earned for that people the claim to be the first potential bringers of unity to Italy. One of these was towards the south into Latium and Campania, the other was northwards into the valley of the Po. Neither is well documented; both ultimately failed. Some scholars have seen a concerted act of the Confederacy of Twelve Cities in both plans for expansion, but it is doubtful how far this can be sustained. It is uncertain whether the Etruscans reached Campania by sea and spread inland from the neighbourhood of the modern Salerno, or whether they went overland and expanded towards the coast from a base at Capua. In either case, the Campanian venture brought them into confrontation with the Greek colony of Cumae. It was also decisive for their relations with Latium, which the Etruscans would now need to hold to secure their communications with the southern venture. The Etruscan foundation of Capua has been dated to 650 B.C., or shortly thereafter; this would fit in well with the traditional date of about 616 B.C. for the establishment of an Etruscan monarchy in Rome and for the foundation, about 600 B.C., of the new

Etruscan city of Veii to contest with Rome for the domination of
the Tiber Valley.

Something will be said later about Etruscan influence on Rome
and Latium. It will here be convenient to summarise the history
of their penetration into Campania. They made a full scale assault
on Cumae in 524 B.C., but were defeated by the forces of that city
under the command of Aristodemus. This defeat really put an
end to their prospects for large scale expansion in Campania and
a further set-back occurred in 474 B.C., when they were defeated
at sea by the combined forces of Cumae and Syracuse. From that
time on their hold on Campania was precarious and in 432 B.C.
the venture came to an end when the Samnites captured Capua.

The northern venture got under way much later, perhaps about
500 B.C. The Po Valley offered splendid opportunities for settlement and for trade with the barbarian peoples of northern
Europe by the routes across the Alpine passes. Certainly the
Etruscans established themselves at Felsina (near Bologna),
Spina and perhaps also at Mantua. A Roman tradition represents
them as penetrating north of the Po to the foothills of the Alps,
but modern archaeology has not substantiated this. In any case,
the Etruscan expansion into the valley of the Po was not destined
to last for much more than 100 years. The great tide of Gallic
invasion swamped them early in the fifth century B.C. and the
land was later re-named Gallia Cisalpina. So ended the two bold
and ambitious ventures for Etruscan expansion in Italy. Had they
succeeded, Rome's unification of the Italian peninsula might
have been anticipated by another people and almost two centuries
earlier in time. But it would have been unification in a cultural
and not in a political sense. Etruscan culture might well have been
spread throughout Italy, as Hellenic culture was spread throughout Ionia. There is no sign, however, that the Etruscans could
ever have advanced beyond the political concept of the autonomous city state, let alone to anything as coherent and
permanent as the system worked out by Rome.

CHAPTER 4

Rome and the Etruscans

THE LITERARY TRADITION gives Etruscan supremacy in Rome a span of little over 100 years, from the coming of the first Tarquin in 616 to the expulsion of Tarquinius Superbus by Brutus and his fellow conspirators in 510 B.C. This marks the end of the monarchy and the establishment of the Republic, but not the end of the threat from the Etruscans. Lars Porsenna of Clusium leads an Etruscan army against Rome in 505(?), but is repulsed, largely due to the heroism of the Horatii. Precise (suspiciously so) in the matter of dates, the traditional account contains many difficulties. Only three kings are mentioned, all of whom come to a violent end. The deeds of the two Tarquins are not clearly differentiated, though both are portrayed as 'bad' kings. In between them comes Servius Tullius, a Latin of mysterious ancestry. He was a 'good' king: indeed, the last such; 'never again was a Roman king to rule with humanity and justice'. But another tradition concerning Servius Tullius—known to the Emperor Claudius—identifies him with the Etruscan Mastarna. Modern opinion inclines to the view that there were more than three Etruscan rulers over Rome and that their rule may have begun earlier; Gjerstad's attempt to bring its conclusion to as late as 450 B.C. has not been generally accepted.

On the effects of Etruscan rule there is more of a consensus. Urbanisation, as understood in the major Etruscan cities, was imposed on Rome. The marshy valley of the Forum was drained by sewers (anticipating the Cloaca Maxima) and the reclaimed ground was paved (about 575 B.C.) to be used as a religious and political centre—the Forum Romanum. The so-called Lapis Niger, with its archaic inscription, is a survival from this early Forum. So too are the names of early streets, the Sacra Via and the Vicus

Tuscus, in which stood a statue of the Etruscan deity Voltumna. The sacred furrow or *pomoerium* was probably traced at this time and the city provided with gates and walls. The course of these latter is uncertain, for the wall which now bears the name of Servius Tullius has been shown to date from after the Gallic invasions (*c.* 390 B.C.).

Temples were built and cult statues provided—the first time, it would seem, that Roman divinities were worshipped in human form. Above all was the great temple of Jupiter Optimus Maximus on the Capitol, with its *cellae* for Jupiter, Juno and Minerva who formed the Capitoline Triad. Down to the end of paganism, this was to be the greatest of Roman cults, the guarantee of Rome's permanence and world Empire. Vowed by Tarquinius Priscus, the temple was built by Tarquinius Superbus, using the forced labour of the Roman people. Roman tradition insists that its dedication took place under the Republic in the consulship of Horatius Pulvillus (509 B.C.). This temple has a stone substructure, supporting wooden walls and columns covered by terracotta painting. Vulca was summoned from Veii to make in terracotta the cult statue of Jupiter, the *quadriga* for the roof and possibly the antefixes to adorn it. Rome was now embellished by one of the noblest of all the archaic temples of Italy which lasted, with some alterations, until its destruction by fire in 83 B.C. Parts of its substructure have been found. But the only surviving example of the artistic splendours of Etruscan Rome is the great bronze Wolf of the Capitol. Another important cult was that of Diana on the Aventine, traditionally established by Servius Tullius as a federal cult of the Latins and later much venerated by the common people of Rome: nothing is known of it archaeologically.

Now, and for the first time, Rome became an important centre of trade. Under Etruscan control, a trade-route from Etruria to Campania crossed the river at the Insula Tiberina. Sea-going ships could discharge their cargoes at Rome, some to be forwarded by land or river up the Tiber. Imports of Greek pottery are one sign of the new phase. Another is the development of the Forum Boarium as a commercial centre which seems to have begun about 575 B.C. In later times the most important cult in this area was that of Hercules, patron of traders, at the Ara Maxima. It has recently been suggested that this grew out of a shrine of Melqart, the Phoenician god of trade and that there may have been a Punic 'factory' on the banks of the Tiber. The gold tablet recently found at Pyrgi, the port of Caere, shows the Etruscan ruler of that city making an official dedication to Astarte at a date which may be about 500 B.C. In this context, Polybius' story of a treaty between Carthage and Rome in the earliest days of the Republic begins to look well founded.

Farming also must have been intensified under the Etruscans. The early farming territory of Rome has not revealed the *cuniculi* (culverts) of drainage schemes on the same scale as those at Veii or on the Alban Hills, but the labour, the know-how and the central direction were there. The records of the ancient festival of the Ambarvalia and of other ceremonies for the lustration of the fields and perambulation of the boundaries, give invaluable evidence for the size of the *ager Romanus*, the cultivable land of the city. Stopping points are known at seven places along certain of the main roads leading out of the city to the south and west; they delimit 'a circular area with a diameter of 16 kilometres and a surface of roughly 250 square kilometres'. Large for a Latin city, it was inferior to that of several Etruscan cities. The *ager Veientanus* was larger than that of Rome, which was little more than a quarter of the *ager* of Tarquinia. These ancient farm lands of Rome have largely vanished within the last few years beneath the urban sprawl of the modern city. But there are still places, notably around Via Appia Antica, where vineyards, fields and gardens extend almost to the walls of Aurelian. No student of Rome should fail to see them. They are the dwindling remnants of the historic nucleus, the narrow base from which the *populus Romanus* set off (to adapt Virgil's words)—*e paupere terra missus in imperium magnum* (from a poor land to a great Empire).

The 'good' King Servius Tullius is also credited with a set of military and political reforms, which included a census, the placing of the obligation to army service on a property footing and the setting up of a new political assembly, the Comitia Centuriata. The problem has aroused endless debate and may in the end be insoluble. Its political details appear in a form far better suited to the class struggles of the fourth century B.C. But, on the military side, it looks as though the object was to enable the Roman army to fight in the way approved by up-to-date Greek tacticians—i.e. with the main reliance on the heavy-armed infantry, or hoplites. And a monarch who favours infantrymen from the middle classes over cavalry from the aristocracy is not acting in a political void.

Rome under the Etruscans was therefore provided with the technology and culture of that civilisation in an advanced form. But she never became an Etruscan city nor joined the Etruscan Confederacy. She was a Latin city under Etruscan or 'Etruscanising' kings, as were many others in Latium, including Praeneste, Tusculum and Satricum. The account of wars and conquest in Latium under Servius Tullius and the Tarquins has led some scholars to think of a kind of Latin Empire under Etruscan Rome. There is not very much to substantiate this. It does look as though Alba Longa and its sanctuaries fell under Roman control about 600 B.C. and the last Tarquin is said to have conquered Gabii and Pometia. More to the point, in the treaty with Carthage already mentioned Rome is stated to have allies (*socii*) at Ardea, Antium, Terracina and other coastal cities of Latium, which implies at least a political hegemony. But in the disturbed state that followed the expulsion of the Tarquins the forces of the Latin League are found capable of military action against an Etruscan army that may well have captured Rome (see p. 15). Whatever her standing vis-à-vis the Latin cities, there can be little doubt that Rome was inferior to Veii. Veii controlled the salt-pans of Ostia and the land route up the Tiber. Her territory was larger and more fully exploited. She built roads and planted colonies. Her temples were more ancient; her artists more sophisticated. Whether it is right to suggest that for a time she dominated Rome is uncertain. But after the capture of Veii by Rome in 396 B.C., followed by the capture of Rome by the Gauls a few years later, a large part of the Roman people thought that migration to Veii was the key to the future. It was a striking tribute to the memory of Veii's greatness.

All Roman writers present the end of the monarchy and establishment of the Republic as one of the fundamental events of Roman history. The traditional account became canonical and the expulsion of Tarquin by Brutus was charged with such potent memories that, nearly 500 years later, it was held up as an example to urge his descendant to an act of tyrannicide. We may if we choose, dismiss Lucretia and her rape as one of those subjects according to Livy, 'more fitted to the romances of poets than to the sober annals of recorded history'. Certainly poets have done well with her. But what really prompted the expulsion of Tarquinius by Brutus and his friends? It was not an isolated act of nationalism, aimed only at driving the foreigners from Rome.

Tarquin was expelled: Etruscans remained. It belongs in a wider context, in which we see the overthrow of kings by aristocratic revolutionaries in several cities of Etruria and Greece. The Peisistratids were driven out of Athens in this same year (510 B.C.) In all such cases propaganda has blackened the names of the kings, accusing them of the crimes and savagery characteristic of tyranny—compare Livy on Tarquinius with Virgil on Mezentius of Caere. The successful oligarchs and the tyrannicides take their place in the ranks of the heroes, Brutus and Collatinus, Harmodius and Aristogeiton. They made their countries a present of *Libertas* (Freedom), that sonorous and ambivalent word that should always prompt the question 'Freedom for whom?' The immediate enlargement of the Senate and the bestowal of *imperium* on the consuls, two annually elected magistrates drawn from that order, leaves the answer in little doubt. In any case, the freedom won was precarious. There was still a party in the city that favoured the monarchy and two Etruscan expeditions are said to have tried to reimpose Tarquin. The first of these was supported by Veii and Tarquinia; the second was led by Lars Porsenna of Clusium. Livy's narrative runs with a deceptive smoothness, embellished by accounts of Roman heroism as displayed by Horatius Cocles at the bridge, Mucius Scaevola, and the brave girl Cloelia. Peace is made finally because Porsenna is so shaken by the revelation that 299 other pledged assassins were ready for him after the failure of Mucius Scaevola. But Tacitus speaks of 'the surrender of the city to Porsenna'. The real check to the Etruscans was not administered by Rome but by Aristodemus of Cumae and the forces of the Latins, who defeated the Etruscans at Aricia in 505 B.C. This victory was decisive in putting an end to Etruscan power in Latium and in preserving the infant Roman Republic against a restoration of the Tarquins.

CHAPTER 5

The conquest of peninsular Italy

FROM THE HILLS above the Tiber the infant Roman Republic looked out on a ring of enemies, actual or potential. Etruscan territory began only just across the river to the north. The mountains that bounded the entire eastern horizon were the home of warlike peoples—the Sabini, the Aequi, the Volsci—ever ready to descend into the plains. Rome was not a sea power and enemies could attack from the sea, unless they were prevented by the friendly Carthaginians. Fortunately the plain of Latium and the Alban Hills were in the hands of people of a kindred stock, the Latins. Throughout the fifth century B.C., the supreme object of Roman policy was to defend her own territory and the plain of Latium, with whatever Latin peoples were willing to stand at her side.

It was an age of small scale wars (hardly more than border raids) and small scale diplomacy. The traditional account has dignified it with such famous names as Coriolanus and Cincinnatus. In fact, personalities are uncertain and details obscure. We do not know what lies behind the story that Attus Clausus brought 5,000 people from the Sabine territory to settle in Rome in 505 B.C. Is this voluntary immigration, or a Sabine conquest in disguise? At any rate, if true, here is the origin of the *gens Claudia* in Rome—with all the consequences, good and bad. Nor do we know why, about a decade later, there was war between Rome and the Latins and the fighting of a battle at Lake Regillus. But

21

with the treaty which brought hostilities to an end (493) we seem
to be on firmer ground. For this is the famous *foedus Cassianum*
and Cicero says that the bronze tablet recording its terms was
still extant in his day. Dionysius of Halicarnassus has preserved
an abstract of these terms, by which the contracting parties make
a permanent peace between themselves and agree not to call in
foreign enemies, 'nor grant safe passage to those who shall make
war upon either, but to assist one another so far as possible when
either is at war, and each to have an equal share of the spoils and
booty taken in wars they jointly fight'. There follows the important
provision that law suits relating to private contracts be judged
within 10 days among the people where the contract was made.
This is clearly a treaty between equals, though Rome is given the
directing share in the traditional account of their joint activities
throughout the fifth century.

It is important to note that the Latins who contracted this
alliance with Rome were a group of the smaller peoples, whose
territories lay in and around the Alban Hills and who had a
common shrine at the *caput Ferentinae* in the lands of Aricia.
Tibur and Praeneste, the most powerful Latin states apart from
Rome, stood aside from the alliance, and their relations with her
were not always friendly. Shortly afterwards Rome appears to
have made a similar treaty with the highland people of the
Hernici. From this time onwards one may speak of a Triple
Alliance of Rome, the Latin League and the Hernici against the
mountain peoples. When we are told of a 'war' lasting for some
50 years (486–431 B.C.) between this Triple Alliance and the Aequi
we have to think of a period of hostilities, with more or less
sporadic fighting occurring every summer. The key to it all was
the famous pass of the Algidus through the mountains just
beyond the modern Grottaferrata. When the Aequi held the
Algidus they were in a position to raid the plains; they were not
finally ejected from it until 418 B.C. when Rome was able to
establish a garrison. It is tempting to call this the first frontier
position or *limes* in the history of Rome. In the next decade, the
southern extension of the Latin plain was liberated from the
menace of the Volsci. With the mountaineers pinned back (for a
time) in the hills, three Latin colonies were planted along the
coast.

During the fifth century B.C., Rome had made systematic but
unspectacular progress against her enemies. The century ended

with a war of a different kind—a fight to the finish against Veii. The dictator Camillus conducted a long siege which ended in 396 with Rome's first conquest of a strongly fortified Etruscan city. Veii was destroyed completely, all her territory annexed by Rome and added to the *ager Romanus*.

Before these successes could be properly exploited, Rome herself was almost paralysed by a sudden and devastating blow. Later arrivals from among the Celts who had won the valley of the Po from the Etruscans had energy left for raiding peninsular Italy. In 390 B.C. one of the more powerful tribes, the Senones, crossed the Apennines and threatened Clusium, who perhaps turned to Rome for help. The Senones advanced quickly on Rome and by the river Allia the Romans had their first encounter with the warriors of northern Europe. It was not an auspicious one; the Roman army panicked and ran away. The joint efforts of Manlius and the geese who gave the alarm are said to have saved the Capitol; at least they preserve Roman pride in the pages of Livy. After the looting and destruction of the city, the Gauls accepted the payment of ransom to go away. But they did not withdraw for good into the valley of the Po. They made many other incursions into Italy, sometimes establishing themselves upon the Alban Hills, sometimes being hired as mercenaries by the Greek cities of the south. But Rome learned from her disaster. She equipped herself with the walls and the tactics which were necessary to withstand attacks of this kind.

For some years after the Gallic siege Rome was preoccupied with her own problems. The so-called Servian Wall seems to have been completed about 378 B.C.; it at once made Rome one of the best defended of Italian cities and one of the largest, for it enclosed an area of 427 hectares. After the settlement of 367 B.C., which had for a time solved her social problems, Rome was ready to move forward again and conquer. She now did so on an unprecedented scale. The work of three generations from about 360 B.C. virtually completed her conquest of peninsular Italy. She had to fight a series of formidable wars which involved maintaining large armies in the field, with all their problems of strategy, tactics and supply. Most of these wars were fought against hostile confederacies, which in their turn kept Roman diplomacy on the stretch. There were allies to be humoured, potential enemies to be won over. There were complex problems of settlement at the end of each of these wars. In a century of hard experience, both military and political, Rome acquired the accomplishments necessary for an imperial power.

The struggle with the Latins produced the most fruitful lessons in politics. In 358 B.C. Rome seems to have been approached by the Latin League for a renewal of the *foedus Cassianum* which would give them an equality adapted to modern conditions. Rome refused and felt free to go her own way, bringing the entire coastal zone of Latium under her own control and making her first effective contacts with the Greeks of Campania. The Latins felt Rome was growing too powerful and in 340 B.C. there was a general Latin alliance againt her. Formidable in themselves, the Latins were joined by the Volsci and some of the cities of Campania. Rome had to fight a gruelling war against odds until 338 B.C. when she was in a position to impose a settlement on her own terms. These were carefully considered, and related to individual cities. Livy gives an account of them, which is of especial interest as it applies to the cities of Latium. Not only does it provide a counterpoint to the *foedus Cassianum*, but it also gives an insight into Roman procedure in handling foreign affairs. In the first place, the Senate refused to deal with the Latin League as a whole and called upon the consuls to introduce proposals for each individual city. In other words, the Latin League was dissolved. The case of Lanuvium was considered first. Its citizens received full Roman citizenship and the restoration, with certain provisions, of their religious rites. Three other deserving Latin cities were treated in the same way. Then came Tusculum, for so long the most loyal of Rome's Latin allies. Its people retained their full citizenship, but a few ringleaders were selected to bear responsibility for the rebellion. Velitrae was a bird of another feather. It had been in rebellion many times and was now due for severe punishment. Its fortifications were thrown down and the senators transferred to live north of the Tiber. A severe fine was imposed on any of them who should henceforth be caught on the wrong side of the river. Roman colonists were now settled on the lands belonging to these senators and, as a result, the city's population was as numerous as before. The Volscian city of Antium was also a special case. The Antiates had been pirates and they were now forbidden to take to the sea. Some of their ships were destroyed, the beaks of others were removed and brought to Rome to adorn the famous Comitia

Rostrata. A Roman colony was settled at Antium; the Volsci were permitted to join it if they liked and were granted Roman citizenship. Then came Tibur and Praeneste, often at odds with Rome and guilty of the heinous offence of employing Gallic mercenaries in the recent war. These offenders lost some of their territory which was added to the *ager Romanus*. Then came a most important clause, depriving the Latin cities of rights of commerce, intermarriage and common council between themselves. Each was henceforth linked direct to Rome. The Senate next turned to the cities of Campania, beginning with Capua. The aristocracy of that city had refused to join the Latins and as a reward the city was given the private rights of Roman citizenship—*civitas sine suffragio*. Two other Campanian cities earned the same rights for services rendered and it was decided that this formula should be extended to yet another two, including Cumae. What these different provisions meant in terms of status is discussed later. Here one should note the Roman method of approach. Individual cases are considered on their merits and a suitable formula devised for each. Where appropriate, a precedent thus established is extended. The whole approach is pragmatic, working from precedent to precedent. Seen in retrospect, it may give the impression of decisions taken on the basis of principle, but this is misleading. The settlement of 338 B.C. is so characteristically Roman that it is well worth while to set it out in detail.

Rome had at last stepped beyond the Mons Circeius, so long her political horizon on the south. She was involved in the destinies of Campania and the control of the best agricultural lands in all Italy. The prize was great, the cost certain to be high. Involvement in Campania made inevitable a conflict with the Samnites, by far the most formidable of all the native Italian peoples. We last saw them as one of the pastoral communities of the central Apennines. When the flocks or the warriors of such communities increased beyond a certain point, it was imperative to win new lands. In a policy of controlled expansion the Samnites had for many years been sending out bands of young warriors in search of new lands and had won for themselves much of Lucania and Apulia. Still more important, they had, after the decline of Etruscan power in Campania, pushed down into the plains and come into contact with the Greek cities there. From about 450 B.C. onwards, a brilliant Hellenic–Oscan culture had developed in

Campania, with flourishing manufacturing cities such as Capua, and also an intensive development of agriculture. Exploiting ampler resources in a richer land, it was culturally far ahead of anything that had so far grown up in Latium.

But enmity had developed between these civilised people of the Campanian plains and the Samnites of the original mountain stock. And it was the Campanians who had summoned Rome to their help. The Samnite Wars were the hardest Rome ever had to fight against an Italian people and in effect were the final struggle for mastery of the peninsula. They lasted for some 40 years (326–290 B.C.), in the course of which the Samnites inflicted on Rome some of her worst defeats—notably the trapping of a Roman army at the Caudine Forks (321 B.C.) and its surrender on humiliating terms. The Samnites forced Rome to learn mountain warfare the hard way. Rome learned to divide her army into mobile columns, able to operate in the roughest country. She learned to control the mountain passes, dividing the enemy up into isolated blocks, driving them off their winter pastures, ravaging their territory without mercy wherever it was profitable. But the Samnites did more than defend their mountain lands with vigour and tenacity. They built up great coalitions, including not only the kindred peoples of Umbria but also the Gauls and the cities of northern Etruria who thought the moment had come to exploit Rome's weakness. Rome was compelled to fight on two fronts and at times was maintaining more than 100,000 men in the field. Her generals during these years of bitter struggle learned to use the advantages of interior lines of communication. Her diplomacy managed to exploit the weaknesses of the loosely organised Samnite confederacy and to win over to her side such doughty people as the Marsi and the Paeligni, besides detaching some of the Lucanians and Apulians to fight as plainsmen against the mountaineers. Victories in the field were slow to come, but they came at last. In 295 B.C. the northern coalition was defeated at Sentinum; two years later a victory was won over the Samnites at Aquilonia. In general, I do not intend to chronicle wars, but when they are fought on such a scale, the names of at least some of the generals should be noted. Such are P. Decius Mus and L. Papirius Cursor on the side of the Romans: on the side of the Samnites there was Gellius Egnatius, who led them in war and diplomacy and who fell in the Battle of Sentinum. It is a pity that all we know of Gellius Egnatius comes from hostile sources, for there are hints that he may have risen above a Samnite patriotism to a vision of the freedom of all Italy.

Operations in the north against the Etruscans and the Gauls formed an aftermath to the Samnite Wars. It was now that Rome came to terms with the northern group of Etruscan cities, granting them treaties that could be renewed and planting colonies on Etruscan soil such as Cosa and Pisa. The Celtic tribes of the Boii and Senones, who had begun to settle in Etruria and Picenum, caused Rome a great deal more trouble and won battles against her. In the end they were both defeated, with heavy losses of their fighting strength; they lost some of their lands and transferred much of their population north of the Apennines. Land taken from the Senones was annexed to Rome as the *ager Gallicus* and in it was planted the colony of Sena Gallica and Ariminum (Rimini). The *ager Romanus* now stretched across Italy to the Adriatic and this factor was to be of vital importance in future wars in the peninsula.

By her successes against the Samnites, Rome had become a south Italian power. As such, she could not long escape being involved in the brilliant and tumultuous world of the Greek cities of Magna Graecia and Sicily. Greek civilisation was planted in those parts as early as the eighth century B.C. and found rich soil for development. In architecture and town planning, in literature and the arts, in science and rhetoric, these Western Greeks had made a major contribution. The names of Pythagoras, Empedocles and Parmenides show how vigorous was the part they played in philosophy. It is right to regard Athens as the supreme example of the Greek *polis* because she was the most creative and the most articulate; but Syracuse was the largest and in many respects the most advanced. At the beginning of the fourth century, Tarentum (Taras) was the wealthiest city on the mainland of Italy with a flourishing trade with the Eastern Mediterranean. Here were cities on a larger scale than Cumae and Neapolis. But these Western Greeks had in full measure the faults and weaknesses of Greek society. Violent class struggles and brutal despotisms had been the mark of their internal politics. Above all, they showed a calamitous tendency to quarrel with each other, instead of combining against their non-Greek enemies. So it was that the Sicilian Greeks, even when Syracuse was at her most powerful, never succeeded in dislodging the hold of Carthage on the western parts of the island—although Agathocles had come very close to doing so. Tarentum, too, although she was able to exercise a hegemony over the other Greek cities of southern Italy, could not protect them from her own resources against the Italic peoples. Indeed, she had of late made little attempt to do so, preferring to hire, in an emergency, the services of one of those mercenary generals who were abundant in the Greek world after Alexander the Great.

Pyrrhus, King of Epirus, was the foremost of these rent-an-army generals and in 280 B.C. Tarentum called him in to break the hold of Rome on southern Italy. Pyrrhus had plans of his own. He wanted to win for himself a western empire—if the cost was not too great. But Pyrrhus and Tarentum alike were anachronisms, as they would soon discover. When Roman resistance made it clear that the cost in Italy would be excessive, he turned to Sicily and tried to revive the plans of Agathocles for an all-Greek Sicily. Rebuffed in Sicily, he returned for a second attack on Rome. Again he failed—thanks to the steady courage of the Roman army and the steady resolution of the Roman Senate, braced by Appius Claudius, 'not to negotiate so long as an enemy remained on Italian soil'. So Pyrrhus returned to Epirus, leaving his name as a by-word for the kind of success that leads to failure—and a daughter married to King Hiero II of Syracuse. In the course of these wars with Pyrrhus, Rome had asserted her hegemony over Italy. Her ability to defeat a professional Hellenistic army under a famous commander had vindicated her claim.

CHAPTER 6

The Roman confederacy— settlement, colonies, roads

By 266 B.C. THE LONG and arduous conquest of peninsular Italy was complete. Unification was to be more difficult: it was not finally achieved until the time of Augustus. But, whether by accident or design, the way Rome organised her relations with the different peoples of Italy did work powerfully to promote unity. Before we look at its most important features, it may be well to repeat that they derived from a pragmatic approach to individual problems and not from any grand design.

A people defeated in war was usually required to make a formal act of surrender—to place itself, in the legal phrase, *sub dicionem populi Romani*. Its citizens were then *dediticii*, entitled to the protection (*sub fide*) of the Roman People. But this was less reassuring than its sounds. For *potestas* (full authority) tended to go along with *fides*—whatever the formula employed—and Rome reserved to herself sole rights of interpreting what *fides* might involve. Sometimes the defeated people would lose part of its lands, which then became *ager publicus populi Romani*. The land so expropriated might be used in a number of ways. Perhaps it was assigned for the planting of colonies, whether of Latin or of Roman citizens, of which more is said later. Or it might be divided individually (*viritim*) to Roman citizens in small lots, often of seven *jugera*. In other cases it might be rented out by the state, perhaps to the original holders. Grazing land especially was treated in this way, the *scriptura* or grazing tax going into the public treasury. Or land might be acquired for some special purpose. When a treaty was made with the Bruttii they gave up to Rome half their mountain lands in the Sila, whose timber

29

resources were enough to supply the demands of the whole of Italy for both ship building and house building.

After the land, the people. With some of the Latin cities, such as Tusculum or Lanuvium, integration was possible; their citizens became Romans with full privileges (*optimo iure*) and their lands were included in the territorial districts of the Roman tribes. A residual local life was left to the people of such communities, but their political future lay as Roman citizens. Other Latin communities received only the private rights of Roman citizenship—those concerned with intermarriage and commerce (*ius connubii et ius commercii*), individuals could migrate to Rome and receive full citizenship. These communities continued an autonomous local life, but were obliged to supply troops to Rome for purposes of joint defence.

The settlement with the Greek cities of Campania provided new problems: they were further away from Rome, had a long tradition of independence and spoke Greek. The solution reached was very like that of the second class of Latin communities. These Campanian citizens acquired a delimited kind of Roman citizenship (*civitas sine suffragio*) and accepted certain obligations or public duties (*munia*). Hence they were called *municipes* and their city became a *municipium*, a status that was to have a wide extension under the Empire. In the course of the Samnite wars many of the highland communities were treated in the same way. Local independence and the private rights of Roman citizenship were valuable, but many of the *municipes* must have felt, at this stage, that they had shouldered burdens rather than acquired privileges. For Rome was acting from enlightened self-interest much more than from generosity. She needed the man-power the peoples of Italy could provide: without them she could probably not have defeated Pyrrhus and would certainly have gone down to Hannibal. But the *civitas sine suffragio* was not a once-for-all grant. Full citizenship was sometimes awarded after probation, as happened to the Sabines. The concept of successful Romanisation as entitling to full privileges was thus early established.

So far, we have considered Latin and Sabellian peoples, close kin to Rome and old neighbours to the Greeks of Campania. With the Etruscans and the Greek cities of south Italy there was felt to be a greater gulf. They were granted the status of allies—*socii Italici*—contributing their own contingents in case of war but not receiving any form of Roman citizenship. For the present, they were content that so much of their independence was retained, but by the second century their exclusion from the Roman *civitas* became intolerable.

The *coloniae* served as a cement for this fabric. The colony as a political device had already had a long history: it had been used by Greeks, Etruscans and Phoenicians ever since the eighth century B.C. And, on a new and splendid scale, it had been deployed by Alexander the Great in the Greek cities he planted in the heart of Asia. But none of Rome's predecessors could match her in keeping her colonies loyal to the mother city, the faithful guardians of her interests. In the early Republic, two types of colony are to be distinguished. Down to 338 B.C., the foundations seem to have been undertaken by the Latin League; while Rome expropriated conquered land, her partner founded citizen colonies, carefully placed in newly won territory where the prospects for growth seemed good. It was open to Roman citizens to join these colonies, which usually began with 2,500 male citizens, or a total population of 7–10,000. From 338 onwards Rome herself produced garrison or fortress colonies at strategic points, such as Antium, Ostia and Sinuessa. These were much smaller (usually with 300 settlers and their families): they had no self-government and were distinctly unpopular to begin with. Latin colonies continued to be founded on the older pattern and scale down to the early second century B.C., and it was not until the settlement of Cisalpine Gaul that large colonies of Roman citizens were established, the forerunners of so many of the famous cities of Lombardy.

All these colonies in Italy served a strategic purpose: some of them also served commercial and cultural ends. A colony of farmer-soldiers is a powerful means of holding down a conquered enemy or protecting a dangerous frontier, as the *kibbutzim* of modern Israel have clearly shown. Both ends were served by the building of strategic roads. Roads and colonies are best understood from a map (see p. 33). Modern archaeology has revealed the physical aspects of some of these Italian colonies, notably at Ostia, Cosa and Alba Fucens. Ostia is the most accessible of these to the visitor, but the fourth century colony there is heavily overlaid by the great buildings of the Augustan and later city. Cosa, easily reached from the Via Aurelia between Grosseto and Rome, is more rewarding. Here the Americans have laid bare the public buildings, streets and walls of a site that occupies

33 acres on a hill rising above the Maremma and overlooking a harbour. It was a colony planted by Rome in 273 B.C. in the territory of the Etruscan city of Vulci. But Alba Fucens in its mountain setting is the most rewarding of all. Planted in 303 after the Second Samnite War, it is sited so as to dominate five valleys; its strongly defensible position (some 3,000 ft above sea-level) was occupied by the unusually large number of 6,000 families of Latin citizens. Here is a truly impressive example of the way Roman engineers handled formidable problems of forti-fication, city-planning and land-distribution. The agricultural features of these colonies are often shown up by air photography, which reveals the pattern of 'centuriation' by which Roman surveyors laid out the land in a grid pattern based on two inter-secting roads (see pl. 3). This system continued into Imperial times and at Arausio (Orange in the modern Provence) there are substantial remains of the original allotment plan recorded on a marble tablet.

The construction of the Via Appia, first of the great strategic roads, was begun in 312 B.C. in the censorship of Appius Claudius. One hundred and thirty-two miles in length, it linked Rome with Capua, the most important city of Campania. It already had the main features that mark Roman roads, standard width and construction, long straight alignments wherever possible, a standard of maintenance and repair that kept it viable in all weathers. Its top-dressing was originally of gravel, but as early as 295 B.C. a programme of paving was put in hand. The crossing of the Pomptine marshes was the chief physical obstacle it had to overcome. It always had a primacy among Roman roads, com-parable to that of the Great North Road in Britain, and its history reflects the growth of the Empire. After the war with Pyrrhus it was extended a further 234 miles to Brundisium (Brindisi): that town in the second century B.C. became the chief port for Greece and the Orient, with Dyrrhachium (Durazzo) and Apollonia as its counterparts across the Adriatic. In 130 B.C. the Via Egnatia was built to connect these Adriatic ports with Byzantium, and the route thus opened was the main artery between East and West throughout the Empire. Other great roads followed the Via Appia to build up a trunk-system in Italy: map 3 shows routes and dates of construction in the north. These roads were built by contractors (*publicani*) working to the specifications laid down by the state. A number of contracts

ARIMINUM 268

■ Sena Gallica 283

PICENUM

UMBRIA

IV

□ Firmum 264

ETRURIA

□ Narnia 299

Hadria 289

Sutrium

□ Nepet 378

III

¯273 Cosa □ □

Pyrgi ■

□ Alba Fucens 303

Carseoli
303

247 Alsium ■ Rome

□ Sora 303

245 Fregenae

LATIUM

I

□ Luceria 313

SAM

326 Terracina

Fregellae 311

388 Circeii □

296 Minturnae □

□ Beneventum 268

NIUM

296 Sinvessa

Capua

Venusia 291

II

Brundisium

□ 244

Neapolis

CAMPANIA

Tarentum

273 Paestum □

LUCANIA

BRUTTIUM

Messana

Rhegium

SICILIA

Syracuse

0   50   100 Miles

2.   Peninsular Italy. Principal colonies and roads with dates (all B.C.)

for repairs survive from the first century B.C.; they record the contractor and the public official who were parties to the contract, the length of road to be repaired, the nature of the works to be undertaken, and the sum of money provided by the treasury. It would be the duty of the official and his staff to inspect the completed work and pass it as satisfactory, as with all such contracts.

The part played by roads in the conquest and settlement of Italy was repeated as each new territory was later brought under Roman control. In Imperial times the *cursus publicus* provided an official transport system, with inns and posting-stations at regular intervals. To this period belong the *itineraria* or road-books for the use of travellers, of which a few examples survive. The road network, fully developed, linked the Roman world together, from Britain to the Syrian desert and from the Atlantic shore of Portugal to the mouth of the Danube. The consular roads of Italy lay at the heart of this huge network. Yet roads formed only a part of the communications of the Empire. It was at all times cheaper to move heavy goods by sea or river: navigable rivers such as the Rhine, the Rhône, the Po, or the Danube played an essential part in transport.

Personal ties must have counted for much in welding together Rome and the peoples of Italy. At the official level, Rome would have had to work closely with local magistrates; it is equally obvious that those known to be *persona grata* at Rome would have stood the best chance of election to office in their own communities. In many cases, they would acquire Roman citizenship after their term of office was over and many became the *clientes* of Roman statesmen. The right of intermarriage was often exercised. Most of the evidence we have for this period relates to upper-class marriages, but no doubt there was intermarriage at all levels of society. Roman citizens were to be found in Latin colonies, for example, and many Latins and other Italians took up residence in Rome: it can scarcely be supposed that their children did not mix socially. Allied soldiers serving with Roman forces and Roman troops on garrison duty in Italian towns must have contracted many unions—legal or otherwise. In all these ways a vast nexus of personal ties was built up, with Rome at the centre. No doubt centrifugal forces were strong, as they always have been in Italy. Etruscan or Greek or Samnite, there was still a local life to be lived and a local culture. Latin was spreading, but it was far from being a master language; Etruscan, Oscan and Greek were still vigorous in their own spheres. Rome as yet had little to offer in the way of culture and nothing in religion, but she was willing to learn from those who had. In such matters she could afford to be open-minded, since in other matters the tide was making towards her.

The polity thus built up in Italy was something quite new in the world. We speak of the Roman Confederation, but Rome herself had no term to describe it as a totality. *res publica populi Romani* is Rome as a city-state: *imperium populi Romani* a phrase only used after the acquisition of an overseas empire. Perhaps it is not surprising that it had no specific term in Latin, for it comprised of Rome, the Latins (including the Latin colonies), and at least 120 allied communities having treaty relations with Rome. The whole is estimated to have comprised of 130,000 sq. kilometres (more than 50,000 sq. miles), of which not more than 30,000 can have been *ager Romanus*, allowing perhaps another 12,000 for Latin colonies, and almost 90,000 for the allies. Allied territory was thus three times as large as that of Rome, with a population perhaps twice as large, giving a total of rather more than four million inhabitants. Commanding resources such as these, Rome was now a force to be reckoned with in the Mediterranean world, and diplomatic relations were established with Rhodes and Egypt. The treaty with Carthage was revised in 278 B.C. (perhaps also in 306). The object, it seems, was to define spheres of influence, and it is probable but not certain that Rome was recognised as having predominant rights in Italy and Carthage in Sicily. If the attempt was made to establish the Straits of Messina as the boundary between the two spheres of influence, it would not last for long.

It must have been some time in the decade following 290 B.C. that the Roman government first set before itself the aim of conquering the whole of peninsular Italy. It is almost certain that, prior to 290 B.C., it had no wish to go further. Yet the clarity of hindsight reveals how her experiences during the conquest of Italy preconditioned Rome for the empire of the Mediterranean world. The partnership with the Latins was fruitful in many ways. It accustomed her to taking the field at the side of allies, in support of their interests as well as her own. 'Our empire', said Cicero in the first century B.C., 'was acquired in defending our allies'— and it is possible that he believed it. With them she learned the concept of a Roman citizenship that could be fully extended to people of a common language and culture, or offered to other communities on probation, suitably graded, and with the prospect of advance. Already it was accepted that a man might have two loyalties—to his own *patria* and to Rome. Already there was a *pax Romana* in the territory under her control, opening new prospects for commerce and development. On the soil of Italy she had encountered cultures higher than her own in the Greeks and the Etruscans. In the struggles with the Boii and the Senones she had learned the strengths and the weaknesses of the barbarian peoples of Central Europe. On the soil of Italy, her armies had learned to fight in different kinds of terrain; her engineers had driven roads through mountains, forest, and swamp. Her dealings with other peoples had developed a pattern which was later enlarged rather than diversified. She could always work up indignation against an enemy whose behaviour might be construed as a breath of faith (*fides*). She could systematically terrorise as an act of policy, witness the ravaging of the lands of the Samnites, and the blotting out of Veii and Fidenae. Yet a defeated opponent—and especially one who had fought well—was often offered surprisingly generous terms. Indeed, in the use of the weapon of calculated generosity, she was more adroit than any other power of classical times.

CHAPTER 7

The Roman Republic— internal politics

DURING THESE YEARS, the political machinery of the Roman state underwent a long and complicated process of development and adjustment. The result was the constitution whose workings Polybius saw and admired in the first half of the second century B.C., though it had been operational since 287. It had three major components—the Magistrates, the Senate, and the People. The magistrates represented the executive; their functions were carefully prescribed, and their powers limited by holding office for a year and working beside colleagues with equal powers. The two consuls were the supreme officers of the state, presiding over meetings of the Senate, holding supreme command in war, and for much of the period actually commanding armies in the field. The praetors had charge of the administration of the law; one of them, the *praetor peregrinus* (created *c.* 242 B.C.), having special responsibility for legal cases in which foreigners were involved. The censor, originally appointed as registrars and mainly for the purpose of assessment of taxes, soon acquired the supervision of public contracts and a wide though vague jurisdiction on questions of morals. The aediles were in charge of public works, streets and buildings within the city of Rome. The quaestors exercised supervision over public finances. The great and growing powers of the Senate rested on its ability to initiate legislation, to prolong the powers of magistrates and to control foreign affairs; they were further enhanced by the collective influence, wealth and experience of its members. The people in their various assemblies elected the magistrates, approved or rejected bills laid before them and decided on issues of peace or war. In theory, the principle of sovereignty was vested in them, but they only met when summoned by a magistrate and voted without discussion on what was laid before them, though they might have heard it explained at a special meeting or *contio*.

Polybius himself was well versed in the theory and practice of Greek politics and his admiration for the constitution of Republican Rome was very high. He saw it as the most impressive example of the virtues of a Mixed Constitution—the people standing for democracy, the Senate for oligarchy or aristocracy and the consuls for monarchy. There was an elaborate system of checks and balances between each of the three components which would make for stability. And in the harmony and stability of its constitution, Polybius saw one of the major factors in Rome's rise to world empire. The analysis is lucid, schematic, and misleading. He was, of course, handicapped by his frame of reference, for he saw everything in terms of Greek politics. We suffer under the same disadvantage when we use political terms of Greek derivation. For example, it can only be misleading to talk of 'democracy' in Rome. Democracy means the rule of the *demos*, or 'people'. But in the first place the 'Roman People' was a much more heterogeneous body than the *demos* of a Greek *polis*. And in the second place the Roman People did not wish to rule the Roman state; rather did they wish to be able to protect themselves against the abuse of power from those who did rule it. Polybius is at pains to compare the Roman constitution with those of Sparta and Carthage. But the comparisons are not very illuminating. The truth is that the Roman political experience can only be understood in its own terms. If we knew more than we do about the politics of the other Latin cities, we might have a clearer picture of at least the early stages of development in the Roman Republic.

As it is, the best approach towards the problem is undoubtedly that of the elder Cato who observed that the Roman Republic 'was not made by the work of one man, but of many; not in a single lifetime, but over many centuries and by many generations'. It was shaped, in fact, through the problems and strains of the long struggle between the Orders—between the patrician aristocracy and the *plebs*. This famous political struggle has occasioned controversy between scholars which has itself been almost as bitter, if not quite so protracted. The trouble is that when we look at the historical accounts of the events of fifth and fourth centuries B.C. we see that they have been written in terms of the political struggle in the times of the Gracchi. It is as though all we knew of the English Civil War of the seventeenth century came from historians who wrote of it in terms of the struggles for Parliamentary reform in the nineteenth. I shall here give no more than an outline of the struggle between the Orders. Details must be sought in the numerous political histories of the period where there is space to analyse the sources.

In the period after the Decemviri in the middle of the fifth century B.C. the patricians had a monopoly of the political, social and economic power. We do not really know the origins of the deep cleavage between them and the *plebs*. The latter represented a broad range of interests, from landless peasant and resourceless debtors to wealthy families who wanted to break into the charmed circle of the patricians. Their first effective demonstration was made when the *plebs* threatened to leave Rome and set up a state of their own. The threat of secession, though repeated more than once, was never carried out. The second effective demonstration was made when the *plebs* set up their own political organisation, the *concilium plebis*, and their own officers, the tribunes, whom they swore to protect against any violence, and who ultimately acquired a power of veto over the acts of any Roman magistrate. Here was a state within the state and political thinkers of the first century such as Cicero saw it as designed for the purpose of sedition. From the time of the Gracchi onwards there was material to support this thesis. But for the *plebs* of the fifth century B.C. the object was to acquire protection against unjust and arbitrary acts of the Senate and magistrates. This protection was made more effective when they had procured publication of a written code of law—the famous Twelve Tables of 450 B.C. Soon after this the rights of the tribunes were legally defined and when in 445 B.C. the right of intermarriage between patricians and plebeians was recognised in the *Lex Canuleia* the wealthier plebeians had a major grievance removed. From this date until the time of the Gallic invasion the heat had been taken out of the struggle between the Orders. In the economic distress after 390 B.C. the question of the just distribution of public lands was one of the main issues. In 367, after a protracted struggle, the *Lex Licinia Sextia* established some limits (the details are uncertain) on the amount of land to be held by any one person. The other main issue was that of admission of plebeians to the highest magistracies—again an objective which could only have been of interest to the wealthier plebeians. Licinius himself became the first plebeian consul in 366 B.C., and by 351 all the magistracies had been held by plebeians. The *Lex Poetelia* of 326(?) abolished imprisonment for debt and opened a system of state mortgages for land. Finally, by the *Lex Hortensia* of 287 decrees (*plebiscita*) of the *Concilium plebis* were to have the force of law.

The various interests represented in the *plebs* had, for the time being, gained all their ends. The struggle between the Orders went into abeyance for a century and a half. When it broke out again, it would be on new issues and with a new alignment of contestants.

Roman sources stress that the entire contest over some five generations was carried out with no bloodshed and with the minimum of violence. It is common to pay tribute to the political good sense of a society in which this could be done. Credit where it is due must not be withheld. But once again the factor of enlightened self-interest can be invoked. Rome lived in a world of enemies, and each of the parties in this internal political dispute needed the other. The patricians needed the numbers and courage of the common people to defend the state in war, the *plebs* needed the leadership and experience of the patricians. It is true that, in the insensate fury of the class struggle, Greek city-states were only too apt to forget an enemy at the gates. But in the Roman Republic, as yet, there was a readiness for compromise and common sense. Furthermore, where the Greeks were fatally apt to conduct their political disputes in terms of principles (and in the spirit which later made martyrs and heresiarchs), at Rome political disputes arose over practical issues.

The sequel to the struggle between the Orders shows clearly how Roman politics can be understood in no other terms but their own. The coalition that had won the victory of 287 B.C. dissolved. The wealthier plebeians 'passed over' to the other side to form a new nobility, comprised of men who had held the high offices of state and their posterity, for a consul ennobled his descendants. It was this new nobility, filling the magistracies and controlling the Senate, that perpetuated oligarchic rule at Rome to the middle of the first century B.C. For although by the settlement of 287 B.C. the *plebs* had gained the means of running the state as a democracy, they did not choose to exercise it. They had neither the wish nor the time to do so; moreover, this situation cannot be explained simply by considering its constitutional forms. Private ties cut across political lines of division: most notably the relationship of patron and dependant that constituted the Roman *clientela*.

CHAPTER 8

The Roman Republic—social and economic conditions

THE CLIENTELA SYSTEM appears among the earliest Roman social institutions, for it can be traced back to the regal period. In its primitive form, it was a simple, personal relationship of mutual obligation between the *patronus*, a powerful aristocrat, and his dependants or *clientes*, men of humble rank. The *patronus* would look after the interests of his *clientes* if they went to law, lend money, give advice, and would act as ward to their children if they were orphaned. The *clientes* would give him political support, attending him on state occasions in visible token of his public standing. It was a kind of extended and hereditary family relationship, and as such, heavily charged with emotion and the sense of duty (*pietas*). Like so many other Roman institutions, its scope was enlarged and its nature altered—but the name remained the same. The political aspects had come to predominate by the third century B.C. and the more powerful noble families organised their *clientelae* as standing political 'interests', ready to deliver a vote when called on.

With the conquest of Italy the *clientela* system was extended to the Italian allies. The overseas conquests of the second century B.C. enabled victorious generals and governors to develop provincial *clientelae*, which included whole communities as well as political leaders. Even this did not exhaust the mutations. Freedmen naturally took as *patroni* the owners who had given them their freedom and by the first century B.C. manumission of slaves was on a very large scale indeed. More important still were the military *clientelae* acquired by such generals as Marius, Sulla and Pompey over their veteran soldiers. By this time the *clientelae* of the leading political figures would reach to every level of society and operate as a fief within the state, as ready to advance personal ambitions as that which sustained the heady career of Essex in Elizabethan England. But this is to anticipate. In the early Republic, the importance of the *clientelae* is that they operated to foster the power of the nobility and to inhibit the growth of a true democratic party. This they did although many of the plebeians were not involved in such a relationship.

The basis of the Roman economy at this time was small-scale farming carried on by family units, the owner and his sons working a few acres (7 *iugera* is a figure often mentioned). Such peasant holdings antedate the agricultural handbooks and so far have not been explored by archaeology. They would cultivate the coarser cereals, especially spelt (*triticum*) and emmer (*far*) and keep a few livestock for milk, wool and hides. It was subsistence farming and not very productive. But one crop did grow well— men. The peasants who worked these lands were the soldiers who served in Rome's army, the *mascula proles* whom Horace rightly saw as the backbone of the old republic. The nobility had larger estates and were putting money into new agricultural methods, but nothing like the *latifundia* of the second century B.C. had developed as yet. Pyrrhus had been impressed by the well farmed land he saw as he invaded Latium in 280 B.C., with vine-yards and orchards and a high standard of farming. This certainly suggests full-time bailiffs and possibly slave labour, but not what Cato was writing about a hundred years later. Even at the start of the second century B.C., such magnates as Scipio Africanus were not above working their own lands.

The surprisingly late development of coined money at Rome argues a primitive economy. Modern research, indeed, puts it even later than was once supposed. Although the appointment of *tresviri monetales* in 289 B.C. attests a mint, they were at first concerned with stamping copper currency bars (*aes signatum*) of six pounds weight. The first true coins, the silver *didrachms* of 269, imitations of Greek issues, were designed for trade with south Italy. The silver *denarius* did not appear till after the Second Punic War.

Very few private inscriptions survive from this period, and almost all the literary evidence we have for social life relates to the upper classes. Here a salient feature is the importance of the *gens* or clan. A man saw himself in terms of the *gens* of which he was a member, measuring his conduct by the standards of his ancestors (*maiores*), hoping by his own achievements to add to the glory of the *gens* and serve as an example to posterity. The *imagines* or portraits of his ancestors were kept in the household as example and witness; worn by mourners, they followed him to the grave. It is something quite alien to our own society, though perhaps it might be understood in the Highlands of Scotland. Achievement was measured almost wholly in terms of public service in peace and war. No class in history can have been so devoted to politics as the nobility of the Republic. To hold office and especially the consulship, to lead armies to victory, to command respect in the Senate, were the objects which generation after generation set before themselves as the *summum bonum*.

The famous epitaphs of the Scipios, which begin with the L. Cornelius Scipio Barbatus who was consul in 298 B.C. and extend over a period of almost one hundred and fifty years, are eloquent of the outlook of the *gens Cornelia*. There is an unchanging belief in inherited virtues, in the prime duty of public service, an insistence on *virtus, gloria, honos,* and *fama*. The semantics of these words in Latin are confused and confusing; a recent study has been of service in showing how their primary meanings are political, to which ethical concepts became attached at a later stage. But the Cornelii Scipiones, for so long the most illustrious of Roman *gentes*, were for that very reason untypical, since they produced brilliant individuals who threatened to break free from the conventional mould. No such charge could be levelled against the Caecilii Metelli, whose combination of high social standing, political power and vigorous conservatism of outlook was impeccable. And, by good fortune, Pliny has preserved the gist of the funeral oration pronounced by his son for the most eminent of the line—the L. Caecilius Metellus, twice consul, and Pontifex Maximus, who distinguished himself in the First Punic War and died in 221 B.C.—'To him, and to him alone since the foundation of Rome, fell the ten achievements, the ten objects which men regard as the most desirable. He was a warrior of the first rank, an excellent orator, a most courageous general: under his auspices deeds of the greatest importance were accomplished: he attained the highest offices in the state: he was distinguished for his wisdom: he held primacy in the Senate: he won a large fortune by honourable means: he left behind many children: he was the most famous man in the Commonwealth.'

It is a purely Roman formulation, untouched by any taint of Greek philosophy or ethics. Of the ten desirable ends, eight are concerned with public, two with private, life. Of the latter, the reference to wealth is worded soberly and discreetly—*magnas res bono modo invenire*. The superlative is carefully avoided, the honourable means stressed; the verb *invenire* in this context means 'to acquire', but carries overtones of stumbling upon or finding. One hesitates to speak of money in so fine a gentleman: enough that it was honourably acquired!

With these values, the Roman nobility was conservative and backward looking, admiring conformity rather than originality in an individual. It was a pattern that proved highly effective in its own context. When Roman expansion brought it into contact with the luxury and sophistication of the Hellenistic world, its limitations would be alarmingly exposed.

Private life was centred on the family—the natural biological unit of husband, wife, and unmarried children, together with the slaves or freedmen who lived with them under the same roof. Within it, law and custom vested an absolute authority in the father (*paterfamilias*). He had control of the family property and his *patriapotestas* gave him powers of life and death over its members. How early and how widely this archaic severity became diluted we do not know. There are improving stories of fathers exercising their rights over disloyal sons in the early Republic, and apparently even under the Empire an unfaithful wife could never be quite sure that the worst might not happen. And in one very important respect—towards new-born children—*patriapotestas* continued to be practised in all its vigour. The new-born child was laid at the father's feet by the hearth: not till he picked it up in token of acceptance was it certain that it would live and be reared. To the father fell the duties of maintaining the family cults, the *Penates* who looked after the house and the store cupboard, the *Lares* and the several agricultural deities who presided over the farm, its animals and crops.

The position of women in Roman life at this time was a complicated matter which we cannot examine in detail here. Legally, a woman did not exist in her own right: as a girl she was under the guardianship (*in manu*) of her father, as a married woman under that of her husband. But there were ways round these legal disabilities, especially for Roman wives. From the third century onwards the commonest form of marriage bond was one which allowed the woman control of her own property after the age of 25 and which made divorce an easy matter. And in its daily life, a Roman marriage was very much a partnership of equals. After the first night with her husband the young bride took part in the religious cults of the family; from then on she was mistress of the house (*domina*). She ran the household, supervised the servants, prepared the food and brought up the children until they went to school. Making clothes for the entire family from homespun wool was general at this period and this was done under her management. *Lanam fecit* is the tribute in many a Roman matron's epitaph. She led an active social life, going about the city to visit her friends and acting as hostess at dinner parties at home. This equality did not, of course, extend to public life. A woman could neither vote nor sit on a jury: it was unthinkable that she should take part in politics. Even in their sophisticated days, the Romans were astonished to find sovereign queens in other nations—a Cleopatra, a Boudicca, or a Zenobia. But women's influence was not determined by their legal status and rights. 'We rule the world', Roman statesmen were to say later, 'and our wives rule us.' A Roman wife might have thought the humour a little forced. But a recent study of Roman women has compared their status to that of women in Victorian England. And in that period, before emancipation, in the full sense, it was usually her own fault if a woman let herself be repressed.

It should again be said that the social life thus described is that of the upper classes for which alone we have evidence. Whether the life of the common people was a diminished version of theirs, or whether it had distinctive features of its own, we do not know.

By contrast, there is a good deal known about Roman religion at this period and its character is well understood. The ancient sacral calendars survive in several versions and many of the archaic features of religious ritual lasted almost to the end of paganism. There is a good deal of literary evidence, notably in the *Fasti* of Ovid and in Varro and Macrobius. The mark of public and private cults alike was the legalistic approach—*ius divinum*, the law of the gods, was very close to *ius civile*. Here again the principle of enlightened self-interest may be invoked. Recognising the existence of supernatural powers, the Roman was anxious to place himself and his country in the right relationship with them and to make a bargain or compact for a mutual exchange of services. 'Enlightenment' was to be derived from a knowledge of how and when to approach a divinity, the correct ritual to be observed, the acceptable sacrifice to be offered. Thus at one end of the scale the Roman State maintained the worship of Jupiter in the most magnificent of its temples, with a permanent priesthood headed by the *Flamen Dialis* and a round of festivals and banquets, most notably the *Ludi Romani*. In return, Jupiter was counted on to secure victory for Roman armies and their commanders and to foster the extension of Roman power. In the greatest of all Roman ceremonies, victorious generals who had been accorded the honour of a triumph offered to him their thanks and the choicest of their spoils. (Of the organisation of these triumphs, their use as political propaganda and their influence on art and architecture, we shall have more to say.) On a humbler level we have the peasant offering a cake to Faunus for the fertility of his flock, or honouring Priapus with a wooden statue on behalf of the vegetables in his kitchen garden.

The State cults were under the general charge of the great priestly colleges, headed by the Pontifex Maximus. As well as for Jupiter, there were special priests (*flamines*) for Mars and for Quirinus, the deified Romulus, besides twelve lesser *flamines* for a minor pantheon of Etruscan and Latin divinities. The cult of Vesta, the living flame that stood for the continuity of the State and was maintained by the only Roman order of priestesses, was unique. There were other specialist priestly colleges such as that of the augurs (*augures*), who sought to interpret the will of the gods from signs, especially the flight of birds; the *haruspices*, whose science derived from the Etruscans, who interpreted the markings on the entrails of victims, and the *fetiales*, who concerned themselves with the rituals for declaring war and concluding peace. Roman magistrates were guided by the advice of these specialists in *ius divinum*. In all these cults, the highest importance was attached to the exact performance of ceremony and to the proper recital of formulae. Any infraction or slip invalidated what had taken place. The Roman respect for the plighted word, and readiness to perform obligations, undertaken on oath, struck Greek observers like Polybius as an admirable contrast to Greek laxity in such matters. But its roots lay in legalism and not in ethics; a bargain had been made, and its terms must be carried out.

The great gods of the Roman pantheon were anthropomorphic:

they had temples and cult statues: they existed in a divine social order and mythology was concerned with their personalities and their deeds. But Roman religion also dealt in relations with another order of supernatural being, the *numina*, depersonalised spirits presiding over some strictly limited field of nature or of human life. A battery of such functionaries looked after cereals; Proserpina presiding over seeds, Nodutus over stems, Patelana over opened sheaths, Flora over the grain in flower, Lacturnus when it was full of milk, Matula when it was ripe, Runcina when it was removed from the ground and Tutilina when it was stored in the barn. St. Augustine describes the workings of this unseen bureaucracy in all its minutiae with frigid contempt. For to him religion must be concerned with morals and with the life of the spirit and the old Roman religion had little to do with either. But at least it was not exclusive; it had from the beginning accepted Etruscan and Greek divinities, as it would later those of the Celtic and the Oriental world. And when, under the later Empire, the great universal religions swept over the Roman world from the East, the moral deficiencies of the native cults provided them with an open field.

The scanty evidence suggests a considerable growth in the urban population of Rome, especially in the early decades of the fourth century B.C. By 264 it may have been in the range 100–150,000, Capua would be about the same size, Tarentum perhaps 200,000, and Syracuse, the greatest Greek city of the West, close to 500,000. But although Rome was the political capital of Italy, her architecture and public amenities did not reflect her position. The rebuilding of the city after the Gallic invasion was left to private enterprise and pushed through at top speed; later generations were to lament the loss of a unique opportunity for town planning. But in fact no great schemes of urban renewal or development were put in hand in Rome before the first century B.C. Building during the early Republic was undertaken *ad hoc*, to serve public utility or the religious and commemorative needs of the State. With the prohibition of private dwellings on the Capitol in 384 B.C., that hill became reserved for temples and shrines, apart from the Citadel. The Forum Romanum was the centre of political life. The Senate met regularly in the Curia Hostilia and the people gathered in the Comitium to be addressed by speakers from the Rostra. Public spectacles, banquets and gladiatorial contests were also held here. Some of the most venerable temples and shrines were in the Forum. At the west end were the Temple of Saturn and the altar of the Fire-god Volcanus. In the centre were the Temple of Castor, the pool and healing shrine of Juturna, the round Temple of Vesta with the House of the Vestal Virgins, and the Regia, the headquarters of the Pontifex Maximus, where the records of the priestly colleges were kept—the whole making a group to rival that on the Capitol.

The Forum was still important as a shopping and commercial centre, though some specialised trades had moved elsewhere—cattle and sheep to the Forum Boarium, vegetables to the Forum Holitorium. The Campus Martius, being liable to floods, was not built upon, but served for sports or for military training. Aesculapius was established in his temple on the Tiber Island in 291 B.C., on a site chosen by the sacred serpent sent to Rome from Epidaurus. The Circus Maximus, in the valley between the Palatine and the Aventine, was the only permanent building for public entertainment. Private houses of the poor clustered thickly in the valleys between the Esquiline and the Quirinal, and slum conditions were already established in the Subura and the Vicus Tuscus. The nobility were moving upwards to the purer air of the Palatine and the Esquiline plateaux, though as yet their houses were neither large nor elaborate. A notable public amenity was the first aqueduct, the Aqua Appia (another great piece of civil engineering sponsored in the censorship of Appius Claudius), bringing water to the city in a covered conduit over a distance of ten miles. A second, the Anio Vetus, followed in 272 B.C. The whole city was included within the Servian Wall and its fourteen (?) gates: there was as yet no settlement across the river.

In so large a city there was obviously work for a wide variety of craftsmen and traders. Unfortunately, in this period there is very little known about their activities. The supply of food and its distribution must have involved butchers, bakers, market gardeners, fishmongers, wine merchants and innkeepers. Stone cutters, masons, carpenters, plumbers, ironworkers, painters, surveyors and carters, were needed for building. Rome was an agricultural centre: there would have been makers of farming instruments of all kinds, leatherworkers, dealers in horses, mules, and donkeys, money-lenders and money-changers. Boatmen, ferrymen, bargees, fishermen, ship chandlers and porters worked on the river and its quays. There were common carriers for the transport of heavy freight by land. It is premature to speak of luxury, but there was already scope for jewellers, goldsmiths, silversmiths, perfume sellers, makers of wreaths and garlands. A few professions were becoming established, notably those of the architect, lawyer, and schoolmaster. Doctors were few and those not highly skilled. As yet there could have been few professionals in sport or public entertainment. There were few slaves and the demands of the market were largely met by free labour. All these occupations—and there must have been many more—seem to have been on a small scale, with little in the way of organisation. We hear nothing, as yet, of the *collegia* or trade associations which were such a feature of the Empire.

One cannot leave this formative period of Roman history without a word of regret that the evidence for it is so meagre, and that so much of it is not first hand. Such as it is, it depicts a society still largely agricultural, narrow and conventional in its outlook, the interests almost wholly directed to practical ends. But can we be sure that this is a true picture? Later writers had a vested interest in purveying just such an idea of archaic simplicity, investing ancestral custom (*mores maiorum*) in the colours of an untainted virtue that may not be authentic. There are at least hints of wider cultural interests. For example, Livy records the stir made by a performance of a ballet by Etruscan dancers in the year 364 B.C. Now enough is known from the tomb-paintings to suggest that Etruscan dancing was subtle, even erotic and sensuous; its appreciation would seem to call for refined taste. But if Etruscan ballet might be thought exotic, Roman oratory was a medium which the native genius had developed to a high level. The famous speech in which Appius Claudius denounced the negotiations with Pyrrhus was still extant in the first century B.C., and is not likely to have been the only example of contemporary oratory to survive. It looks as though the Romans, for public purposes, had evolved an artistic prose before there were Greek rhetoricians in Rome to tell them how to do it.

At a much lower level, the complete disappearance of the Atellane farce and the popular performances known as *satura* have left us bereft of what would have been valuable evidence for social life. The Atellane farces were of Oscan origin, and seem to have been an adaptation of the 'Doric' comedies of Sicily and Magna Graecia. They were masked performances, presenting stock characters in comic and bawdy situations. The *satura* was of Roman origin (or so we are told) and perhaps the music-hall of nineteenth century England comes closest to what is known of it. Unfortunately, it was too ephemeral and casual to be thought worth preserving. But any possibilities of development latent in these forms of popular entertainment were not to burgeon. For the great change of taste was impending which resulted from contact with Greek literature in all its plenty. The full impact was not to come until the second century, but its beginnings fall within this period. Among the spoils of war sent from Tarentum in 272 B.C. was a 12-year-old boy called Andronicus. He was sold as a slave into the household of M. Livius Salinator and became a tutor to the boys of the family and their friends. Greek boys for centuries had been brought up on the poems of Homer, and Andronicus decided to introduce this best of all school books at Rome, though it meant making his own translation. Why he chose the *Odyssey* instead of the *Iliad* we do not know. But Livius Andronicus' Latin version of the *Odyssey*, the first work of literature to be translated into Latin, appeared in 240 B.C. From this school book derives the whole corpus of Latin literature written on the Greek model.

PART III · ROME AND THE CONQUEST OF THE MEDITERRANEAN WORLD
(264–133 B.C.)

THIS SECTION COVERS a period of a little more than 130 years, which may fairly claim to be the most decisive in the whole of Roman history. When it began Rome was in control of peninsular Italy and had just defeated Pyrrhus. When it ended she was a super-power, in direct control of much of the Mediterranean world and able to enforce her will in any part of it. In military terms, indeed, the decisive period was shorter still; as the Greek historian Polybius rightly said it was the 50 years between the outbreak of the Second Punic War in 218 and the defeat of Macedon at the battle of Pydna in 168 B.C. We have seen that the Romans had no collective label for what we now call the Roman Confederacy in Italy. But they had no doubt as to the nature of the Mediterranean Empire that succeeded it. It was *imperium populi Romani*, the Empire of the Roman People. Yet modern concepts of imperialism do little to explain it. There was no grand strategy of acquiring territory to serve the prestige of Rome. Where economic motives can be identified, they seem to come into play after expansion, not before. The struggle between Rome and Carthage was a straight fight in which victory went to the side that could hold out longer: its only peculiarity is that it was fought to the death. It is the ease with which Rome overcame the great Hellenistic powers that has surprised observers, in ancient as in modern times. Whatever the reasons, in this period Rome discarded the role of an Italian power and became the ruler of a Mediterranean Empire. The consequences were to be worked out over the next three centuries. Slowly and painfully, the political institutions of Rome were transformed from those of a city-state to a world empire. Less painful, because partly unconscious, was the change by which Roman society acquired the features of a universal society. Cultural change was more rapid. During this period Rome received the full impact of Hellenism, and her response was such that a new Greco-Roman civilisation came into being.

53

CHAPTER 9

The struggle with Carthage

SO FAR AS IS KNOWN, Carthage had no literature or historians; posterity can only see her through the eyes of her enemies, even though something of the pro-Carthaginian Greek historian Philinus has filtered through to the narrative of Polybius. But at least the main features of the maritime empire of Carthage are known and they reveal a society almost unique in the classical world. In the eighth century B.C. the ancient Phoenician cities of Tyre, Akko, Sidon and Byblos had been among the most vigorous colonisers in the Western Mediterranean, to which it seems they were originally drawn by trade with Tartessos, the mysterious kingdom which was the first to exploit the mineral wealth of Spain. A string of Phoenician colonies and trading posts was planted along the coast of North Africa from Tripoli to Morocco, in Corsica and Sardinia, western Sicily and at Gades (Cadiz) beyond the Straits of Gibraltar.

Carthage soon became the most flourishing of these colonies, no doubt because of her superb position commanding the 90-mile-wide sea passage between Cape Bon and western Sicily (a little less than the distance from Southampton to Cherbourg). Virgil was right in describing Carthage as situated 'opposite Italy' (*Italiam contra*): with a strong navy she could shut off the Western Mediterranean and turn it into a Carthaginian lake. By the fourth century B.C. she had virtually achieved this. Her only challenger at sea was the powerful Greek city of Massilia, which kept open the important sea-ways to the mouths of the Rhône. But Carthage had the monopoly of trade with Spain, and control of the approaches to the Straits of Gibraltar and the exit to the Atlantic. She had all but strangled the Greek colonies in Spain, and would probably have done the same to Massilia but for the fatal clash with Rome. While her navy policed the Western Mediterranean, the merchant fleet of Carthage carried on a highly lucrative commerce in which the raw materials of Spain and Africa were exchanged for the manufactured goods of Egypt and the Levant. The profits thus earned made Carthage the wealthiest mercantile city (it is said) in the Mediterranean world, and while some of her money went to finance spectacular voyages of exploration around Africa, most of it was used to extend her trade, to develop high farming in the Bagradas Valley, and to assert her control over the native African peoples of the hinterland.

Carthage proper was a city of perhaps 400,000 inhabitants, protected by a belt of powerful fortifications more than twenty miles in length, longer than the Wall of Aurelian which protected Rome in the Late Empire. Little is known archaeologically of the Punic city; the literary sources speak especially of the two splendidly equipped harbours and the wealthy shrines of Tanit and Eshmoun. Her hegemony over the other Punic colonies was loyally accepted—a contrast to the relations which usually prevailed between Greek cities in the West. But her relations with the indigenous peoples (the Libyans and Numidians) were notably poor: she was successful neither in conquest nor assimilation. Here her record compares unfavourably with that of Rome and reveals her great military weakness. Her armies were made up of mercenaries, not of her own citizens. She could afford the best mercenaries, it is true—Spaniards, Gauls, Africans—but money cannot win the loyalties of a mercenary army. They can be won only by the personality of a great commander, and in Hamilcar, Hasdrubal, and, above all, in Hannibal, it was lucky indeed for Carthage that she produced a succession of generals of the stature required.

Such was the adversary with whom Rome was about to enter on a protracted struggle, with life or death as the stakes. Its nature is, so far, unparalleled in history. In less than 120 years Rome and Carthage fought three great wars, and there were 42 years of actual hostilities. The First Punic War (264-241 B.C.) was the greatest war yet fought, notable for its huge naval battles and enormous losses of manpower. The Second (218-202 B.C.) was on a yet greater scale: at one stage Rome seemed almost defeated, but she rallied to defeat Carthage overwhelmingly and reduce her to impotence. The consequences of this war left an indelible mark on the victors. The devastation of southern Italy was such that never again has that area been the most advanced and civilised part of the peninsula. The Third Punic War (149–146 B.C.) was a tragic finale in which Carthage, reduced and humiliated as she was, was provoked to war and annihilated by her pitiless adversary.

These dire consequences cannot, of course, have been foreseen when the two powers first clashed in 264 B.C. The immediate issue was a trivial one, whether Rome should protect some disreputable Campanian mercenaries who had settled at Messina and appealed for her help against Carthage. Behind it lay the larger but not insoluble problem of the control of Sicily. The Senate, uncharacteristically, made no recommendation but left the decision of peace and war to a vote of the Popular Assembly. In voting for war, that body had as little idea of what it would mean as did the cheering crowds in the capital cities of Europe in August 1914. And indeed, as so often in the history of wars, the reasons for the appalling mutations they undergo are to be sought less in any rational considerations of interests or strategy than in the psychology of the combatants. It is easy to see that Carthage felt that the successful challenge to her sea power by Rome in the First Punic War threatened the whole basis of her existence. As for Rome, she had put forth such efforts to eject Carthage from Sicily that she was glad to take the chance that presented itself, shortly after the peace treaty, to push her out of Sardinia and Corsica as well. This opportunity arose when Carthage was engaged in the Truceless War against her own mercenaries—a struggle whose atrocities were without parallel in ancient times. Having learnt in this war to stick at nothing and embittered by the loss of Corsica and Sardinia, Carthage was obsessed with a war of revenge, which became the prime object of her policy between 241 and 218 B.C. The great work of colonisation carried out in Spain during those years (under the leadership of the generals of the House of Barca, Hamilcar, Hasdrubal, and Hannibal), provided the means and the strategy. Spanish wealth and Spanish manpower went to provide an army which could be led overland to smash Rome. In the Second Punic War this grand strategy came so near to success that Rome was left with a neurotic fear of Carthage. Fifty years later this neurosis found an outlet and Carthage was wiped out.

T.R.—F

The Second Punic War was the greatest of all wars fought in antiquity. It is probably the best recorded and certainly the most dramatic in the variety of its battles and sieges, as in the vicissitudes of the fortunes of war. All this and its long duration give it an epic quality. The finality of its outcome is that of some great and inexorable tragedy. No summary can fully bring out these qualities; they are best apprehended from the reading of a good and detailed account. I shall here attempt no more than to indicate some of the main themes.

From first to last, this great war was dominated by the military genius and indomitable energy of Hannibal. He had trained, assembled and led from Spain the great army of 40,000 men which was to crush Rome. He put into practice the daring plan of invading Italy from the north, breaking through the barrier of the Alps which had been thought impassable for a large army. In the great campaigns of his first three years in Italy he won a sequence of classic victories—Trebia, Trasimene, Cannae—a devastating *crescendo* of offensive power. Later, he maintained himself for 14 years in his base in southern Italy in the face of vastly superior numbers and never lost the loyalty of his polyglot army. Even when he was in exile after the defeat of Carthage, his name could make the Roman Senate shake in its resolve.

On the Roman side, one should first remark on the adoption of 'Fabian tactics' (a scorched earth policy and avoidance of pitched battles), when it was realised that Hannibal could not be faced in the field. Next, the firm resolution shown in the darkest hours of the war after the defeat at Cannae. Rome maintained several fronts, in Spain, in Sicily and finally in Africa, as well as containing Hannibal in Italy. It is impressive to see how men and supplies went to Spain and Sicily, when the obvious but more timid approach would have been to pull back everything for the defence of Rome. In siegecraft, where Hannibal met with little success, Rome was able to take Capua and Syracuse, the best defended city of the time. When at long last Rome was able to pass to the offensive (after 211 B.C.) her generals showed boldness and enterprise, and in the end she produced in Scipio Africanus a commander who, after brilliant victories in Spain, dealt the *coup de grâce* to Hannibal himself in Africa. Nor is the interest of the war confined to the military side. The strength and the weakness of the Roman Confederacy were revealed. The Campanians, the Samnites and the Lucanians went over to Hannibal when he seemed victorious. In Rome's worst hour, 12 out of 30 Roman colonies refused to send their quota of soldiers to the Roman armies. But the rest stood firm, and nothing could shake Rome's hold on Central Italy and the loyalty of the Latins, Sabini, Marsi, Umbri and the people of Picenum. The military alliance between Carthage and Philip V of Macedon seemed to pose a fearful threat, but it was not to prove effective. And Carthage herself showed less resolution than Rome; she failed to reassert her old supremacy at sea or to reinforce Hannibal when the result might have proved decisive.

The last act of this tragic conflict is best told here. The terms of the settlement after the Second Punic War left Carthage deprived of her overseas empire and commerce and virtually disarmed. She retained her territory in north-east Tunisia with its rich possibilities for agriculture. But even in Africa a thorn was carefully planted in her side. The kingdom of Numidia, under its able and ambitious King Masinissa, became an ally of Rome, who claimed to arbitrate disputes between Numidia and Carthage. Roman diplomacy could play them off against each other. Masinissa was encouraged to encroach on the territory of Carthage, but not too far: he was credited with plans for a North African empire which would not have suited Rome. This situation lasted for more than forty years. Then for reasons which are hard to understand Rome made the decision to destroy Carthage. Cato was the champion of this policy: his opponents led by Scipio Nasica argued that it was healthy to have a potential enemy. Cato prevailed. The Carthaginians were manœuvred into a situation which enabled Rome to declare war. Against all odds, Carthage resisted for three years against a Roman army led eventually by Scipio Aemilianus. In the spring of 146 B.C. the city fell, after six days of desperate street-fighting in which every one of its tall houses had to be stormed like a fortress. The 50,000 survivors were sold into slavery, the site of the city was ploughed over and a curse pronounced on it by Scipio. The territory of Carthage became the Roman province of Africa. 'Henceforth', said Scipio Nasica, 'we need know neither fear nor shame.'

CHAPTER 10

Provinces in the West

THE PEACE TERMS after the First Punic War provided for the evacuation of Sicily by Carthage and, as we have said, she was shortly afterwards forced out of Sardinia and Corsica. By the settlement of 201 B.C. she gave up Spain, retaining only her possessions in Africa. So the Carthaginian Empire had come to an end and Rome was heir to her position in the West. The Roman provincial system arose from the need to provide for the administration of those lands taken over from Carthage—or rather, in retrospect it is seen that this was so. In fact, in each case there was an *ad hoc* response to an immediate problem, and it must be noted that the newly won lands differed very widely in their development, both actual and potential.

As first established in 241 B.C., the Roman province of Sicily was confined to the western part of the island. It included the Carthaginian colonies of Panormus, Lilybaeum, and Soloeis, a number of Greek cities, notably Segesta and Selinus, and some backward Sicel communities. Rome had to provide for its defence (the cost of which she naturally expected to be met from provincial taxes), and for the law suits between the different communities. This latter need had been met in Campania by the appointment of special praetors: it was really an enlargement of this idea that a praetor was to govern Sicily, with quaestors to assist with finance. The most advanced cities were allowed varying degrees of local autonomy. The kingdom of Syracuse, the most highly civilised part of the island, remained independent until 211 B.C., when after the aberration which led it to join the cause of Carthage it was incorporated in the Roman province. Its much admired tax system with its famous *decuma* or 10% tax on the production of grain, which was a model of the most advanced Hellenistic

techniques, was taken over in full working order and extended
to the rest of the province. Sicily made a rapid recovery from the
damage caused in the Second Punic War, largely owing to Roman
encouragement of its grain production, and its economy (if not
its social life) was flourishing until the great slave rebellions of
135 B.C.

Corsica and Sardinia, the other two large islands, were far
more backward. Urban life was almost unknown, the inhabitants
warlike and rebellious, the economic prospects uninviting. They
were united into a single province in 227 B.C. but Rome put
very little into their development and got almost nothing out of
them, except (from Sardinia) corn and slaves.

Spain was another matter. Impressive though Punic colonisation had been under the Barcids, it had only been in operation
for some twenty years and had just begun to tap the resources of
the huge Iberian peninsula—which was twice as large as Italy—
and its heterogeneous peoples. It was to take Rome two centuries
to complete the conquest of Spain, which was the historic grave-
yard of the reputation of Roman governors of the second century
B.C. In 197 the Romans set up two provinces in Spain—Citerior
or Nearer Spain with its capital Nova Carthago (New Carthage)
and Ulterior or Further Spain, ruled eventually from Corduba.
Initially, these two provinces covered the fertile coastal belts
of southern and eastern Spain which extended almost 1,000
miles: control over the central plateau and its proud and independent peoples had still to be asserted. The Punic city of Gades
became a Roman ally, as did the little Greek cities of Emporiae
and Rhode. Scipio's foundation of Italica, intended for his
wounded veterans, was to grow into one of the finest cities in
Spain. The silver mines of Sierra Morena were in full production
and Polybius records that in his day they employed 40,000 men.

But it was not primarily as El Dorado that the Romans of
this period thought of Spain. The combination of inefficient
Roman governors and fierce Spanish resistance and rebellion led
to a series of ill-conducted wars and disasters. Spain came to be
thought 'a rough and warlike province' (*horrida et bellicosa
provincia*) offering neither booty nor glory: service there was
unpopular among the troops and their commanders. On the
native side, the Lusitanian War (154–138 B.C.) produced Viriathus,
one of the finest of all the patriot chiefs who fought against
Roman imperialism. The Celtiberian War (143–133 B.C.) was

remarkable for the ferocious resistance of the mountaineers in such strongholds as Numantia, whose 4,000 defenders were finally conquered by Scipio Aemilianus in command of an army of 60,000 men, after a siege in which they were reduced to starvation and cannibalism. The Romanisation of Spain was later to become one of the proudest and most fruitful episodes of Rome's work in the West, but it made very little advance before the first century B.C. Earlier than that, its record in Spain is one of the most telling indictments of provincial government under the Republic.

A more commendable story is disclosed by the Romanisation of Cisalpine Gaul, whose main outlines are shown in Map 3. The annexation of the Po Valley effected between the end of the Second Punic War (202 B.C.) and about 150 B.C., was part of a grand design for enlarging and protecting the frontiers of Italy on the north, securing land communications with Spain, and giving Massilia security against her Celtic neighbours. The first of these needs had become urgent before the Second Punic War, for the Gallic tribes of the Po Valley had mounted a formidable attack on Italy in 225 B.C. which was finally halted by a hard-won Roman victory at Telamon. The reprisal had been the planting of colonies at Placentia and Cremona. Any further advance was cut off by Hannibal's invasion of Italy; but then his penetration of Italy and the readiness of the Gauls to join his army made it imperative to take up the project again, as soon as possible. Indeed, there were times during the Second Punic War when it seemed that a Carthaginian province might take shape in Cisalpine Gaul and Liguria, cutting Rome off from Massilia and posing a standing menace to Italy. In 203 B.C., therefore, Rome mounted a double offensive against the Gallic tribes of the Po Valley and the Ligurians of the Maritime and Apuan Alps. Both led to long and difficult wars: the Po Valley was not won till 191 B.C. and the Ligurians held out in their mountains until *c.* 155.

In the Po valley, conquest was followed by the building of roads such as the Via Aemilia, the founding of cities, the clearing of forests, the draining of swamps and the control of flooding by the Po and its tributaries. There was a rush of immigrants from Italy, mostly peasants who had lost their lands in the devastations of war. Indeed, the old Italian peasant farming was virtually re-established in this new land, itself two-thirds the size of peninsular Italy, and reclaimed from Nature by the work of the Roman soldier, engineer and farmer. Polybius, who

passed through Cisalpine Gaul in 151 B.C., was much impressed
by the rich corn yield on drained land and by the extensive vineyards; we know too that Parma and Mutina were beginning their
careers as important wool-towns. As for the Gallic peoples, the
most intransigent of them, the Boii, seem to have been driven
north of the Alps, save for a few who lived in a much reduced
territory. The other great peoples, the Cenomani and the Insubres,
came to terms with Rome and kept local autonomy. The Veneti
had always been friendly, and the establishment of a colony at
Aquileia in 181 B.C. served both to protect them from the Alpine
peoples and to advance their Romanisation. It is to be noted that
Cisalpine Gaul was not organised as a province until (perhaps)
78 B.C.

To trace the beginnings of Roman supremacy in the lands
beyond the Alps will take us a few years outside the chronological
limits of this section. Once again, there was the factor of bringing
aid to an ally. Massilia had always been a faithful friend of the
Roman people, but her inability to maintain herself in the face
of opposition from the Celtic peoples of the hinterland recalls the
besetting weakness of the Greek cities of southern Italy. And
from about the middle of the second century B.C. Massilia was
exposed to threats from two quite distinct quarters. To the east,
the Ligurian peoples were becoming a menace, their hostility
no doubt exacerbated by the harsh treatment of their kinsmen by
Rome. A much more dangerous threat was developing in the
north-west where the Arverni of the Massif Central had built
up a powerful empire which might have been the first power
to unify the peoples of Gaul. The first Roman intervention
in 154 B.C. checked but did not end these anxieties. A generation
later they were taken in hand. In 122 B.C. Sextius Calvinus
defeated the Salluvii and their allies and captured their capital at
the hill of Entrêmont, near Aix-en-Provence. The work of
French archaeologists has shown in fascinating detail the features
of that Celto-Ligurian culture with its grim cult of the severed
head, yet showing a smattering of Hellenisation in the regular
planning of the streets of the *oppidum*, and in the sculptures of its
gods and heroes. Next year (121 B.C.) Cn. Domitius Ahenobarbus
gained a great victory over the Arverni and eventually captured
their king Bituitus. But it does not seem likely that (as was once
thought) the next step was to organise the Roman province of
Gallia Transalpina. Massilia was thought to be strong enough to

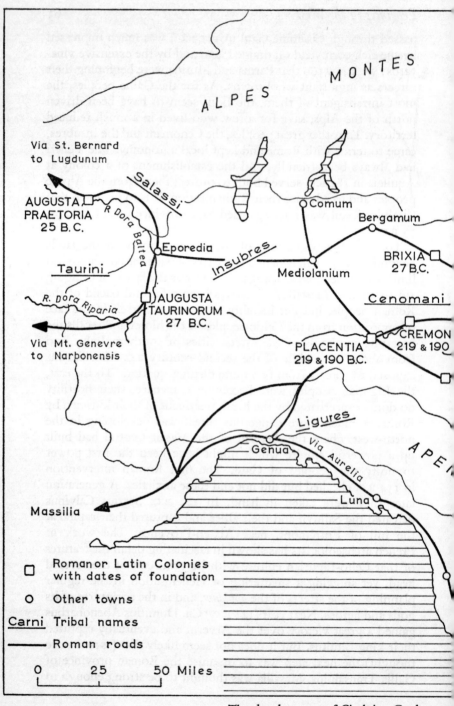

ALPES MONTES

Via St. Bernard
to Lugdunum

Salassi

AUGUSTA
PRAETORIA
25 B.C.

R. Dora Baltea

Comum

Bergamum

Eporedia

Insubres

Taurini

BRIXIA
27 B.C.

Mediolanium

Cenomani

R. Dora Riparia

AUGUSTA
TAURINORUM
27 B.C.

Via Mt. Genevre
to Narbonensis

PLACENTIA
219 & 190 B.C.

CREMON
219 & 190

Ligures

Genua

Via Aurelia

A P E

Luna

Massilia

☐   Roman or Latin Colonies
     with dates of foundation

O   Other towns

Carni Tribal names

——   Roman roads

0   25   50 Miles

3.   The development of Cisalpine Gaul

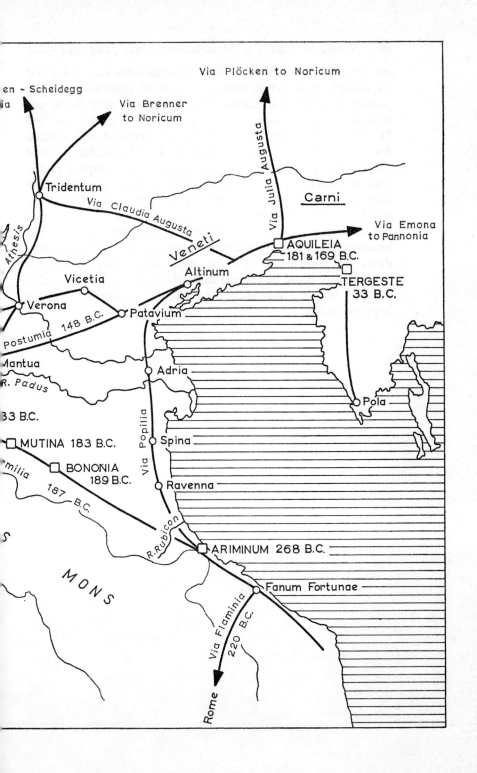

Via Plöcken to Noricum

en - Scheidegg

Via Brenner
to Noricum

Tridentum

Via Claudia Augusta

Carni

Via Julia Augusta

Via Emona
to Pannonia

Veneti

AQUILEIA
181 & 169 B.C.

Athesis

Altinum

TERGESTE
33 B.C.

Vicetia

Verona

Patavium

Postumia 148 B.C.

Mantua

R. Padus

Adria

Via Popilia

Pola

33 B.C.

MUTINA 183 B.C.

Spina

Aemilia

BONONIA
189 B.C.

187 B.C.

Ravenna

R. Rubicon

ARIMINUM 268 B.C.

MONS

Fanum Fortunae

Via Flaminia

220 B.C.

Rome

protect the lower Rhône Valley; alliances with the Aedui and Allobroges gave Rome effective means of intervening in the politics of the Celtic tribes. Communication with Spain was assured by the building of a great strategic highway, the Via Domitia, which crossed the Rhône at Tarascon and entered Spain east of the Pyrenees. A fort at Aix (Aquae Sextiae) and other military posts guarded this road, whose purpose recalls that of the Via Aemilia in the Po Valley. There was one other measure of security—the founding (118? 115? B.C.) of a Roman *colonia* at Narbo (Narbonne), situated to the west of Massilia and not, as yet, an economic rival. Rome had shown that she could intervene effectively in the Rhône Valley and she had the means to do so even more decisively in the future. Meanwhile, it was hoped that pressure could be exerted through her allies and annexation avoided. Within a very short time it would be obvious that this hope was false.

CHAPTER 11

Rome and the Hellenistic world

AT THE OPPOSITE END of the Mediterranean events took a very different course. Here Rome found herself in contact with the Hellenistic world—a world which had been brought into being by the career of Alexander the Great and modified by the struggles and rivalries of his successors over more than a century. The term Hellenistic denotes a new phase in the story of Greek civilisation. Macedonian arms and Greek technology had enormously enlarged its field of operations and a vigorous policy of colonisation had established it in many new parts of the territory of the old Persian Empire. This had led to the growth of a grandiose political concept—that of the entire *Oikoumene*, or inhabited world, being united in a single polity, enjoying a common culture and a common language and forming a single vast economic unit. It is uncertain how far such ideas originated with Alexander himself, as his admirers like to suppose. But in the successor States the possibility of a unified world Empire attracted rulers and political thinkers, far though it was from realisation. In Syria, especially, the memories of Persia and the deeds of Alexander combined to set the goal of world Empire before many a Seleucid king. But in fact, the Hellenistic world was one of great political diversity and another older idea was still potent. This was the idea of freedom and independence as expressed in the city-state of classical Greece. There is a paradox in the relations between Rome and the Hellenistic states in the first half of the second century B.C. Rome entered the Hellenistic world as the champion of liberty. That championship led her to destroy the stronger powers, one after the other; in the end she herself stood forth as, potentially, the heir to the world empire

67

of Alexander, and she came closer to achieving it than did any other power in the ancient world.

Polybius, and indeed a number of earlier Greek observers, credited Rome with a grand design for world dominion formulated at least as early as the Second Punic War. Modern scholars show little inclination to believe this. To judge from their actions, the two great Hellenistic monarchs with whom Rome was to clash in the first years of the second century B.C. (Philip V of Macedon and Antiochus III of Syria) did not feel that the rise of a new power in the West represented a menace that they would be unable to contain. In 200 B.C. the Great Power status of the three Hellenistic kingdoms seemed assured, to be challenged only among themselves. All three still retained something of the charisma of Alexander. The Antigonids commanded the fierce loyalties of the warlike peoples of Macedonia; they had rich resources of minerals, timber, corn and wine. The Macedonian phalanx was still thought to rule the battlefields of the world. But Macedonian hegemony over historic cities such as Athens and Corinth was really a source of weakness—the prestige it conferred was outweighed by the opportunity for a liberator to appear from outside and overthrow it.

The Seleucid monarchs had tried to create a new Macedonia in Syria as the heart of a vast Empire which in theory at least stretched from the Mediterranean to the Indus. Potentially the richest of the three Hellenistic kingdoms, it was also the most difficult to organise. The heterogeneous peoples ruled from the new world capital of Antioch ranged from primitive nomads to the highly sophisticated peoples of the Tigris and Euphrates valleys, the homes of the earliest urban civilisations. There were among them the same centrifugal tendencies that had marked the history of the Persian Empire. Independent or semi-independent Greek kingdoms arose in Bactria and India. More important, the strong oriental cultures of Persia and Media contained latent forces deeply hostile to Hellenism. The Syrian hegemony over the Greek cities of Asia Minor was again something that could be turned to account by a liberator. But in times of peace the great caravan routes that connected Europe with Central Asia, India, and China offered an economic potential without parallel in the world. While Rome was at grips with Hannibal, Antiochus III had been busy reasserting Syrian supremacy in Central Asia; on his return to Seleuceia in 205 B.C. he received the title of 'The

Great King'. It only remained for him to assert some outstanding claims at the expense of Egypt and Macedonia and the primacy of Syria was assured.

Egypt was the most highly organised of the Hellenistic kingdoms, though the reign of Ptolemy V Epiphanes (204–181 B.C.) saw the beginnings of a decline in her political power. The enormous riches of the Ptolemies derived from a carefully planned and far-reaching system of monopolies, which diverted the profits of the main natural resources of the land into the royal treasury. Salt, nitre, alum and papyrus were treated in this way. Beer was sold at fixed prices through licensed retail traders. The king took a percentage of the profits on the sale of oil and linen. The main product of Egypt, corn, was controlled in every detail, from the annual sowing plan to the disposal of the harvested grain. The taxation system of the Pharaohs had been detailed and comprehensive, but it was further tightened by the Ptolemies, under whom Egypt experienced the most rigorously controlled state economy of ancient times.

Larger and richer than Antioch, Alexandria was the true capital of the Hellenistic world. Its splendidly planned harbours attracted trade from all parts of the Mediterranean, the Red Sea and the Indian Ocean. The Nile was a great highway of commerce, bringing goods from Ethiopia and Central Africa, as well as Egypt herself The royal foundations of the museum and library were the most important scientific and cultural centres in the world. The city itself was the best example of Hellenistic town-planning on the grand scale, though unfortunately it is known to us only through descriptions in literature. The final distinction of this great and splendid city was that it was the burial place of Alexander. The splendour of the royal tomb and its attendant cult had by now erased the memory of what was an opportunistic piece of body snatching by the first of the Ptolemies. Had its military strength equalled its economic resources, Egypt might have been the most powerful of the Hellenistic kingdoms. As the weakest, it sought and received the protection of Rome; there was to be no military conflict between them until the time of Julius Caesar.

For the historic cities of mainland Greece it was a time of poverty and decline. The population was falling, land was not cultivated and there were threats of famine. The yoke of Macedon was heavy; domestic politics were largely given over to a ferocious class struggle (both were to be important factos in relations with Rome). Literature, science and the arts had moved away to new centres. Athens still taught philosophy, though even there creative activities had almost ceased. In politics, however, there was some originality, most notably in the promotion of federal unions with some rudimentary form of representative government, thus achieving polities larger than the city-state but less autocratic than the monarchies of the day. The most important of these were the Achaean League in the Peloponnesus and the Aetolian League among the less developed peoples north of the Gulf of Corinth. Both have a place in the history of political thought and their constitutions were eagerly studied at the time of the founding of the United States of America.

In Asia Minor the rivalry between Macedon and Syria made it possible for other cities and kingdoms to exist in freedom and prosperity. Trade, banking and industry flourished in the Greek cities of the Aegean coast, notably at Miletus, Smyrna and Ephesus. The excavations at Miletus and Priene have shown how their wealth had been poured out for temples, public buildings and cultural amenities: they were as well equipped as Alexandria and Antioch, though on a smaller scale. Along the shores of the Sea of Marmara and the Black Sea there was a string of wealthy commercial cities—Cyzicus, Byzantium, Heraclea Pontica and Sinope. A feature of the third and fourth centuries B.C. was the rise of Asian kingdoms under ambitious philhellene monarchs, modelling themselves on the rulers of the great Hellenistic kingdoms, but steadily asserting their independence until, one by one, they eventually came under the sway of Rome.

Pergamum was the most important of these; the energies of the able dynasty of the Attalids, and later her alliance with Rome, expanded the Pergamene kingdom far beyond her original territory in north-west Asia Minor. It has been observed that the Attalids based many features of their policy on the model of Ptolemaic Egypt—not least in the munificence they showed to scholarship and the arts and the construction of a splendid capital with an imposing royal quarter as a showpiece to the world. But the Kings of Pergamum had another exemplar— Athens. They stood for the protection of Hellenism against the barbarian, as Athens had done in her greatest days against Persia. Again and again this motif is repeated in the official monuments, most notably on the great Altar of Zeus. The kingdom's economy was rich and varied. Mount Ida produced silver and copper: grain, horses and cattle were important products of the land. Her textile industry flourished, later to become of world-wide importance, as did the production of the writing-material parchment, which still preserves its name. The trade of Pergamum reached south Russia in the East and Italy in the West. No Hellenistic state was to profit more from alliance with Rome— and none to pay a higher price for it.

The neighbouring kingdom of Bithynia had a similar but less spectacular rise. Here the people were, basically, of Thracian stock. Their country was rich in timber, agriculture and building stone, though it never developed industry and commerce on the scale of Pergamum. But it, too, had a new capital city in Nicomedia, which was later to become one of the greatest cities of the Roman world.

Next was the kingdom of Pontus, famous for the earliest production of iron and steel, rich in timber, crops, and fruits and terminus for important caravan routes into the heart of Asia. The capture of the Greek city of Sinope gave it a ready-made capital: otherwise, there was little growth of urban life. Culturally and historically its links were with Persia, and in the first century B.C. it was to be the base for a violent Greco-Oriental reaction against Rome. Mention must also be made of the stable and powerful kingdom of the Bosporus (the modern Crimea), though this remained on the periphery of the Hellenistic world.

Finally, in the heart of the Anatolian plateau, around the modern Ankara, an exotic and maverick power had taken root— that of the Galatians. Few chapters in the history of the Celtic peoples are more remarkable than the story of how these people migrated from their homeland in the Danube Valley in the third century, fought and plundered their way to the Hellespont (sacking Delphi in 279), and finally settled in Asia Minor. Here they kept their Celtic speech and tribal system, and in their ancestral fashion enriched themselves by plundering their more civilised neighbours. The latter regarded them sometimes as rude barbarians, sometimes as noble savages, and always as excellent mercenary soldiers. Rome, too, was to use them in her armies.

Surveying Hellenistic civilisation, Rostovtzeff pointed to the predominance of *homo technicus* and *homo economicus* over *homo politicus*. At Rhodes, since the fourth century B.C. the greatest maritime and commercial centre of the Aegean, the first two were certainly to the fore. Technology had produced the three spacious harbours of Rhodes, the famous Colossus—prototype of the Statue of Liberty—which greeted incoming ships, the Exhibition Grounds for the display of the products of all nations and the town planning of the three cities which had united to found the island state. The trade of Rhodes reached Numidia in the west and the Crimea in the east, the famous Rhodian stamped jars are found in the Carpathians and in southern Arabia. Since commerce depends on credit, Rhodes became the chief banking and financial centre of the world. Now that Egypt had lost naval control of the Eastern Mediterranean, the Rhodian navy took over the vital task of policing the seas, protecting commerce from the raids of pirates from other strongholds in Crete and Cilicia. Service in this highly organised and efficient force was the proudest duty of a Rhodian citizen. The Rhodian code of maritime law became the foundation of all such later legislation. But *homo politicus* also played his part with a vigour that recalls an older Hellas, with the important difference that aristocracy and people seem to have found a way of working together for the common good. When one adds that literature and the arts, rhetoric and philosophy all flourished, it is tempting to see in Rhodes a unique blend of the best features of classical and Hellenistic Greece—or, indeed, as something akin to Venice in her golden days. But Rhodes was not the only flourishing commercial centre in the Aegean. The Macedonian kings had established a port on the island of Delos with the idea, it would seem, of threatening Rhodes with a rival if need be. It would be for Rome to turn this threat into actuality.

The impact of Rome on this Hellenistic world was sudden, violent, and in different ways destructive to all parties. It need not have been so. The alliance which Philip V of Macedon made with Hannibal at the worst moment of the Second Punic War had aroused deep suspicion in Rome: it had forced her to open another front in Greece to forestall a Macedonian attack on Italy. When Antiochus III of Syria and Philip made an agreement between themselves for the carving-up of the possessions of Egypt, Rome was alarmed once more. Her suspicions were fostered by Pergamum, Rhodes and the Aetolian League and she was induced to declare war on Macedon, using the time-honoured slogan of 'freedom for the Greeks'. Freedom for the Greeks would leave them independent of Macedon: independence would

leave them weak and probably quarrelsome: with Roman agents
in control of the Greek states things could be ordered as Rome
wished. These were the war aims which, after an unpromising
beginning, Titus Quinctius Flamininus was sent out to achieve,
and he did so with style and panache during a memorable four
years in Greece. He generated confidence in the Greek cities
friendly to Rome and detached others from the support of
Philip. Eventually, the main Macedonian army was brought to
bay and defeated at Cynoscephalae (June 197 B.C.): the peace
concluded between Rome and Macedon in the following winter
put an end to Philip's hegemony in Greece, broke his naval power
and saddled him with a war indemnity. In the summer of 196,
Flamininus delivered his famous proclamation at the Isthmian
Games, conferring liberty on the Greeks. Rome was not to
replace Macedon. But it was not liberty as the Greeks understood
it, for in the settlement of claims and counter-claims that followed
Rome decided as she wished. Some were disappointed, notably
the Aetolians. So was born the policy of 'a protectorate over the
Greek world' (*patrocinium orbis Graeci*). Carrying as it did overtones of the relationship between *patronus* and *cliens*, it was to
prove much less benevolent than it sounded. In 194 Roman
troops were withdrawn from Greece: they could always return
if needed. As early as 192 B.C. the need arose.

The war which Rome fought against Antiochus III of Syria
had a diplomatic prelude too complex to set out here. Enough to
say that once again Pergamum and Rhodes urged Roman intervention and again the issue of Greek freedom was raised—this
time pertaining to the Greek cities of Asia Minor. On his side,
the Great King acted for a while with caution, which in the end
gave way to a surprising sequence of misjudgements. The first
of these, undoubtedly, was to receive at his court no less a
person than Hannibal, forced from Carthage by his political
opponents in 195 B.C. After this, Rome would believe Antiochus
capable of anything. The second was to accept the invitation of
the Aetolian League to intervene in Greece on behalf of the
proletariat of the Greek cities which Rome had left in the control
of their opponents. (An invitation which the Aetolians were
very stupid to send.) The third was for Antiochus, having
decided to intervene, to arrive in Greece with an army of only
10,000 men: this initial error was fatal to the Great King's plans
in Europe and a Roman army defeated him on the field of

Thermopylae. The second round of the war was fought in Asia and at sea. The Roman army was under the command of Scipio Africanus, once more an effective counter to the great name of Hannibal. Pergamum and Rhodes were useful allies. Late in the year 190 a decisive battle at Magnesia-ad-Sipylum showed again that the legion was master of the phalanx. The new order of things in Asia was defined by the treaty of Apamea in 188 B.C. Antiochus was to withdraw beyond the Taurus mountains and a line of demarcation was defined. He had to submit to a degree of disarmament and pay the huge indemnity of 15,000 talents. Syria had, in effect, been pushed out of Asia Minor. The beneficiaries were primarily Pergamum and Rhodes, with Pergamum getting the lion's (or as some would have it, the jackal's) share. Rome kept nothing for herself, but she had given a compelling demonstration of her power. For good measure, an army under Gnaeus Manlius Vulso had stormed through Anatolia, chastised the Galatians, and robbed them of their accumulated plunder. In 188 Rome withdrew from Asia, as she had done from Greece. She had shown up the Great King as a paper tiger, and the Galatians as second grade robbers.

But in neither Greece nor Asia could Rome refrain from intervention. Power determines the arbiter and the next 20 years were filled with the comings and goings of diplomatic missions—the Greeks to Rome to advance claim and counter-claim, Roman commissions going east to investigate and award, and then aggrieved Greeks returning to protest against the arbiter's decision. The Senate during these years must have got very tired of Greek problems.

Others, too, were discontented with the general settlement imposed by Flamininus. Philip of Macedon disliked his cramped horizons and set about reviving his kingdom as a military power. The policy was continued by his son Perseus, who succeeded him in 179 B.C. Enemies of Macedon, especially King Eumenes II of Pergamum, lost no chance of denouncing them to Rome. It became taken for granted that Rome and Macedon were on a collision course. Yet the collision did not come till 171 B.C. The Third Macedonian War (171–168 B.C.) was a hard-fought struggle for Rome, until finally the lightning campaign conducted by Aemilius Paullus led to the great Roman victory at Pydna in 168. Pydna was decisive on both military and political planes. The Macedonian monarchy was swept away and with it the

Macedonian phalanx. The country was divided up into four cantons, each of which was given a republican constitution. As a measure of disarmament, the mines were closed down, though they were reopened within a decade. Rome had smashed the most famous of the Hellenistic kingdoms. Small wonder that the survivors in every state of the Hellenistic world came to the conclusion that (in the words of Polybius) 'for the future nothing remained but to accept the supremacy of the Romans and to obey their commands'. Only a few weeks after Pydna the Seleucid king himself got a sharp lesson in obedience when the Roman commissioner, C. Popilius Laenas, sent to stop him from war against Egypt, drew a circle round him with a stick and demanded an answer before he stepped out of it. Harsh lessons, too, were visited on Rome's principal allies, for Rome disliked an over-powerful ally only a little less than an enemy. Rhodes had compounded her sins in trying to mediate in the Third Macedonian War. Rome detested interference. So Rhodes lost her possessions on the Asian mainland and Rome struck a hard blow at her commerce by deliberately fostering the trade of the free port at Delos. As for Pergamum, her king was out of favour and neighbours were allowed (perhaps even encouraged) to attack him.

Yet, even now, Rome showed no wish to acquire any territory in Greece or Asia. The patronage was to continue, even though the patron was a good deal more overbearing. This anomalous situation went on until 148 B.C. when a succession of attempts to restore the monarchy in Macedonia led Rome to establish a province there. Two years later the Greeks were shown, unmistakably, how Rome meant to go on. When the Achaean League rashly defied Rome in arms, the city of Corinth was blotted out and its people sold into slavery. The authority of the governor of Macedonia was extended to cover mainland Greece whenever Roman intervention was required. *Patrocinium*, as Flamininus had conceived it, was over: what would succeed it would be Roman rule. Sooner or later the entire Mediterranean world would be covered by the *imperium populi Romani*—the Empire of the Roman People. Attalus III, the last King of Pergamum, read the signs of the times. When he died in 133 B.C. it was found that he had bequeathed his kingdom to the Roman People.

From this outline of Rome's dealings with the Hellenistic East it will be obvious that modern concepts of imperialism do little to explain them. Neither annexation of territory nor obtaining economic advantages seem major factors in Roman policy. Again, we must look for an explanation in purely Roman terms, remembering that foreign policy was in the hands of the Senate at this time. The major object was to prevent the rise in the East of any power strong enough to threaten Rome. This was achieved. In the process, men such as Flamininus, Aemilius Paullus and Manlius Vulso could acquire *gloria* in the field and the armies they commanded could win rich booty. War could be made to pay. Such was the booty brought back for the triumph of Aemilius Paullus—of which Plutarch gives a splendid description—that it was possible to bring the *tributum* or property tax levied on Roman citizens to an end. Nor can we suppose that Roman diplomatic missions in Greece failed to pay for themselves; there was a good understanding there of the rôle of the *douceur* in negotiation. Prominent Romans acquired in Greece wealth, clients, prestige, honorific titles and occasionally the bonus of divine honours. There must have been many in Rome who found the whole situation highly satisfactory. Roman policy could usually be enforced: when it could not, the supremacy of the Roman army enabled policy to be continued by other means. Yet, in fact, it was deeply corrupting, as power without responsibility can only be. The relationship of the two peoples was such as to foster the worst qualities of both. The Greeks showed increasing subservience, factiousness and venality; the Romans increasing brutality and greed. The difference between Flamininus, the affable philhellene, and Lucius Mummius, the despoiler of Corinth, is a measure of Roman moral deterioration. And the Roman soldiers who fought in these Eastern wars thought of plunder and booty rather than the defence of their country. The Roman provincial system as it worked in the second century B.C. had many defects, but at least it fastened responsibility on Rome. Perhaps this is what Attalus III of Pergamum had in mind when he bequeathed his kingdom.

CHAPTER 12

Social and economic consequences of the wars

THE CONSEQUENCES OF THE great wars against Carthage and of expansion in the Mediterranean were such as completely to transform the social and economic life of Italy. In loss of life and in devastation the Second Punic War was one of those traumatic experiences which nations survive only with difficulty. Fighting had been more or less continuous for eighteen years, for the last fifteen of which much of southern Italy was in enemy occupation. In central Italy, Fabius Maximus had started a scorched earth policy to prevent Hannibal living off the land. The same policy had of course been employed by Hannibal to weaken the resources of Rome. As Rome slowly regained lost territory in the South she inflicted the harshest punishment on allies who had seceded to Hannibal. The consequences in Apulia and Bruttium were appalling. Never again did the cities of Magna Graecia recapture the prosperity they once enjoyed. The countryside became almost denuded of inhabitants, and immigrants imported from the north to resettle it failed to restore the former level of population. Indeed Toynbee contends that even in 1962 the traces of Hannibal's occupation were discernible, and will not be eliminated unless and until the modern policy for the development of the Mezzogiorno by the Italian government is a success.

It is not easy to give an estimate for the loss of life during the war. The ancient sources give casualty lists for the major battles but they are always suspect. Toynbee's conclusion is that the loss of life among Roman citizens may be set at somewhere between 66,000 and 90,000 and that of the allies at about 100,000. What is certain is that the worst of the losses fell on the Roman peasant

77

farmers who had done most of the fighting. Those who survived
were scarcely more fortunate than the dead. Too many of them
would come back from the war to find their homes destroyed,
their land uncultivated, the farm animals killed, the vineyards
and olive groves uprooted or burned. What alternatives were
open if they lacked the heart or the means to start again? Some
might hire themselves out as labourers to contractors in their
own neighbourhood, to work on public contracts or to meet
the seasonal demands of agriculture. But such work was chancy
and ill paid and increasingly met by the use of slave labour. Many
more would drift away to the towns, especially to Rome, there to
find what work they could, or to live as the dependants of some
rich *patronus*. Others would join the armies engaged in almost
continuous fighting overseas. What this might mean is illustrated
by the much quoted case of Spurius Ligustinus. According to
Livy, at a time when army recruiting was going badly that
articulate soldier had come forward to address the Roman People
in full assembly. Of Sabine origin, his father had left him a single
jugerum of land with a cottage on it; 'and there I am living today'.
Here he and his wife had raised a family of four boys and two
girls, but not of course on the produce of the land. For Ligustinus
had first joined the army in 200 B.C. and had served in the war
against Philip of Macedon. After discharge, he again volunteered
to go to Spain under the command of Cato, a commander with
a keen eye for a brave soldier who singled him out for promotion.
Four years later he was back in the Eastern Mediterranean serving
in the wars against Antiochus. Ten years later there was another
and longer period of service in Spain (before 180 B.C.) Altogether,
says Ligustinus, he has served for 22 out of his 50 years as a
soldier; he has received 31 awards for bravery and six times
saved the life of a fellow soldier. Legally, he is exempt from
further obligations to the army, but he will always gladly
volunteer so long as he is fit for service, and so he implies, should
all men . . . Meanwhile, he is back in the ancestral cottage; the
four boys are ready for the army when the day comes and the
two daughters are married off. It is an improving story, though
Ligustinus has omitted to tell us what booty he collected during
these 22 years of service. Not much perhaps in Spain, but there
will have been rich pickings in the East. And perhaps some
improvements will have been introduced in the cottage.

For those who remained faithful to the land there were (and

increasingly as the century went on) new opportunities in Cisalpine Gaul. But in peninsular Italy peasant farming had been drastically cut back, though by no means eliminated. Where once it had been the backbone of the Roman state, it was now recessive and obsolete. The growth of towns opened up a wider market for the produce of the land which was met by new and specialised forms of agriculture. In Apulia and other parts of the south, cattle and sheep ranching developed on a very large scale. The herdsmen on these ranches were slaves, working under the direction of an overseer or bailiff (*vilicus*), for an owner who was often an absentee. Such ranches met the demands for leather, hides, wool, cheese and (to a minor extent) meat; a great deal of money was put into them in the period immediately after the Second Punic War. We lack a contemporary picture of them, but about a century later they are vividly described in the works of Varro.

About cash-crop farming, the other new development, we are very much better informed thanks to Cato's work *de agricultura*, published about 160 B.C. What Cato there describes are the possibilities for those with money to invest of medium-size holdings with access to urban markets, particularly in Campania, Latium and southern Etruria. The most profitable use for an estate of 100 *jugera* is for high quality vines, then, in descending order, for a kitchen garden, a willow plantation, an olive orchard, pasture land, arable land, timber, coppice plantations, and finally a wood for acorns. He gives a detailed list of the labour force, plant, tools, and equipment required for an olive orchard of 240 *jugera* and for a vineyard of 100. For the olive orchard (*oletum*), one would need an overseer and his wife, five field hands, three oxherds, one swineherd, one donkey driver and one shepherd. This human labour force of 13 slaves would be supplemented by nine oxen, three donkeys for carrying manure, one donkey to work the mill and 100 sheep. (The latter to graze the land between the olive trees.) The vineyard (*vinea*) would need a bailiff and wife, 10 field hands, one oxherd, one swineherd, one donkey driver and one willow-tender—a total of 16 slaves. Fewer animals are required—only two oxen for ploughing, two donkeys for drawing carts and one donkey to work the mill. Toynbee notes that this is the minimum labour force required on an all-the-year-round basis. At heavy working periods such as harvest contract labour would be employed. The estate would support itself in food and clothing as far as possible. The best markets for the purchase of various kinds of farm equipment are noted. The overseer is the key man in the whole operation, for it falls to him to assign work to the slaves and to drive them as hard as he can. The more the owner keeps his eye on him, the better he will carry this out. The owner, in fact, is to treat the estate as an investment unit and he will no doubt acquire others depending upon available funds. Economic efficiency no doubt was served, but at the usual high price in human happiness (and on the great ranches the cost was higher still). Yet Cato has the effrontery to preface his cost-conscious handbook with some moralising on Farming as a Way of Life!

The importation of slave labour on a large scale to Italy and Sicily was an enormous social disaster. It has been estimated that 250,000 prisoners of war were brought in as slaves in the first fifty years of the second century B.C.; thousands of others must have come through the ordinary commercial channels. Like the trade in African slaves to the plantations of America this brought in its train evils which were to continue at work over many centuries, whose consequences fell heavily on the exploiters. Immediately, it provided a new and sinister motive for Roman wars of aggression. Thus we hear of the 150,000 Molossians sold as slaves by order of the Senate, and of the swamping of the market by the thousands of Sardinians captured by Sempronius Gracchus in 177 B.C. But Roman campaigns were not the sole source of supply. A new stimulus was given to the pirates of Crete and Cilicia, who worked hand in glove with the slave dealers of Delos, the Liverpool of the time. At full stretch, we are told the Delian slave market could handle 10,000 purchases a day, though we do not know how often this limit was reached. But like Liverpool the trade of Delos was not confined to slaves. From 166 B.C. onwards, it rapidly developed as the most important entrepôt of the Aegean, and attracted a large and flourishing colony of Roman and Italian business men. Their inscriptions provide us with the richest evidence for the economic life of the time. Much of the trade between Rome and the East passed through their hands, and the island became an important banking centre—all of course to the detriment of Rhodes. The Delian slave trade was diversified as well as highly organised, dealing with slaves who had specialist skills such as doctors, cooks, musicians, entertainers and artisans of various kinds. Italy soon learned the evil effects of slavery. The herdsmen on the great ranches had plenty of opportunity for brigandage, which they were not slow to take. Insurrections were numerous, and sometimes developed into full scale wars, notably in the two great Servile Wars in Sicily (135–132 and 104–100 B.C.) In the first of these the insurgents captured several of the most famous cities of eastern Sicily before they were suppressed. In the second they were at one point in control of almost the whole island. The brilliant account of Diodorus Siculus shows that the energy and ferocity displayed by the slaves in these great risings were comparable (in everything but success) with those in Haiti against the French.

During the Second Punic War large fortunes had been made out of contracts for supplying the Roman armies. Lacking any organisation of its own, the State had been obliged to turn to private contractors to supply the troops with food, clothing, equipment and even on occasion with pay. Some of the contractors were patriotic and honest, others were not; the most flagrantly dishonest were publically broken as soon as opportunity allowed. At the end of the war there were large sums of money in the hands of *publicani*, individuals and corporations employed on government contracts. Peace did not put an end to their opportunities. Polybius notes the vast number of government contracts, covering the whole of Italy, for work on harbours, mines, roads, public buildings, bridges and the like. The *publicani* handled the collection of pasture dues and port charges. Expansion in the Mediterranean opened richer prospects still. Besides government contracts, men could put their money into banking, money lending, shipping or trade. So this period brought the growth of a new business class (the *equites*) whose individual wealth often exceeded that of the Senatorial aristocracy. Politically they had yet to make their weight felt, but this would come in the revolutionary period of the Gracchi. When it did, it seems to have been a surprise to the senatorial class whose judgement was affected by their own success in keeping their hands for so long on the levers of political power.

CHAPTER 13

The Roman oligarchy

NEVER HAD THE POWER of the Roman Senate seemed as firmly based as during the first 70 years of the second century B.C. The prestige it had won from its conduct during the Second Punic War was enhanced by its new position as the virtual ruler of the Mediterranean world. In the East great Romans such as Lucius Aemilius Paullus or Scipio Africanus appeared as the rulers of men and nations, the superiors of the Hellenistic kings. In Rome they were treated as equals by their fellow senators, their powers were no more than those of whatever magistracy they held; their personal influence what their own *auctoritas* could command. But that could indeed be very great, for the notion of republican equality between senators—however dear to their hearts—was in fact an illusion. The great families were dominant as never before and held a near monopoly of the highest offices of the State. The head of a great house such as that of the Fabii, Valerii, Metelli, or Cornelii Scipiones, stood at the centre of a nexus of political interests whose strands extended to every grade of Roman society and beyond it to Italy and the provinces. They talked in terms of friendship, service and obligation: they meant political office, favours and power. Annual elections for all the regular magistracies maintained their rivalry at full tension. Advantage was to those with the standing and money to build up the most powerful political machine. These political factions might form temporary alliances or bargains for this or that end, not always readily perceived by us. It might be expedient from time to time to let in a new man—a *novus homo* often from one of the local aristocracies. Such a man was M. Porcius Cato from Tusculum taken up as a protégé by the Valerii. But from such a milieu there could never develop

82

anything remotely resembling a modern political party, that is to
say an organisation with a corporate personality greater than
that of any of its members, and having (or affecting to have) long
term political ideals.

Unaccustomed to ideals, the Roman nobility was strongly
attached to conventions. One such was their instinctive hostility
to the concentration of power for too long in the hands of any
individual, whatever his record of service to the State. This is
best noted in the treatment of Scipio Africanus who was prema-
turely driven out of Roman politics in 187 B.C. The younger
Scipio came in for similar though less drastic treatment. Another
convention was the reverence incessantly expressed for '*maiores
nostri*' (our ancestors), and the standards of personal and political
conduct which they were supposed to have handed down. To
the Romans themselves, this was an aspect of *pietas*, the reverence
due for example from a son to his father. Politically, as recent
studies have shown, it was a clever piece of dissembling, intended
to conceal the fact that the political power of the Roman aristocracy rested on no constitutional foundations but merely on a
set of practices which for some time had been allowed to pass
unchallenged. But the challenge was soon to come.

Once again the *gens Cornelia* will provide the fullest evidence
for the history of a great patrician family. At the end of the
Second Punic War Scipio Africanus stood on a pinnacle of
prestige and authority such as no Roman had hitherto attained.
As a result, Scipionic influence was dominant in politics for the
next decade. The wars against Macedon and Syria were the result
of their policy, and they or their protégés such as Flamininus,
Manlius Vulso, Acilius Glabrio, commanded the armies in the
various theatres of war. But their enemies led by Cato were
powerful and watchful; campaigns in the wealthy lands of Asia
were fruitful in scandals, and a series of trials in 187 B.C. involved
both Scipio Africanus and his brother Lucius as well as their
supporters. The day of glory was ending for the victor of Zama.
He withdrew from Rome to his estate at Liternum, and as he
lay dying in 184 B.C. gave the order that he was to be buried
there 'lest my funeral should be held in my ungrateful country'.
Only his statue was placed in the family monument outside
Porta Capena at Rome. He had married Aemilia, sister of Aemilius Paullus, a Roman matron austerely old-fashioned: her
magnificent gowns and jewels were on display only at state

religious ceremonies. There was nothing opulent about the
villa at Liternum, which later generations would find small
and mean. There were four children of this marriage. The
boys must have been a disappointment. The most positive
achievement of Lucius was to get himself captured by the troops
of Antiochus in Syria. He probably died young. Publius suffered
from bad health and could not hope for a public career, though
he was a good orator and historian. It seemed unlikely that he
would have an heir and this led to the adoption of his cousin, son
of Aemilius Paullus, who took the name of Scipio Aemilianus.
The energy and brains of the family seem to have gone to the
girls, especially to the younger Cornelia. She married Tiberius
Sempronius Gracchus bearing him six daughters and six sons:
among the latter were the famous revolutionaries, Tiberius and
Gaius Gracchus. She possessed all her mother's virtues and more
than her fecundity, but belonged to a new generation in her taste
for the things of the mind. She took charge of her sons' education—a task usually left to the *paterfamilias*—and chose for them
the best Greek tutors of the day. She was the first Roman lady
(so far as we know) to hold a *salon*, the resort of statesmen, poets,
and philosophers. A widow, and the mother of twelve children,
she was sought in marriage by the King of Egypt, Ptolemy VII.
She refused him. It was her choice that she should be known as
'the mother of the Gracchi'—but she should be remembered
in her own right.

The fortunes of the Scipionic house were at a low ebb when
Scipio the Younger was adopted, for in 184 B.C. it had suffered
not only the death of Africanus but the degradation of the elder
Lucius Scipio. A famous passage of Polybius tells how the young
Aemilianus confessed that he found the hopes reposed in him an
almost intolerable burden. His distinguished and many-sided
career restored the Scipionic influence and (to later ages) set him
beside Africanus. The destruction of Carthage in the Third Punic
War, it is true, was less arduous than the defeat of Hannibal in
the Second; the siege of Numantia falls short of the victory over
Antiochus. But his political career was longer, more distinguished
and commanded wider support. Time and again the State turned
to him in a crisis. He undertook a major diplomatic mission in
the East. Perhaps the greatest of all Roman politicians who tried
to work within the framework of the Roman constitution, it is
not surprising that he was portrayed as the ideal statesman by

Cicero in the *De Re Publica*. In this we need not follow Cicero. Scipio showed the traditional Roman ruthlessness to a defeated enemy. In the early stages of the Gracchan crisis he looked for what was expedient. But there was a real greatness about him perhaps never fully realised. Sudden death cut him down in 129 B.C. as he was about to face the supreme test of his career— the crisis brought about by the agrarian legislation of Tiberius Gracchus. Fortune, invoked by Polybius to account for so many of the events of that period, saw to it that neither of the two greatest Scipios should reach the age of sixty.

Scipio Aemilianus left a lasting mark on the cultural history of the Roman world. He was brought up in a family devoted to Greek culture. Aemilius Paullus brought back the royal library of Macedon for the use of his sons and the young Aemilianus was familiar with Greek statesmen and savants. Later he himself became the patron of the famous Scipionic Circle, in which philhellene Roman statesmen and Greek and Roman writers and philosophers encouraged each other in the development of their talents. In Lucilius they had a major satirist—the first great writer in that distinctive Roman genre to lash out at the follies of contemporary society. Terence, writing in pure and graceful Latin, brought the refined subtlety of Greek New Comedy to the Roman stage: too often his plays went above the heads of a popular audience. But more important still were two Greeks—the historian Polybius and the philosopher Panaetius. The intimacy of Scipio Aemilianus and Polybius was of mutual profit. Through it the historian was able to be present at some of the crucial occasions in Roman history and to gain that knowledge of 'cities, places, and battlefields' which he regarded as indispensable to his trade. He was certainly at Scipio's elbow when Carthage fell; he probably accompanied him to Numantia and on his mission to the East. He had a first-hand knowledge of the western parts of the Empire, Gaul and Spain: he had sailed through the Straits of Gibraltar and up the Atlantic coast of Portugal. Largely through Scipio and his friends he had come to know the Roman aristocracy and how it looked at the world. But he had also much to give—a lofty view of history and its value, and above all the concept that universal history was what mattered, now that the whole civilised world had been brought under the domination of a single power.

How that power would be judged would depend on whether

Roman rule turned out to be for the benefit of the governed. In 146 B.C., the year of the brutal destruction of Carthage and Corinth, this must have seemed open to doubt. One of the chief defects of the Roman aristocrats who now ruled the world was that they lived by an inherited code of conduct, rather than by any reasoned philosophy of life. Panaetius set himself out to provide just such a philosophy, and succeeded as perhaps no other Greek philosopher of the day could have done. It was significant that he came from an aristocratic family of Rhodes, whose free political life gave him an interest in politics very different from that of the Asiatic Greeks who had founded the Stoic system. He saw the necessity for restyling Stoicism if it was to win converts at Rome. The logic and metaphysics of Zeno and Chrysippus would bore a Roman statesman; but the austere code of morals they enjoined could be presented as akin to the *mos maiorum* of the Roman nobility. Hence the Middle Stoicism taught by Panaetius concentrated on ethics and politics providing rules of conduct for public and private life. From Panaetius to the last days of the Empire, Stoicism kept a footing at Rome.

It is not too fanciful to credit members of the Scipionic Circle with a vision of a world order based on justice, and including the peoples of Western and Northern Europe, as well as those of Italy, Greece and the Orient. It would be administered by enlightened Roman nobles and its security would be guaranteed by Roman armies. It is true that the course of Roman politics— and especially the fatal schism which developed after the revolution of the Gracchi—was soon to stultify these high prospects. Such successes as were achieved were mainly due to jurists like Q. Aelius Tubero and Mucius Scaevola, who tried to extend Roman law into an international code. But it was valuable to have the concept, and it would be taken up later by the more enlightened Roman emperors.

To turn to Cato, the great enemy of Scipio Africanus, is to enter another kind of world. It is probable that some features of his narrow and chauvinistic outlook may well have derived from the Tusculan farming stock from which he came. But some of it looks like a pose, designed to provide this *novus homo* with a political persona acceptable to the conservatives in the Senate. And indeed, Cato has been persistently misjudged by modern critics. Because his book on agriculture is one of the earliest pieces of Latin prose and is in an archaic style, they have attributed

old-fashioned and even endearing qualities to the author.
'Quaint and entertaining' is the verdict of one distinguished
scholar. His contemporaries did not find Cato quaint and
entertaining. The book *De Agricultura* is written in the spirit of
inhumanity that produces modern factory farming. Avarice, his
outstanding characteristic marks him as a man of the new age.
Ruthless, litigious and a vindictive personal enemy, even the
strict line he took as censor may be due to the wish to ensnare
his enemies rather than to uphold a code of morals.

The Roman aristocracy was ceasing to conform to type at this
time. A rich and many-sided personality is brought out in
Plutarch's *Life of Aemilius Paullus*. His father had been killed in
battle at Cannae, and the son set out to prepare himself for a life
of public service, especially in war. Through popular favour he
came early to various magistracies and he won notable military
successes in Spain and Liguria. It was by popular choice that he
took command of the war against Perseus at the age of sixty.
He was a strict commander, 'thinking it his business as much to
train citizens as to defeat the enemy'. He could, if required, treat
a defeated enemy with full Roman ferocity, as he showed to the
unfortunate people of Epirus. In everything he did he showed
meticulous attention to detail, whether performing the duties
of an augur, or mustering an army for battle, or entertaining
Greek notables to dinner with the liberality proper to the victor
of Pydna. He was, says Plutarch, a poor maker of money, and a
generous spender of it. He took for himself no part of the
Macedonian booty except the royal library. On his death his
estate was worth no more than 370,000 drachmae (about £12,000).
A devoted philhellene, he saw to it that his sons received a
Greek education which he had not experienced himself. They
were surrounded 'not only with sculptors and painters, with
riding masters and dog trainers and teachers of the art of hunting,
all of whom were Greeks. Unless some public business intervened, the father himself would always be present at their
exercises and studies, for he had now become the proudest
parent in Rome.' His experiences of war left him deeply impressed
with the inscrutable workings of Fortune in human affairs. The
night after the surrender of Perseus he took his sons, his sons-in-
law and other young officers into his tent. There he sat for a
long while in silence meditating with himself. Then he began
to talk of Fortune and of human affairs . . . 'The successor of

Alexander the Great, who attained the highest pinnacle of power, has in the space of a single hour fallen and been put beneath your feet. You see kings who recently were surrounded by thousands of infantry and cavalry, receiving from the hands of an enemy the food and drink they need for a day. Do you suppose that we ourselves have any guarantee from Fortune that will avail us against the attacks of time? Young men, abandon empty insolence and pride of victory. Humble yourselves as you confront the future, expecting a time when God at last shall launch against each one of you his jealous displeasure at your present prosperity.' Young Scipio Aemilianus was to remember these words when more than 30 years later he watched the destruction of Carthage and was filled with a sudden foreboding for the fate of Rome. Aemilius Paullus was to learn soon enough how Fortune intended to strike at him. As he celebrated his famous and resplendent triumph in Rome his two younger sons both died. Since the two older boys had been adopted into other houses he was now left without an heir at the age of sixty. Plutarch gives the substance of his noble address to the Roman people on this theme, in which he reflects that the blows of Fortune having fallen on his own house in the hour of triumph will spare the City itself. 'But Perseus, though defeated, has his children, Aemilius the conqueror has lost his.' So spoke the proudest father in Rome. It is this blend of the old Roman fortitude with the new culture of the Hellenistic world that makes Aemilius Paullus one of the representative figures of the age.

CHAPTER 14

The Roman army

THE ARMY WHICH HAD given Rome supremacy in the Mediterranean world was still substantially the citizen militia of the Roman Confederacy, levied (in theory) in equal numbers from Roman citizens and allies. By virtue of their military command, the consuls held the levies as emergencies arose; for much of the second century B.C. that meant every year. In the Second Punic war, tactics, training and equipment had been improved and standardised. As described by Polybius, the Roman army had many features of a long term professional service. He notes with approval the rigorously standardised system of pitching and breaking camp. A Roman camp was like a city and in it each soldier knew exactly the position of his own house. The night watch was scrupulously observed; inspection and punishments fell heavily on anyone who forgot the password or fell asleep on duty. The whole army was kept together by the centurions, men chosen for steadiness rather than dash, the sort of men 'who will hold their ground when worsted and hard pressed, and be ready to die at their posts'. He praises especially their readiness to adopt new fashions and to imitate what others do better. So they had taken the *gladius* or stabbing sword from the Spaniards, the *scutum* or shield from the Greeks, and carried throwing spears (*pila*) of improved design and in two makes—heavy and light. A carefully planned system of rewards and punishment operated for all ranks. 'No wonder', Polybius concluded, 'that the wars which Rome undertakes come to such a successful and brilliant conclusion.'

No army of ancient times, and few of modern, can match the record of the Roman Republican army between the victory at Zama in 202 and that at Pydna in 168 B.C. In this period of 34 years—roughly two generations of serving soldiers—it had met and defeated the greatest military powers of the world, Carthage, Syria and Macedonia. But the armies of the Republic were not always successful. There were mutinies in Scipio's armies in Spain; Aemilius Paullus led back from Pydna an ill-tempered army, resentful of strict discipline and meagre booty. In the later wars against the native peoples of Spain the Roman military record, as we have seen, was usually deplorable. At the end of the second century B.C. there were military disasters in Africa against Jugurtha and in the North against the invading Germanic tribes—until matters were taken in hand by a brilliant general in the person of Marius. For Roman troops were very dependent on the personality of their commander and the commander had to acquire his experience in the field. Another limiting factor was the number of men eligible for conscription. Both Rome and the allies ran into serious difficulties over recruiting in the middle of the century. Some recent studies have suggested that the legislation of Tiberius Gracchus was intended to increase the number of men liable to military service rather than to solve an agricultural crisis.

The soldiers returning from service in the East brought with them many new-fangled commodities and notions, most of them disapproved by the old fashioned moralists. Livy tells us that Scipio's army brought back from Asia to Rome the first bronze couches, bed-covers, bed-curtains and other fabrics, elaborate tables and sideboards. They introduced for the first time the art of cooking, costly banquets and cabaret girls for entertainment. There was a recurrent outcry against *luxuria*; action was taken by the censors; there were sumptuary laws, with no more than the usual success. But after all luxury is a relative term. By the standards of the first century B.C. those of its predecessor were modest indeed. Elaborate town houses and luxury villas were yet to come. And indeed much of Roman life was still on a surprisingly simple level. Plutarch describes how Quintus Aelius Tubero lived with fifteen of his relatives and all their wives and children in a little house, supported by the revenues of a poor farm. For his valour at the Battle of Pydna, Aemilius Paullus presented him with a silver bowl weighing five pounds. This was the first piece of silver that had ever entered the house. Yet one of the wives in this overcrowded place was Aemilia, daughter of Aemilius Paullus—'she was in no way ashamed of her husband's poverty, but admired the virtues that kept him poor'.

CHAPTER 15

Art, architecture, and literature

By ABOUT 150 B.C. Rome may well have had a population of half a million, and was for the first time a cosmopolitan city. Besides immigrants from every part of Italy, the urban population included large numbers of slaves and freedmen, notably from Greece and the Orient. Scipio Aemilianus, addressing the Roman people, could refer to them as 'the step-children of Italy!' Building activities during these years were mainly to serve the needs of this growing population. So we hear of improved harbour works along the Tiber, new markets, warehouses, shopping centres and colonnaded streets. Rome was beginning to take on some of the aspects of a Hellenistic city, though scarcely as yet one of the first rank. No fewer than three basilicas were built in the Forum Romanum for legal and commercial business between 184 and 169 B.C. The Forum was still the centre of political life and funeral games and gladiatorial shows continued to be held there. Indeed, there was little specialised provision as yet for public entertainment apart from the Circus Maximus. Although this was the heyday of the Roman stage, there was no permanent theatre, a proposal to erect one having been defeated on grounds of public morality in 154 B.C. The Campus Martius provided an open space for military training and for sports. There were no gardens, public or private, and of course nothing like the great *thermae* or bath buildings of Imperial times.

It was possible to admire in Rome the products of Greek art and sculpture, but they had come as spoils of war and not collected by *dilettanti*. The two richest hauls were those brought by Marcellus from Syracuse in 211 and by Mummius from Corinth in 146 B.C. None the less, the foundations for the growth of connoisseurs were being laid. We have seen how the sons of Aemilius Paullus were taught to appreciate painting and sculpture. Visiting Olympia, Aemilius Paullus himself made a comment on the famous statue of Zeus (saying that Pheidias had portrayed the Zeus of Homer) which won approval and was frequently repeated. But, world capital though she was, the amenities of Rome fell as yet short of those of the great cities of the Hellenistic world.

We may note an efflorescence of Latin literature during these years. Critical appraisal is another matter, since so much is lost. Of all the plays written for the Roman stage we have only the 21 comedies of Plautus and the six of Terence. Of the three great tragedians, Ennius, Pacuvius and Accius, we have only fragments. The orators' works have virtually disappeared; so have the historians: Cato's book on agriculture is the sole surviving prose work. Two things stand out above all from a survey of this considerable literature. First, that the writers are drawn from all parts of Italy, but that they write largely for an audience at Rome. From southern Italy came Ennius and Pacuvius. Ennius, who knew Greek, Oscan and Latin, said of himself that he had *tria corda*. The words are usually translated as 'three hearts', but they really mean three minds, an insight through language into three cultural worlds. Naevius and Lucilius came from Campania: from the North, Umbria produced Plautus and Accius: Caecilius is said to have been an Insubrian Gaul, perhaps from Milan. Terence is said to have been bought as a slave from Carthage, hence his name Terentius Afer. Secondly, none of these writers could escape the pervasive influence of Hellenism, though some of them might react strongly against it. This should occasion no surprise. Greek literature had behind it more than six centuries of brilliant achievement. Its greatest authors seemed unrivalled— many of them are so still. It established the scope and conventions of all the major literary *genres*—except satire. No Roman author could ignore its standards. But the common criticism that Latin literature was second hand and derivative lacks critical insight. This is clearly seen in the example of Plautus and Terence. The raw material for both was the Greek New Comedy from which they drew their plots, their characters and in many cases whole plays. Yet no two writers could be more different. Plautus gave careful thought to which Greek plays would appeal to a Roman audience. He then cut down the dialogue, introduced songs and burlesque scenes, infused the whole with his characteristic bawdy and knock-about humour and finally wrote in a racy contemporary Latin. Terence in contrast took his plays largely from Menander, the most refined of the Greek authors of New Comedy. He carefully preserved the Greek setting of the original, and represented the Attic simplicity of its style with his own pure and limpid Latin—the diction favoured by his patrons and their friends of the Scipionic Circle. In Plautus we see that gift of creative transformation which is so characteristically Roman, in Terence the highly sophisticated reproduction of the original in another language. The people of Rome knew which they preferred—Plautus.

Another contrast is seen in epic. Naevius wrote his *Bellum Punicum* in the old Saturnian metre. The concept of an epic poem on an historical theme was Greek but he meant to give it an Italian form. The set of the tide towards Hellenism depressed him and he thought that Latin poetry would not survive his death. That it did so was largely due to his great successor Ennius and his master work, the *Annales*. Here, too, the theme was the national history of Rome, culminating in the Second Punic War. But, by the choice of the Homeric hexameter as his medium, Ennius was able to invest his noble theme with a grand if archaic dignity. The Father of Latin poetry, he had domesticated the metre best suited to its genius. If we had the *Annales* of Ennius, together with the *Satires* of Lucilius, we should better understand the mind of Rome at this time.

CHAPTER 16

The crisis of the Gracchi

As THEY LOOKED BACK on the period of the Gracchi, later generations saw it as the great divide in the political history of the Republic. 'The Gracchi', it was said, 'gave the State two heads.' Nothing afterwards was the same. Yet it is improbable that the tribune Tiberius Gracchus when he presented his Land Bill to the people in 133 B.C. had revolution in mind. The need for agrarian reform was widely admitted; Laelius, friend of Scipio Aemilianus, is said to have introduced a measure for the redistribution of public land when consul in 140 B.C., but he dropped it in the face of opposition from within the Senate. In 133 B.C. Tiberius had the support of Mucius Scaevola, one of the consuls of the year, and of his own father-in-law, Appius Claudius, who commanded a powerful *clientela*. Scipio Aemilianus was away in Spain. Would the Senate be reactionary enough to reject a Land Bill endorsed by the Assembly, and not ultra-radical in its terms? For the Bill proposed to revive a law that had fallen into disuse, limiting the amount of public land occupied by any one person to 500 *jugera*, with a further 500 for each of two sons. There would be compensation for improvements to those dispossessed, land recovered would be redistributed in lots not exceeding 30 *jugera* and a Land Commission would supervise the entire operation. They would face severe problems. Some of the land had changed hands many times, some of it had been pledged as security. Some of the Italian allies seemed hard done

95

by, since they had acquired public land in good faith and yet were excluded from the redistribution.

The Senate decided to kill the Land Bill and induced another tribune, Octavius, to interpose his veto at the moment when it had won a majority of votes in the Assembly. Tiberius Gracchus had him removed from office, on the ground that he had opposed the will of the sovereign people. It was a head-on collision on constitutional issues. According to Roman practice a veto must prevail, according to Greek theory the will of the people must not be thwarted. Meanwhile the Bill had passed, and the Land Commission began its work. But it needed money, and just at this moment there came the bequest of the kingdom of Pergamum. Tiberius Gracchus put to the Assembly the proposal that the royal revenues should be diverted to the Land Commission—another blow at the Senate who normally ruled on money matters. His plan to stand for re-election as tribune was a further breach of the conventions, and a party of Senators, headed by the younger Scipio Nasica, killed him and 300 of his followers on the day of the election. It is uncertain whether the murder was deliberately planned or stemmed from a riot which got out of control. However that may be, blood had been shed in civil strife and a vicious precedent set for the future.

Yet the Land Commission continued to work, though on a restricted scale, from 133 to 118 B.C. Inscriptions show that conservative Senators, such as Popilius Laenas, took part in its work and tried to claim credit for it. 'I was the first', he proclaimed in an inscription from Forum Popili in Lucania, 'to make the cattle-breeders give way to ploughmen. I built a market and public buildings here.' Another inscription testifies to the re-establishment more than forty years later of boundary-marks determined by the Land Commissioners. Modern scholars estimate that between 7 and 10 per cent of the public land was redistributed to about 75,000 smallholders.

Tiberius' younger brother, Gaius Gracchus, who had taken an active part on the Land Commission, set himself a much more ambitious plan of reform. To avenge the murder of his brother he saw as a duty to his family, to smash the power of the Senate as a duty to the State. For all his Greek education Gaius Gracchus was a Roman who worked in a pragmatic fashion towards an immediate goal. Hence he built up a vast coalition of all interests opposed to the Senate and got himself elected to the tribuneship for 122 and again for 121 B.C. With the support of the Assembly, he turned that office into the control-point of Roman politics, pushing through his own measures and those he owed to his heterogeneous supporters. It did not bother him that their interests were incompatible in the long run, nor did he consider whether some of his measures might not bring evil consequences. He did what he had to do for he did not expect to live long. So the *equites* were granted the Asian tax-contracts, the richest pickings ever leased out by the State. In case provincial governors tried to hamper them, they were also granted control of the courts set up to try cases of extortion. They also benefited from a huge programme of public works on roads, harbours and colonies. The Italian allies were to get Latin rights, the Latins, Roman citizenship—sensible and enlightened measures, which the Assembly refused to support. For the Roman people there was the guarantee of corn at reduced prices, improved conditions of military service, land-distribution, and the foundation of colonies, notably at Capua, Tarentum, and also Carthage, despite Scipio's curse. But Gaius Gracchus thought it necessary to go out to Africa himself, and during his absence the Senate undermined his support through the use of a dummy tribune proffering a dummy programme of reform. When he returned and stood for a third year as tribune they plotted his murder, beyond doubt with full deliberation. So he was assassinated like his brother before him. (There are modern parallels.) For good measure, this time, they killed 3,000 of his followers. Scipio's curse was perhaps potent, after all.

The episode of the Gracchi laid bare ugly realities beneath the surface of Roman political life. The selfishness of the oligarchy was revealed, and its readiness to resort to murder when its position was challenged. The power that the tribuneship could confer on an ambitious politician stood out in its positive aspects as never before. Perhaps most alarming of all was the naked clash of interests, political and economic, which had opened between the various elements of the body politic. After the murder of Gaius Gracchus the Temple of Concord in the Roman Forum was restored by his chief murderer L. Opimius. But to restore her former powers to the divinity was to prove another matter.

CHAPTER 17

From Marius to Sulla

THE CAREER OF GAIUS MARIUS shows new forces at work in the State. He was the first to organise the Roman army as a professional long term service; what is insufficiently stressed is that he was the first professional military commander in Roman history, in the sense that his standing rested on his military attainments and nothing else. A 'new man' from Arpinum, he had served with Scipio at Numantia and later became tribune of the *plebs*. His opportunity came with the wars fought against Jugurtha, King of Numidia and mishandled by a succession of senatorial generals. Marius was elected consul for 107 B.C. to put an end to a scandalous situation: he enlisted an army from the Roman poor, led it to Africa, trained it in the tactics required by the terrain (not unlike Rommel) and laid Jugurtha by the heels.

The African scandal was succeeded by a graver danger from the North—the startling invasion of Gaul by the Cimbri and Teutoni. The northern barbarians were, in fact, whole peoples on the move in search of lands, like those barbarian invasions which later broke up the Empire. Tacitus rightly saw them as the first clash between Rome and the Germans which had continued for more than two centuries in his day—'so protracted is the conquest of Germany'. The first clash went wholly in favour of the Cimbri, with the annihilation of two Roman armies whose generals refused to co-operate, near the modern town of Orange in 105 B.C. Gallia Narbonensis lay at their mercy: if they turned to Italy, there was very little to stop them. Why they decided to invade Spain instead is not clear. When they returned Marius was ready to meet them with a trained and toughened army— whose labours are even today visible in the *Fossa Mariana*, the canal that connects Arles directly with the sea. The next years were marked by two great victories; over the Teutoni at Aquae Sextiae (still commemorated by the name Mont St. Victoire), and over the Cimbri at Vercellae in the Po Valley. The emergency brought Marius four successive consulships, and he was to have a sixth in the year 100 B.C.

But what was to be done for Marius' veterans, to whom the State owed so much? It was the tribune Saturninus who came forward with proposals for colonisation on a lavish scale in both Numidia and Gaul. The first was carried out, the second obstructed by the Senate. Here was the concomitant of the professional army—the veteran soldiers looking to their commander for reward. It made for a *clientela* of a new type, which was to be a determining factor in the last phase of the Republic. After Marius no one won supreme power at Rome without an army to back him.

Little more than a decade after the defeat of the Cimbri, Rome had to fight in a grim struggle known as the Social War against her Italian allies. That such a situation should come to pass was a startling indictment of Roman selfishness, in which the *plebs* show up just as badly as the Senate. The Gracchan land laws brought to a head the grievances of the allies, but their roots went back much further. The Italians had been bearing more than their fair share of the military burden of Rome's expansion and getting much less than a fair share of the rewards. Since 188 B.C. there had been no extension of Roman citizenship to Italian communities, as distinct from individuals. Roman magistrates had taken to behaving with arrogance in the allied states. Roman citizens followed their example and acted in disregard of Italian pride and susceptibility—a point that will be readily understood in Scotland or Wales. In 91 B.C. the position had become intolerable and there was a large scale secession led by the Oscan-speaking peoples, notably the Samnites in the south and the Marsi in the north. They set up an Italian Confederacy with a Federal capital at Corfinium, and for three years there was a bitter struggle. The Latins and Campanians did not secede nor did the Greeks of southern Italy: some of the Etruscans and Umbrians joined when the tide was running in favour of the Italians, but essentially it was a struggle between 'the Sabellian Bull and the Roman Wolf'. By weight of numbers, and by a timely concession of Roman citizenship to individuals and communities that laid down their arms, Rome prevailed. Henceforward Rome and

Italy were legally united, though two generations later, in the time of Augustus, local loyalties were still strong, and Virgil is careful to point out that Rome grew great by Italian valour. By then the most valiant of all Italian peoples, the Samnites, were no more than a memory: their last fighting men were butchered by Sulla as prisoners-of-war after the Battle of the Colline Gate in 83 B.C.

The foundations of Roman power were shaken both in the East and West by the violent events of these years. In Mithridates VI Eupator, King of Pontus, Rome met her most formidable opponent since Hannibal. His challenge was maintained for 25 years (88–63 B.C.), and tried the skill of three of Rome's most able generals in Sulla, Lucullus and Pompey. Mithridates himself was undoubtedly the most remarkable of the many Oriental princes who rose to power on the Asian fringes of the Greek world. He came from a line of kings who held the throne of Pontus for more than two centuries, and were connected with the old Royal House of Persia. A man of large ambitions, he had extended his rule over the Crimea and much of southern Russia, and it was as a great Black Sea power that in 88 B.C. he assaulted the whole Roman position in Asia and the Aegean.

In Asia Rome was highly vulnerable, in Greece hardly less so. The *publicani* in Asia had fleeced the provincials and made themselves hated; upright governors like Mucius Scaevola and his deputy Rutilius Rufus had been ruined when they tried to restrain them. They were abetted by the *negotiatores* or moneylenders. Mithridates' first political act on entering Asia was to arrange for a general massacre of 'Romans and Italians', in which 80,000 are said to have perished in one day. (The 'Italians', it is thought, were mostly Greeks from southern Italy.) In both Asia and Greece Rome had favoured the oligarchies in the cities: Mithridates' appeal to the democrats met an enthusiastic response. He also posed as the champion of Hellenism against the Romans, 'the common enemies of mankind'. In this capacity he was less impressive at close quarters as some of the Greek cities found. At first his military gains were spectacular for his forces overran Asia, sacked Delos and invaded Greece. Sulla could do no more than restore the military *status quo* and punish the cities of Asia according to their demerits. To levy fines of five years' arrears of taxes payable at once was his favourite measure. The moneylenders reappeared, and the ruined cities paid their fines by pawning their public buildings and other assets. Asia had good powers of recovery, but Greece and much of the Aegean were permanently damaged by the first Mithridatic War.

In 83 B.C. Sulla returned to Rome to exercise his considerable talent for restoring order. His immediate problems were to put an end to the rule and indeed the personnel of the party which, under Marius and Cinna, had dominated Rome in his absence and to provide rewards for his own veterans and political supporters. Sulla saw how these two problems could be made to dovetail—kill or exile his opponents, confiscate their lands and goods and use them to reward his followers. This formula, applied on a gigantic scale, was the basis for the infamous *regnum Sullae*, the personal rule of Sulla, long remembered as one of the most sinister episodes of Roman history. The device of the proscription, an official list of men declared outlaws to be murdered with impunity, was an evil precedent—40 senators and 1,600 *equites* were liquidated by this means. Immense fortunes were built up on their ruin, notably by Sulla's wife Metella and his freedman Chrysogonus, the first of his class, it would seem, to attain wealth and power. Sulla then turned to his long term objective, which was to reform the constitution so as to set the power of the oligarchy on a lasting and unchallengeable basis. For this purpose he was made Dictator, an office that had not been employed since the Second Punic War. Under the constitution he produced (and set his name to) every office or device that had challenged the Senate since the time of the Gracchi was abolished or emasculated. The office of tribune became a political dead end. The Assembly was confined to voting on measures laid before it by the Senate. Ambitious politicians were curbed by a careful control of the stages of an official career and of the minimum age at which various magistracies could be held. The Senate was enlarged and men from the equestrian class added to it: it recovered control of the courts dealing with extortion. No army was to be stationed in Italy. Such provisions would have made impossible the political careers of the Gracchi, Marius, Saturninus, Cinna, and indeed Sulla himself. They would make Roman politics once again the preserve of the great nobles, like Q. Lutatius Catulus or the Metelli, who doubtless supplied the ideas behind Sulla's constitution.

And yet, though Sulla's reforms were almost wholly reactionary, his career and personality belong to a new age. He recognised no divinity except Fortune, whose favourite he believed himself to be—Sulla Felix Epaphroditus. His political ideals are well summed up in the epitaph he chose—that no man ever did more good to his friends, nor more harm to his enemies. It is honest but it marks a decline from the epitaphs of the Scipios.

CHAPTER 18

Pompey, Crassus and Caesar

SULLA HAD TRIED TO CONFINE Roman political life into a strait-jacket. Within ten years of his death it had broken free. Above all, he had left no scope for men to follow his personal example—men whose goals and methods are described in Lucretius' famous lines:

> *noctes atque dies niti praestante labore*
> *ad summas emergere opes rerumque potiri*

('To toil night and day with vast exertions, in order to heap up great wealth and to attain supreme power').

Such men were Pompey, Crassus and Julius Caesar. The story of the last thirty years of the Republic is basically that of the conflict between their ambitions and the attempts of the Senate's leaders to keep the political machinery working in what they regarded as the normal way.

The Senate held the advantages that belong to a corporate body in its struggle with war-lords. It could hope to see them—even as with Caesar to thrust them—into their graves. But the times made it impossible to avoid granting extraordinary commands: from 74 to 48 B.C. there was always at least one war-lord at large and sometimes more. And while the leaders of the Senate could hope to play them off against each other, there was always the threat, realised in the First Triumvirate of 60 B.C., that they would combine against the Senate and make normal government impossible.

The career of L. Licinius Lucullus is revealing. When the

Kingdom of Bithynia was bequeathed as yet another legacy to the Roman People, Mithridates took alarm and renewed hostilities against Rome. Lucullus was given the three provinces of Asia, Bithynia and Cilicia, and placed in command of the Roman forces for the Second Mithridatic War. Lucullus was one of the best generals Rome ever produced, and he was one of the most public-spirited of her great servants. The campaigns (74–67 B.C.) in which he drove Mithridates out of Pontus, followed him into Armenia and captured the new and splendid capital of Tigranocerta, were not to be matched again by a Roman general in the East until Corbulo—more than four generations later. But Lucullus was a disciplinarian of the old school and the new Roman armies would not stand it. Nor would Roman financial interests tolerate Lucullus' attempts to mitigate the worst features of Sulla's settlement in Asia. Complaints were laid against him in the Senate where financial interests were now dominant. The troops mutinied: Mithridates got back to Pontus: Lucullus was recalled. He gave up his command to Pompey, 'the carrion bird', as he bitterly remarked, 'that flocks to other men's killings!' The settlement for his veterans and his triumph were held up for years. A century earlier, a man of Lucullus' qualities might have vied with the Scipios.

As for Pompey, he certainly acted the vulture's role in the war in Spain against Sertorius and in stamping out the slave rebellion of Spartacus. But in the war against the pirates he gave a formidable demonstration of his own powers of organisation and the resources at the command of Rome. Endemic in the Mediterranean throughout antiquity, piracy flourished as never before after the decline of Rhodes and during the civil wars of Rome. From their lairs in Cilicia and Crete the pirates expanded into a Mediterranean thalassocracy, treating as a sovereign power with Mithridates, capturing and sacking Roman cities, raiding the coast-line of Italy right up to Ostia, bringing sea-borne traffic to a standstill and threatening Rome with starvation. The *Lex Gabinia* of 67 B.C. gave Pompey the extraordinary powers he needed to cope with this dangerous emergency. He had command of the entire Mediterranean and of adjacent lands to a distance of 50 miles from the coast. He had an army of 120,000 infantry, 4,000 cavalry, and a fleet of 270 ships, besides those from allied sources. Twenty-five senators acted as his deputies. Pompey divided the Mediterranean basin into 25 sectors, placing a deputy in command of each, with a balanced naval and military force. Each had the duty of exterminating piracy in his own area. Pompey retained supreme command at the head of a mobile force. The Western Mediterranean was cleared in 40 days: after which Pompey returned through Rome to Brundisium for a tour of the eastern sectors. Forty days saw them swept clear in their turn; and Pompey prepared for what was expected to be the most difficult operation—the assault on the pirate head-quarters in Cilicia. But, by this time, the pirates had had enough. They surrendered in the hope of lenient treatment and (surprisingly, with Pompey) they received it. He sent them back to their own countries where most of them settled down as useful citizens. It was the last great outbreak of piracy until the decline of the Empire.

In the war against Mithridates and the subsequent reorganisation of the East, Pompey showed his talents on an even more impressive scale. The *Lex Manilia* of 66 B.C. had given him the most extensive powers ever conferred on a Roman commander—for he had taken over Lucullus' powers in addition to those he already held. He had a free hand over war and peace and the making of treaties. No senatorial commission hampered him, as it would have done a century earlier. Once Mithridates was defeated, he was able to survey and settle the entire area from the Eastern Aegean to the Caucasus Mountains, from the southern Black Sea to the frontiers of Egypt, in what he deemed to be the best interests of Rome. A huge new province, consisting of Bithynia and Pontus, was organised in northern Asia Minor and a determined effort made to promote the growth of cities there. Cilicia was enlarged. The last of the Seleucids was expelled from his shrunken kingdom and Syria became a Roman province. Further East Pompey organised a belt of client kingdoms, ruled over by monarchs favourable to Rome—Armenia, Cappadocia, an enlarged Galatia and many minor realms. Among them we must mention Judaea, whose stubborn people were to preserve at all times a hard core of resistance to Greco-Roman civilisation. How they did so was not revealed to Pompey—he entered the Holy of Holies in the Temple at Jerusalem and found it empty. In its main outlines, Pompey's Eastern settlement, with revisions carried out by Mark Antony, determined the structure of the most flourishing part of the Roman Empire. Immediately, its greatest beneficiary was Pompey himself; he accumulated a huge

fortune in those years, and the client kings were in his pocket.
Nothing could have stopped Pompey from making himself master
of the Roman world when he came back from the East in 62 B.C.
had he so desired.

Ten years earlier, it must be noted, Pompey had done Rome's
long-term interests a disservice by the war he fought in Spain to
crush the Marian governor, Q. Sertorius. For, unless the ancient
sources, notably Plutarch, are unduly biased, Sertorius was by
far the most enlightened of Republican provincial governors—
a class in which it was not hard to excel. The chances of the Civil
Wars determined Sertorius' career in Spain: ousted by a Sullan
governor, he was recalled to head a native rebellion. His objective
was to use Spain as a base for the revival of the Marian fortunes,
but he had to weld Roman and Spanish supporters to make this
possible—and he was granted nine years to do it. He established
a senate of 300 members, raised and trained a fine army in which
Roman discipline and Spanish flair for guerrilla warfare were
nicely balanced, opened a school for the sons of Spanish nobles
and showed himself sympathetic to the native cults of Spain.
With the possible exception of the older Tiberius Sempronius
Gracchus, he seems to have been the first Roman to try to discover how the peculiar gifts of the Spanish peoples might be
developed. Small wonder that they responded so warmly.

This is perhaps the moment to raise the question of provincial
administration under the Republic. Despite apologists for the
Roman Republic, its typical representative was probably closer
to Verres the notorious despoiler of Sicily, rendered infamous by
Cicero, rather than to Sertorius. We hear of Q. Mucius Scaevola
in Asia, it is true: he enunciated principles of provincial government that the Senate officially commended as a guide to practice.
But he and his deputy, Rutilius Rufus, fell foul of the financial
interests and ended in exile. So even more strikingly did Lucullus
at the peak of his success. Cicero, if we may believe him, did his
best in Cilicia, but his letters make it plain that there were limits
beyond which he dared not go and he expects that his brother
Quintus will find the same in Asia. But there is much evidence on
the other side—Aquillius in Asia, Appius Claudius in Cilicia,
Verres in Sicily—to support the general assumption that Roman
officials in the provinces, of whatever rank, could expect to
fleece their charges. Moreover, the short term of office of a
provincial governor, his small and largely amateur staff, and, by

contrast, the permanent and well organised position of the *publicani*, can be seen as factors making administration impossible in any real sense.

To return to Pompey. His refusal to seize supreme power on his return to Rome in 62 B.C. opened up a new situation. If Pompey expected gratitude he got little. The oligarchy, for whom 'back to normal' had become a political programme, saw the chance of asserting power over a former war-lord by delaying land-grants to his veterans and confirmation of his actions in the East. Caesar and Crassus, the ablest of those who wished to follow Pompey's example, saw the chance of a coalition: Pompey was persuaded. So was born the First Triumvirate of 60 B.C. which has stirred so much indignation in historians sympathetic to the Republic, from Pollio onwards. In so far as it was a faction, formed for the joint pursuit of personal interests, it had precedents in Roman politics. What distinguished it was the ability of the partners and the scope of their plans. Certainly Caesar, probably Crassus, and possibly Pompey aimed at supreme power. Where earlier coalitions had worked for advantages within the framework of the Republican institutions, the effect of the Triumvirate, renewed in 56 B.C., was to bring the machinery of the Republic to a halt and then shatter it beyond repair.

The consulship of Caesar in 59 B.C. is commonly regarded as a turning point. Elected in the teeth of opposition from the Senate, Caesar regularly took his proposals to the Assembly if the Senate disliked them. Pompey was given what he had been promised: Crassus got a revision of the Asian taxes: Caesar, at the end of his year, gained a five-year command covering Cisalpine Gaul, Narbonensis and Illyricum. Here was his chance in a new arena to surpass what Pompey had done in the East.

In 58 B.C. Caesar set off for his province. In the next seven years he conquered the whole of Gaul, suppressed the great national uprising led by Vercingetorix and won the personal devotion of the most effective army Rome had so far put into the field. In appraising these momentous events one must distinguish sharply between motives, methods and consequences. A more or less respectable case can be made out for the campaigns against the Helvetii and for the defeat of the German king Ariovistus. Any Roman governor of Narbonensis would have had to act in this way. But the subjugation of the rest of Gaul, including that of the Veneti in Brittany, of the Belgic peoples in the north-east, and the Aquitanians in the south-west, was undertaken solely for Caesar's military glory. Furthermore, the considerable spoils from these campaigns largely went to enrich, or at least redeem from bankruptcy, the members of his staff—as seedy a pack of adventurers as those who earlier followed the revolutionary plans of Catiline. The whole episode forms one of the most sordid chapters in the history of Roman Imperialism. As to method, Caesar and his army have possibly been over-praised for professional competence. The great sieges of Gergovia and Alesia, the campaigns in the north against Indutiomarus and Ambiorix, and the naval defeat of the Veneti in the Gulf of Morbihan, have so dazzled students of military history that they have sometimes been prone to overlook the two unnecessary and (except for purposes of propaganda) ill-conducted expeditions to Britain. In all these undertakings the commander and his soldiers must often have showed a devotion beyond the call of duty—but the same could be said of Rommel and the Afrika Korps. On the other hand, Caesar was ruthless and without scruple in his dealings with the Gauls: the *clementia* (mercy) which he later showed to Roman nobles was seldom extended to them.

Sympathy and admiration should go to those who fought for the freedom of Gaul—above all to Vercingetorix. The consequences are another matter. For in the long run, the Gauls were to prove themselves splendid material for the civilisation which Rome offered them from the days of Augustus onward. The provinces of Tres Galliae, together with parts of Spain and the old province of Narbonensis, became the most highly Romanised lands in the Latin West. In its turn, this Gallo-Roman civilisation provided the historical basis for the rise of France, and of all that France has meant for Europe and the world. Such were the distant results that would follow from Caesar's dash, in the late March of 58 B.C., to demolish the bridge over the Rhône at Geneva in the path of the advancing Helvetii.

The free society of Celtic Gaul which Caesar was about to demolish was the most advanced culture which had yet appeared north of the Alps. It was commonly underestimated by classical writers, since it lacked some of the features which they regarded as essential for civilisation. It had no cities, for example, in the classical sense of the word, although centres of population had begun to grow up round the dwellings of powerful nobles, or for purposes of trade and industry—such as Bibracte (Mont-

Beauvray), capital of the Aedui. Caesar calls such places *oppida* (towns), but it is clear that Celtic society was in a pre-urban phase. Again it was not a literate society in the classical sense. The Greek alphabet was used for inscriptions and coin-legends, written in Celtic (a number of these inscriptions survive such as the famous Calendar of Coligny). But its literature which seems to have been extensive was an oral one: we do not know how long it survived when the Gauls became Roman provincials and learned Latin in Roman schools. It does not seem to have been written down at this stage, and nothing of it has survived. It is reasonable to suppose that much of it was heroic poetry of the kind produced in the Dark Ages by similar societies in Wales and Ireland.

Socially, the Celtic world was dominated by great nobles living on their country estates with their kinsmen and vassals. They had long valued the luxury products of the classical world, especially its wine and metalware. But the Celts were themselves skilled workers in metals—iron, bronze and gold. Within the limits of a strict and formal canon of art, they could produce superb objects for the luxury trade—brooches, mirrors, cauldrons, decorated weapons and shields. Such things have a freshness and vitality that we do not find in the contemporary products of the classical world. Moreover, the Celts were skilled agriculturists and pastoralists, feeding the very large population of Gaul on the produce of the land. They were especially skilled with horses, their breeding, and their use in war and for transport. Their cavalry was always superior to that of the Romans, and they had a great variety of carriages and wagons, whose Celtic names were taken over into Latin. Small wonder that the cult of Epona, Goddess of Horses, was one of the most widespread. The Veneti of Brittany had evolved a sturdy type of ship which was suitable for Atlantic conditions—something the Romans never did. Divided though they were into tribal communities, there were some features of their society which were pan-Celtic. Language was one—Celtic seems to have been spoken with only minor variants from the south of Scotland, through Britain and Gaul, and then across Switzerland and far down the Danube Valley. Another was the organisation of an order of priests, law-givers and teachers known as the Druids; Caesar's succinct account (and he probably did not find out much about them) has served as a starting-point for much fanciful speculation. But

we know that they penetrated into every tribe in Celtic Gaul and
Britain, that they met annually at a sacred place in the territory
of the Carnutes (near the modern Orléans), and that they inspired
resistance to Rome both in Gaul and later in Britain.

The weak point of Celtic society was its political organisation.
Gaul at this time was divided into some sixty states. Some of
the more powerful, like the Aedui, Arverni and Remi, were the
leaders of a group of allied states, but there were no longer great
empires ruled by powerful kings like Luernus and Bituitus in
the second century B.C. Nobles had largely ousted kings and each
state was a prey to bitter party strife. A century later, as we learn
from Tacitus, the Roman reply to Gallic complaints about loss
of freedom was to say: 'We gave you peace, instead of continued
warfare between yourselves. We allow you to share the benefits of
Roman civilisation. Above all, we have protected you against
the Germans, who would certainly have conquered Gaul but for
us.' The first two claims have substance, the last is speculation.
In fact, we cannot know what might have happened had the Gauls
been able to remain a free society on the periphery of the classical
world.

While Caesar was in Gaul his rivals and partners in the Triumvirate pursued their own ambitions. Those of Crassus took him
in the end to disaster and death beyond the Syrian desert at the
head of an army of seven legions. Crassus, who called himself the
richest man in Rome and was certainly its ablest financier, stood
out as champion of the political interests of the commercial
classes, especially the *publicani*. After his consulship in 55 B.C. he
had obtained the province of Syria, and from there had launched
his fatal attack on Parthia. Since men of his kind do not nowadays
die on the battlefield, modern scholars have looked for economic
motives to explain his action. It seems more likely that the action
was guided by what had become the accepted pattern of Roman
politics. Supreme power went to the commander of a victorious
army: Pompey had set the pattern in the East, and now Caesar
in Gaul; a war against Parthia was the last great prize left. But
as a general Crassus could not claim to rank with his fellow triumvirs. Hence the disaster of Carrhae in 53 B.C.—the worst inflicted
on a Roman army since the time of Hannibal, and one that would
have to be avenged.

Pompey and Caesar were now left face to face, and for some
time the Senate leaders—notably Cato—had been doing their

best to estrange them. The death of Julia, Pompey's wife and Caesar's daughter, which took place in 54 B.C. had severed personal ties. From 52 to 50 B.C. a great political coalition was building up against Caesar in Rome with the object of crushing him as soon as his Gallic command ran out. Caesar's agents worked for a prolongation of his present *imperium*, allowing him to run for another term as consul with a further great command beyond it. Various attempts at reconciliation, in which Cicero took a hand, came to nothing and the Senate eventually moved to open hostilities against Caesar on 7th January 49. On January 10th, Caesar crossed the river Rubicon to enter Italy. The Civil War had begun.

The struggle between the two ablest generals of their day ended with Caesar's victory over Pompey at Pharsalus in Thessaly on June 6th, 48. Pompey fled to Egypt but was murdered as soon as he set foot ashore. The republican cause was maintained in several theatres of war and Caesar had to visit Egypt, Asia, Africa and Spain before it was stamped out. The African campaign was marked by the suicide of Cato at Utica, to be exploited by republican propaganda as a kind of political time-bomb. In 48 Caesar had been made Dictator (for the second time): in July of 47 he received the Dictatorship for ten years. Such a term of supreme power was something that Sulla and Pompey never had and Caesar was known to have studied their mistakes. What would he do with the Roman world now that he was sole master of it?

He would not relinquish power as Pompey did, nor like Sulla, liquidate his enemies by proscriptions, nor retire from the Dictatorship. But the question cannot really be answered. Caesar was to be granted little time before the Ides of March in 44 B.C., and much of that was devoted to the *ad hoc* solution of immediate problems. Caesar never published a political programme; his much-quoted phrase about working for 'the tranquillity of Italy, peace in the provinces, the well-being of the Empire' is too vague to be illuminating—who would not subscribe to such generalities? The measures he is known to have taken during his short period of supreme power may be set out. But to project them forward, as scholars have done, and to deduce from them a set of principles which he might have used to solve the deeper problems of the Empire, is to go beyond what the evidence will bear. Nor is much help to be gained from the

4. Rome's northern frontier in the second century A.D.

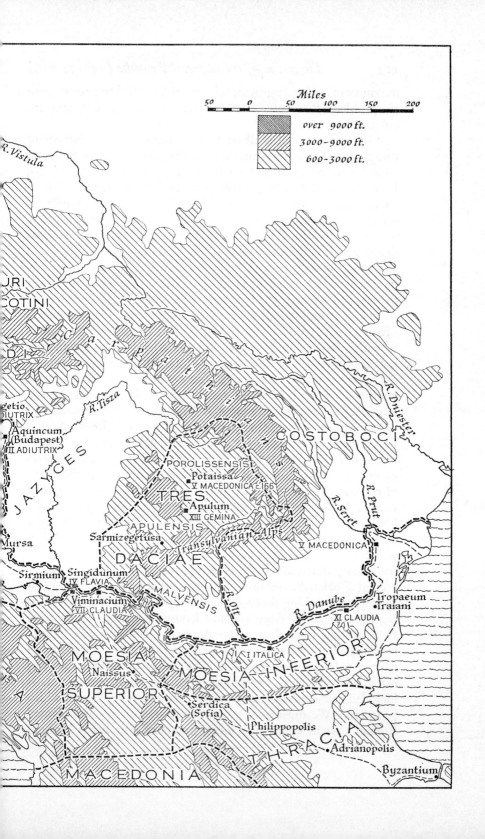

Miles

50   0   50   100   150   200

over 9000 ft.

3000–9000 ft.

600–3000 ft.

R. Vistula

URI

COTINI

DI

C a r P a t h u s

etio
IUTRIX

Aquincum
(Budapest)
III ADIUTRIX

R. Tisza

COSTOBOCI

R. Dniester

JAZYCES

POROLISSENSIS

Potaissa
V MACEDONICA c.166

TRES

Apulum
XIII GEMINA

APULENSIS

Sarmizegetusa

Mursa

Transylvanian Alps

R. Seret

R. Prut

V MACEDONICA

DACIAE

Sirmium

Singidunum
IV FLAVIA

MALVENSIS

Viminacium
VII CLAUDIA

R. Olt

R. Danube

Tropaeum
Traiani

XI CLAUDIA

MOESIA

Naissus

SUPERIOR

MOESIA INFERIOR

I I ITALICA

Serdica
(Sofia)

Philippopolis

THRACIA

Adrianopolis

MACEDONIA

Byzantium

measures taken by Augustus; it is true that he had to grapple with the problems that would have faced Caesar, but in vastly different circumstances.

With this caveat, I shall try to summarise the most important things Caesar was concerned with as Dictator. First, the policy of *clementia*, of trying to win over the nobility by calculated kindness. It promised well to begin with, but in the long run it failed to pay. Caesar's own supporters did not like it: to the nobility it must have seemed arrogant, an insult to their dignity; besides, the policy was more than counterbalanced by his contemptuous disregard of republican conventions. 'The Republic,' he is quoted as saying, 'is only a name, without form or substance.' Certainly he behaved as if he thought so. The Senate was enlarged to 900 and packed with Caesar's adherents. Caesar's proposals were sometimes forced through it without any discussion. He often nominated the magistrates; he had taken over the public treasury. Before long Cicero and his friends were grumbling that they were living like slaves with no law-courts or Senate.

Caesar's settlement of Spain, after a renewed outbreak of civil war in 46 B.C., does afford some clues to his outlook on the administration of the provinces. It was marked by the foundation of new colonies, both for veterans and Roman citizens: about a dozen such foundations are known and the charter of one of them, *Colonia Genetiva Julia* (Urso), has survived. The famous cities of New Carthage and Tarraco were also raised to the status of colonies, and Roman citizenship was granted to the people of Gades. In Gallia Narbonensis he founded a colony at Arles (Arelate) and a new port at Fréjus (Forum Julii); other cities such as Nîmes (Nemausus) received Latin rights. Gallia Cisalpina, which had given Caesar such loyal support in his proconsulship was incorporated into Italy, now extended to the Alps. Here was a great if belated extension of Roman citizenship. All this seems to imply a breaking down of exclusiveness, an attempt to incorporate new talent from outside Rome and Italy. There were Celts among Caesar's new senators (and the fact was bitterly resented), but most of them have been shown to be landowners from the Italian municipalities. The policy of colonisation was extended to Achaea, Syria, the Black Sea coast and Africa. It included new foundations at Carthage and Corinth both of which prospered. We must note the two-way traffic: colonies planted Roman citizens in the provinces, grants of citizenship brought provincials into the service of Rome. How much of all this was the reward of support given to Caesar, how much deliberate planning for the future is not easy to say.

Nor is it easy to say whether Caesar had any long-term plans for the central problem of Roman politics, which was to supersede the institutions of a city state by a firmly based government suited to the needs of an Empire. Such a government would have to be an autocracy. But on what would it be based and how would it be perpetuated from autocrat to autocrat? The old Roman office of Dictator gave Caesar himself the powers he needed, but to have it extended to ten years was unprecedented; to accept it for life (as he did in February of 44—his life was to have one month to run!) unconstitutional. Monarchy then as in the Hellenistic world? Caesar flew several *ballons d'essai*; hostile propaganda, playing on these as firm intentions, revived all the deep-seated Roman prejudice against kings. If there was a Tarquin in the State was there not also a Brutus. . .?

If Caesar had any answer to this fundamental problem, we do not know it. It is not indicated by the fact that at the time of his assassination he was on the point of leaving Rome to take charge of a great army raised for war against Parthia. Revenge for Crassus, yes; but a war against Parthia had nothing to do with what ailed Rome. The plan to assassinate Caesar, in which Brutus and Cassius were the ringleaders of some 60 senators, seems to have developed with great rapidity after Caesar accepted life Dictatorship on February 15th. The world knows how it was carried out at a meeting of the Senate in the Curia of Pompey on the morning of March 15, 44 B.C. After the murder the assassins ran through the streets waving their bloody daggers and shouting 'Liberty!' Like many who raise that cry they had little idea of what they had just done nor what they should do next.

CHAPTER 19

Antony, Cleopatra, and Octavian

CAESAR'S MURDER LEFT THE fundamental problems untouched. As one of his followers, Gaius Matius, wrote to Cicero,
'If Caesar, with all his genius, could not find a way out, who is
likely to do so?' Seventeen years and two more rounds of Civil
Wars had to be endured before that question could be answered.
For a little while, there was a chance that the Caesarian party and
the Republicans might be reconciled under the leadership of some
respected elder statesman such as Cicero. But a breach soon developed and continued to widen at the same time as a struggle went
on for the leadership of the Caesarians. Mark Antony, consul for
the year 44 B.C. and a leading supporter of Caesar, was the obvious
man: there was also Marcus Lepidus, who had been Master of
Horse in Caesar's dictatorship. There was also a boy of 18, Gaius
Octavius, Caesar's grand-nephew whom he adopted and made
his personal heir; although hardly a serious contender he could
not be left wholly out of account. By the early months of 43 B.C.
the Senate had embroiled the young man with Antony, meaning
to drop him as soon as convenient. By October of that year the
three Caesarians had formed a new Triumvirate, with the object
of punishing Caesar's murderers and then dividing up the Roman
world. They began inauspiciously with proscriptions on the
Sullan pattern. The proscription edict, according to Appian,
alludes to their duty to avenge the treacherous murder of Caesar,
and goes on to say that proscriptions will be necessary, since they
have to take their armies to the East to confront Brutus and
Cassius. They promise not to kill more men than Sulla had done
—although, as they point out, three men are bound to have more
enemies than one! The qualifying clause was what counted—
their victims were in fact more numerous than those of Sulla. At

116

the insistence of Mark Antony they included Cicero. His head
and hands were cut off and displayed on the Rostra in the Forum
Romanum where he had made so many of his speeches. In 42 B.C.
Brutus and Cassius were defeated at the two battles of Philippi.
Except for the fleet of Sextus Pompeius, the Republican cause
was finished.

Antony—still very much the senior partner— was the obvious
choice to take over Caesar's unfinished project of a Great
Parthian War. It brought him another of Caesar's legacies, for in
40 B.C. the Queen of Egypt, Cleopatra VII, sailed for Cydnus to
meet Mark Antony. In beauty, high spirits, and ambition,
Cleopatra was indeed what Shakespeare called her—'a lass
unparallel'd'. She had ensnared Julius Caesar after Pharsalus,
nearly brought him to ruin in the foolish war of Alexandria, and
had born him a son; these were her salad days. But now she had
to face the vicissitudes of Roman politics and the rivalry of a
virtuous woman before she could wholly win Mark Antony.
The Triumvirate was renewed in the next year and Antony
married Octavia, sister of his rival Octavian. Until 37 B.C. there
was peace in the Roman world. Antony organised the eastern
provinces and prepared for the Great Parthian War: Octavian
resettled the veterans in Italy and quietly mustered support in
Italy and the West. Antony had the more glamorous role in every
sense of the word. But his Parthian campaigns went badly and
their failure was crucial. Antony began to fall more and more
under the influence of Cleopatra with whom he contracted some
form of marriage. The chaste Octavia was put aside for the
delights of Alexandria and the 'Inimitable Life' which he led
there with Cleopatra. There was talk according to Octavian's
propaganda of an Eastern Empire with Alexandria as the capital.
But, as Caesar and Pompey had shown, the Roman world could
not endure two masters. So for the third time, the forces of the
East (Antony and Cleopatra) were arranged against those of the
West (Octavian) and they clashed in a naval battle fought at
Actium in 31 B.C. No account of this decisive battle makes
military sense, but the facts seem to be that Cleopatra's fleet sailed
away, that Antony joined her and they sailed for Egypt. There
for a few more months, the 'Inimitable Life' continued, but its
practitioners took a new name—the 'Companions of Death'.
Then Octavian caught up with them: Antony committed suicide
after one more futile battle, and Cleopatra took the asp. All this is

in Plutarch's *Life of Antony*, later to be transmuted by Shakespeare in *Antony and Cleopatra*. Octavian was now sole master of the Roman world.

Such, in the baldest of outlines, is the narrative of the decline and fall of the Roman Republic over the 100 years or so from Tiberius Gracchus to the Battle of Actium. Telescoped in this way and concentrating on the history of war and politics which are the themes of the classical writers, it seems a story of unrelieved horror and disaster. But what sort of picture should we get, under that formula, from a comparable period between say the American Civil War and the War in Vietnam? Yet as we know, even in this horrendous century there have been interludes of peace and prosperity and many millions have known personal happiness. So it was in the Roman Republic. There is a very significant passage in a letter of Cicero's, written from Formiae in Latium on March 1st, 49 B.C., as Caesar was preparing to enter Rome and Pompey to withdraw from Italy. 'The country people and farmers talk to me a great deal. All they care for is their lands, their little farms, their petty incomes. Consider how public opinion has changed. They fear the man they once trusted [Pompey], and admire the man they once feared [Caesar]'. This is a phenomenon that has never ceased to amaze politicians, though Cicero had the good sense to add: 'It grieves me to think of our errors and wrongdoings that have led to this reaction.' A man who understood those petty individual hopes and fears might have the answer to the question of Gaius Matius (p. 116).

CHAPTER 20

Rome and Italy—social and economic conditions

AN INTIMATE, BRILLIANT PICTURE of Roman society at this time is afforded by Cicero's letters. There are more than 800 in the surviving collection, covering the years 68 to 43 B.C. (the majority not earlier than 54 B.C.). Their value is that they were not written for publication. As a good photograph conserves the fleeting moment, so these letters reflect the hopes and fears, the preoccupations and amusements of Cicero and his friends in the last agonies of the Roman Republic. Pompey, Caesar, Crassus and Mark Antony all appear—sometimes in an unfamiliar light. What was it like to entertain to dinner the Dictator Julius Caesar, as Cicero did in his villa at Puteoli? 'Nerve-racking', says the host: 'he travelled with a bodyguard of 2,000 soldiers. But it passed off tolerably: he was in a very good humour: the talk at table was all of literature and serious subjects were avoided. All the same, once is enough.' Cicero's social circle was a wide one though he was never at ease with the great nobles. He shows a respect for the rank of Appius Claudius that he cannot have felt for the man; there is an astringent letter from Q. Metellus Celer, rebuking Cicero for want of the proper regard 'for the standing of our family'. Such fine gentlemen never let him forget that he was a *parvenu*.

With his intimates Cicero is relaxed, his mood nicely adjusted to theirs. Thus he writes of politics and scandal to the young rake-hell Caelius Rufus, of dinners and menus to the Epicurean Papirius Paetus, of art collecting and prices to Fadius Gallus. His own family stand out with all the realism of a Roman portrait. With his first wife, Terentia, affection cools and there is a divorce after 30 years. His last letter to her would be offhand even to a housekeeper (. . . 'see that there is a hand-basin in the bathroom'). But she was a nagging woman, and, as Aemilius Paullus had said in a similar case, only the wearer knows where the shoe pinches. His brother Quintus is shown as a good man of affairs, but touchy and henpecked in private life: Pomponia, his second, moody wife is the cause of painful scenes. Then there is young Marcus, a student at Athens, getting through an allowance of £1,000 a year with the help of his tutor, but promising to do better in future. Cicero's real love—like that of so many Romans —went to his daughter, Tullia. Her death in childbirth left him desolate, hoping for but not believing in the immortality of the soul. In general, we are shown an urbane and civilised society, passionately absorbed in politics, finding pleasure in country houses, in dinner-parties and in literature. Rome is the centre of the world. Her citizens are often in debt but credit is easy. They long for security but it is an age of civil wars. The resemblance to Renaissance Italy is striking. There too, a sophisticated society lived under the shadow of sudden and violent death.

For the workaday life of the Italian countryside we may first turn to the three books on agriculture by the great polymath, M. Terentius Varro. Published in 37 B.C., their dramatic setting is earlier and they reflect farming practice in Italy before the Civil Wars. Varro wrote as an expert. He had kept large flocks of cattle and sheep in Apulia, which were driven north for summer pasturing to his own district of Reate in the Sabine country. His villa at Casinum had a famous aviary which was something of a showpiece: its features included a 'bird theatre' full of singing birds, a 'harbour' with pens for ducks, an orrery, and a wind-and-water clock. But the aviary is described as a plaything only: his main task is to deal in a practical and methodical way with all the main branches of farming. The headings are cereals, animal-husbandry and farm feeding, which includes poultry and other table-birds, bees, hares and rabbits, fish-farming in ponds or *vivaria*, snails (the *escargot* is not the least of Rome's legacies to France), and dormice—the last a Roman delicacy not now in vogue. The book starts with the claim that farming should be both for profit and pleasure and that Italy is the best farmed of all countries. This is easy to believe, if indeed Italian farmers followed the precepts set out so elaborately and for such a wide range of specialised activities. For cereals, viticulture and orchard fruits there is a systematic account of methods of sowing or planting, care needed during growth, harvesting and storing. In properly built granaries wheat can be preserved for 50, millet for 100 years. There are special fruit stores (*oporothecae*) for the preservation of apples, pears, grapes, quinces, pomegranates and sorbs. Other things to be preserved or pickled are olives, walnuts, dates and figs. Everyone knows about olive oil, but not about the lees (*amurca*), which should be stored and used as a weed killer.

Animal husbandry displays the same system and care. Each of the main domesticated animals—sheep, cattle, horses, goats, pigs, asses and dogs—is treated under the headings of points of the breed, mating, period of gestation, birth, care of the young and rearing. Then there is the optimum size of the herd—50 or 100 for goats, 700 or 800 for sheep, 100 or 150 for swine, 100 or 120 for cattle—and the ratio of males to females. Varro has much to say about asses—the speciality of the Reate district—and there is a long passage on the breeding of mules. The herdsmen's duties are carefully described. The head herdsman must be able to read and write since he must keep the herd book, describing animal and human diseases and their remedies. Women should be allowed to go along with the herds to the mountain pastures, as happens in Illyricum. Sturdy girls they are too—they will step aside to have their babies and bring them back as if they had found them! In general, Varro's attitude to slaves is markedly more humane than that of Cato—he maintains it pays to treat them well, and their breeding can be a source of profit. But, he says, don't keep too many of the same nation together; it leads to quarrels. Spartacus had not fought totally in vain.

Varro has some fascinating asides. Sheep dogs, we are told, are attached to shepherds and not to the sheep. To illustrate— 'Publius Aufidius Pontiarius, of Amiternum, had brought some flocks of sheep in northern Umbria: the purchase including the dogs but not the shepherds, though the latter had to take them to pasture at Metapontum and to market at Heraclea (in Apulia). The men returned home; the dogs turned up a few days later in Umbria, of their own accord, simply out of longing for their masters, and living off the country, though it is a journey of many days.' (And of more than 300 miles.) And yet he adds, none of the shepherds had used the infallible recipe for attaching a dog to its master by giving it a boiled frog!

On profits, we learn that 5,000 fieldfares ought to fetch 60,000 sesterces (about 2,400 dollars, or £950). As for bee-keeping, Varro knew two brothers from Falerii who never made less than 10,000 sesterces (a year?) from this source—but they always waited for the best time to sell their honey, rather than rushing to catch the early market. We hear of the excellence of Gaulish hams and of the flitches annually sent to Rome. There is talk of remarkable sows: one from Portugal had 15 inches of meat between the skin and the bone: Varro caps this with the claim to have seen in Arcadia a sow so fat that she could not rise to her feet, and a shrewmouse had made a hole in her side and there raised her young. Finally, there is the picture he gives of Q. Tremellius Scrofa, the leading Roman authority on agriculture, whose highly cultivated estates are more worth seeing than the villas of Lucullus. He speaks with the authority of an expert, and is accorded the deference due to one.

To Varro's list of specialities we may add oyster-farming, for which the Lucrine Lake won a name among epicures. Trout, mullet and lampreys were also reared in *vivaria*, and Roman practice seems to have been ahead of modern in this respect. The luxury trade also created a market for flowers and garlands which was met by highly skilled gardeners. Roses and lilies were chiefly cultivated, and the *rosaria* or rose gardens of Paestum became famous. Many new varieties of flowers and fruits were brought into Italy from the East. Lucullus who introduced the cherry was one of the leading experts, and his famous gardens on the Pincian Hill in Rome, and also his luxurious villas in Campania, were of scientific as well as aesthetic importance. The vine and the olive were by now the staples of Italian agriculture. Italian vintages, especially those of Campania and Sicily, could challenge the noblest products of Greece and won a rich market. Both wine and olives travelled up the Rhône Valley to the wealthy chiefs of Gaul, across the Alpine passes into Germany; through Aquileia they reached the peoples of the Danube lands and Eastern Europe. The wine growers of Campania became wealthy and built themselves fine houses in town and country. The sudden growth of urban elegance in Pompeii later in the second century B.C., and again after the Social War, was largely due to them. Some fifty *villae* or country-houses in Campania have now been excavated: while some were the property of wealthy Romans, others belonged to the nobility of the Campanian towns. The ancient world had an insatiable demand for olive oil, and here too the *olearia* of

Italy, most notably those of Venafrum, won a large slice of the world trade. Many varieties of olives were cultivated, some for eating, others for oil of many grades. Despite the lament of the moralists about imports of foreign corn, in fact cereal production continued in Italy. Rome had a special corn dole but other parts of Italy had to feed themselves. In some of the estates in Etruria and elsewhere in northern Italy cereals were grown on a very large scale.

No doubt much of the work was done by slaves, but on the estates of Domitius Ahenobarbus we hear of *coloni* or tenants. Like the great feudal magnates, landowners such as Domitius and Pompey could raise whole armies from their estates. As we have seen, peasant farming found new scope in Cisalpine Gaul and we must not forget the many thousands of veterans settled on the land in other parts of Italy. There is little evidence of how they fared for we seldom hear of them after they get their grants of land. The general impression of Italian agriculture in the late Republic is one of prosperity and diversification. To quote Varro once more: 'What useful product is there which not merely does not grow in Italy, but which does not grow to perfection? What spelt (*far*) can I compare with Campanian? What wheat with Apulian? What wine is equal to Falernian, what olive oil to Venafran?' And for good reason, he says, since the Italian farmer judges by two criteria—will the land give a good return for money and labour, and is it a fertile soil or not? In default of either of these, anyone who wishes to take up farming is out of his mind and should be locked up by his family and relatives. How far the Italian farmers were successful in keeping the land fertile we cannot judge. Varro's insistence on the importance of manuring shows that the problem was recognised, and we also hear of crop rotation.

CHAPTER 21

Trade and commerce

THE EMERGENCE OF A WEALTHY business class in Rome has already been noted, and its influence on politics. It remains to say something of how activities were organised. This can best be done by studying the *publicani* who farmed the taxes of Asia. Not only were they the most elaborately organised, but their operations gave rise to so many complaints and scandals that they are unusually well documented. In their heyday (between the Gracchi and Sulla), these tax farmers were organised in companies (*societates*) with headquarters in Rome. How many shareholders (*participes*) they had we do not know, but we must not think in terms of the large limited-liability company of today with shares on the open market. Their affairs were in the hands of a manager (*magister*), whose chief duty was to negotiate with the Roman government, and especially to enter bids for the collection of the three kinds of tax (agricultural tithes, pasture dues, harbour taxes) which were let out for four-year periods. It is to be presumed that the highest tender was accepted, since this was the amount the contractors would pass on to the government, keeping any extra amount collected as their own profit. At the Asian end was the working organisation, consisting of a large staff of clerks and agents under a deputy manager (*promagister*). Their headquarters were apparently at Ephesus. They did not collect the taxes directly, these being sub-contracted to the various communities by agreement (*pactiones*) probably on an annual basis. The companies' agents saw to it that nothing taxable escaped the net, that the assessments were as high as possible, that amounts due were handed over and that interest (a very high one) was collected on arrears.

The possibilities for abuse are obvious, especially where the governor of the province was complacent. Together with their natural allies, the money-lenders (*negotiatores*), the *publicani* bled Asia white as long as they were allowed to do so. That Gaius Gracchus should have given their order control of the courts which dealt with financial abuses in the provinces was a monstrous piece of political opportunism. While the companies were nominally rivals, they could act together if their interests so demanded. Thus we hear of at least one occasion when they asked for the cancellation of contracts, and exerted very heavy political pressure to that end without immediate success. Another and perhaps commoner practice was for companies to form a ring and agree in advance on the tenders to be made. While Asia offered the richest pickings (until Sulla and Lucullus), we also hear of *publicani* in Cilicia and other Eastern provinces, Gallia Narbonensis and Africa. It must be remembered that tax collecting was only one of the activities open to the *societates*; we have noted Polybius' passage about their operations in Italy in the previous century, and the great increase in public land in the provinces must have enlarged their scope.

The term *negotiatores* covers men engaged in a wide range of services such as banking, money-changing and money-lending which offered a good field for investment, both in Rome and in the provinces. The cities and kings of Asia borrowed on a very large scale; aspiring Roman politicians especially at the start of their career were always short of money; countless individuals needed loans, whether to expand their business or to pay off tax arrears. There is a famous passage of Cicero's about the situation in Gallia Narbonensis in 74 B.C. 'The province', he says, 'is packed with traders, full of Roman citizens. No Gaul ever does business independently with a citizen of Rome; not a penny changes hands in Gaul without the transaction being recorded in the books of Roman citizens.' But here again Asia offered by far the richest field, and Tenney Frank has collected the evidence for Italians engaged in Asian business, such as M. Cluvius, banker of Puteoli, who had lent money to five Asian cities. Rates of interest varied widely according to conditions: one of the most outrageous was the 48 per cent charged by that paragon of virtue M. Junius Brutus. But 12 per cent seems to have been recognised as the norm in the Eastern provinces; if this seems high, it is lower than the rates of most modern hire-purchase companies. (In Italy rates were lower usually at 6 per cent and occasionally as low as 4 per cent.) But while at times the money-lenders deserved the description of 'harpies that snatch at the people's food', some of them were recognised as benefactors by the Asian cities themselves and were honoured by inscriptions and statues. Magie has sketched the career of a certain Aulus Aemilius Zosimus who rose to the highest office at Priene, 'loving the city as his own fatherland and showing all the devotion of a native-born citizen'. Besides the professional *negotiatores* there were very many amateurs including senators. This may sound inconsistent with the high moral line often taken in that body about the evils of usury, but it is not surprising when one reflects that, in the absence of any proper system of stocks and shares, money-lending was by far the easiest means of putting spare capital to work.

It is not possible to document the trade of the late Republic in the same detail as the early Empire. No doubt there was a large expansion—especially in the period between Sulla and the Civil War. Even the pirates attest the volume of the trade which was their prey. We know of the luxury goods brought to Italy from the East—Greek wines, *objets d'art*, marble, textiles and furniture. The ship wrecked at Mahdia off the coast of Africa whose cargo of marble columns and statues was discovered in 1907, dates from this period: her contents were evidently for the antique trade in Rome. Then there were the regular imports of grain from Africa, Sicily and Sardinia, most of which at this time came through Puteoli. A fleet of Egyptian ships in 55 B.C. brought to that port 'cheap and flashy goods of paper, linen and glass'—the Alexandrian junk-trade, in fact by shiploads. Italy exported wine, olive oil and the metal ware of Campania. Very little of the merchandise, it would appear, was carried in Roman ships' bottoms. Even for her naval campaign in the Aegean Rome seems to have relied on the ships of the allies. And she seems to have been content to let the profits of the carrying trade go to the captains of Gades, Massilia, Alexandria or Syria.

We can to some extent follow the fortunes of individual ports. The rise of Puteoli was spectacular and it handled most of the Roman as well as the Campanian trade to and from the East, equipped as it was with the facilities of a major Hellenistic port. It had a younger rival in Ostia as terminus for the trade from Spain, Gaul and Liguria, but there the advantage of being closer to Rome was offset by the disadvantages of a poor anchorage. In the Western Mediterranean Gades (Cadiz) throve famously:

she seems to have succeeded to the Carthaginian trade in the Atlantic and Mediterranean. The rich merchant of Gades became a familiar and welcome figure in the night life of Rome. Massilia, on a lesser scale, also did well until she chose the wrong side in the wars between Caesar and Pompey. A second Gallic port developed at Narbo reflecting the economic growth of Narbonensis. Brundisium and Dyrrhachium became busy channel ports for the crossing of the Adriatic. In the Eastern Mediterranean, Alexandria retained primacy. But Rhodes was in decline and Delos never recovered from its treatment by Mithridates. Ephesus was the chief port on the western coast of Asia Minor, followed closely by Smyrna. When Caesar refounded Corinth the natural advantages of the site quickly asserted themselves. A chain of important ports catered for the Black Sea traffic— Cyzicus, Heraclea, Sinope and Trapezus. Pontic timber was highly valued for ship-building, and was used for the yacht in which Catullus journeyed (so it would seem) from Bithynia to the head of the Adriatic, up the Po and the Adige, to Verona and to a final resting place on Lake Garda.

CHAPTER 22

Art, literature, and thought in the late Republic

THE TIME FROM SULLA TO CAESAR may fitly be called the first great age of Roman architecture. Sulla provided the conditions from which that art has so often found a stimulus—dictatorship, money and disaster. The Temple of Jupiter on the Capitol was destroyed in the fighting with the Marians: it fell to Sulla to commission this greatest of all building projects in Rome, although the dedication in 69 B.C. was by Q. Lutatius Catulus. We know nothing of this temple, itself destroyed in the Great Fire under Nero. But at the foot of the Capitol, and comprising a monumental backcloth for the Forum Romanum, there still stands a great building of Sullan inspiration—the *Tabularium* or Record Office. Michelangelo raised it by a storey and altered some of its fenestration: now entered from the Piazza di Campidoglio, it serves as the City Hall of Rome. Its austere and massive dignity is still compelling, a credit to its two great architects. Who the earlier one is we do not know, but it seems all but certain that he is responsible for the remarkable complex of buildings at the shrine of Fortuna Primigenia at Praeneste, the modern Palestrina. This project arose from the destructive siege of Praeneste by the troops of Sulla; the Allied bombing and shelling of the Second World War disclosed the full scale of a splendid conception. Its hemicycles, terraces and ramps take up the entire slope of a 600 ft. hill, with the oracular shrine at its summit not violating the natural skyline and commanding a superb view over the Campagna to the sea. It was possible to build because of the recent discovery of concrete, a spectacular advance in building technique, making for the use of new shapes and the covering of very large spaces. It has rightly been called 'perhaps the most seminal architectural complex in the whole Roman world'. Other famous Italian shrines embellished by Sulla were those of Hercules Victor at Tibur and Jupiter Anxur at Terracina. There too great buildings were carefully sited and integrated into noble landscapes. We cannot doubt that the same union of the architect's and the landscape-gardener's art was seen in the splendid country houses of Lucullus, Sulla and Julius Caesar. It was not to be repeated until the villas of the Italian Renaissance, or the country houses of eighteenth-century England with their landscaped parks. We can judge of it now only in a single and much later example—the Villa of Hadrian near Tivoli.

Pompey's enormous spoils were brought back from the Hellenistic East and his conquests were given a worthy commemoration in the building that bore his name. Situated on the Campus Martius and begun in 55 B.C., the Theatre of Pompey was set in a kind of art centre, for the *opera Pompeii* included a Temple to Venus Victrix, a *Curia* for the meetings of the Senate and a colonnaded square which served as an open-air art gallery.

Caesar who outdid Pompey in everything was not to be outdone in building. He was not granted time to complete the great programme of building and urbanisation which he planned for Rome and some of the schemes which he did begin were completed by Augustus. We hear of a scheme to canalise and straighten the Tiber, which would have enabled the development for building of the Campus Martius, whose sporting activities would have gone across the river. Augustus embanked the Tiber but left it in its natural channel. 'There was to have been a huge theatre built into the side of the Tarpeian Rock, and a Temple of Mars, the largest in the world . . .', says Suetonius in the *Life of Caesar*. Neither saw the light of day. But Caesar has left his mark on classical Rome as we know it. The Basilica Julia occupies much of the western part of the Forum Romanum, and from its ground-plan can be seen to rival the Tabularium in scale. Opposite is the Curia Julia, Caesar's Senate House; its noble and spacious proportions, preserved by the rebuilding under Diocletian, have now been disengaged from a medieval church. We can also appreciate how the Forum Julium, with its Temple of Venus Genetrix, set the pattern for the series of five imperial *fora*, from Caesar to Trajan, which form the most magnificent piece of town planning in ancient Rome.

The site for the Forum Julium is said to have cost 100,000,000 sesterces (£2,000,000). Land was dear in Rome, and the urban poor were increasingly housed in *insulae*, high buildings of nine or more storeys which were rented out in flats. Through building cheaply, charging high rents and skimping on maintenance, the landlords of these buildings made good profits. Living conditions for the poor were deteriorating. They may not have reached the squalor depicted by Juvenal rather more than a century later, but there were as yet few of the public amenities so lavishly provided by the emperors. At the other end of the social scale, the wealthier senators and merchants lived in opulent private houses in favoured quarters such as the Palatine and the Carinae, above the mists of the river and the stink and heat of the slums. We first hear of these town mansions late in the second century B.C. but increasing opulence soon made the prototypes out of date. In his day, according to Cicero, there were a hundred mansions in Rome that were finer than any at the beginning of the century.

Our knowledge of Roman thought and literature during the last century of the Republic is curiously uneven. Little survives of any author between the Gracchi and Sulla. From Sulla to Caesar come some of the greatest names—the poets Lucretius and Catullus and the historians Sallust and Caesar himself. Then there is Cicero, most versatile of Roman writers, vying with Demosthenes as the greatest orator of antiquity, Lucretius as expositor of Greek philosophy, and unrivalled as a writer of letters, the great exemplar of Latin prose style—and injudicious enough to venture into poetry. Because of these men and their lesser contemporaries, this period is recognised as the first phase of the Golden Age of Roman literature. But the earlier period was not unfruitful, and scholars have shown that its authors were interesting in their own right and as pioneers of trends others brought to fruition.

The violent political struggles of the period of the Gracchi led to an outburst of propaganda, expressed in histories and justificatory memoirs. Rutilius Rufus in exile at Smyrna wrote five books of *Memoirs* in Latin and a *History of Rome* in Greek. The first was, no doubt, an *apologia* for his political career, especially for his period in the province of Asia and the events of his trial. The *History* seems to have continued the work of his friend Polybius and is thought to have expressed the views of the Scipionic moderates on the great crises of the age. The Gracchan viewpoint is known to have found expression in the *Annals* of

C. Fannius, friend of Tiberius Gracchus and the probable source
of the favourable picture given in the *Life* by Plutarch. The
writing of memoirs engrossed the later years of many politicians,
notably the prominent senator Aemilius Scaurus and even Sulla
himself. Sulla indeed though ruthless and violent was no philistine.
He is credited with a thorough knowledge of Greek and Latin
literature: he was interested in Greek philosophy, bringing back
from Athens a library that contained all the works of Aristotle.
He is also said to have been a connoisseur of Greek art, though
his method of art-collecting was on a par with that of the late
Marshal Goering.

Perhaps the taste of the age is best seen in the figure of Q.
Lutatius Catulus, a leading champion of the Senate and consul in
the year 102 B.C. He was joint commander with Marius when the
Cimbri were defeated at Vercellae, fought in the Social War and
was driven to suicide in 87 B.C. by the victory of Marius' party.
Cicero, who introduces him as a figure in the dialogue *De
Oratore*, shows him as a man of wide and deep culture. His skill
in Greek commanded the admiration of Greeks; his Latin speeches
were marked by pure and graceful diction. He had studied the
Greek Sophists, especially their work on rhetoric, esteemed
Aristotle above any other Greek philosopher and was familiar
with Greek painting and sculpture. It was natural that such a
philhellene should have been the patron of Greek poets, and we
hear of his kindness to Antipater of Sidon and to Archias,
writers well represented in the classical Greek Anthology.
Lutatius Catulus wrote poetry (two minor samples survive); a
history of his own times is mentioned, though it had become a
rarity by the age of Cicero. This combination of man of action,
patron and writer recalls certain of the Elizabethans.

Such Roman gentlemen seem intellectual lightweights beside
the great Greek savant Posidonius (*c.* 135–*c.* 50 B.C.), the pupil of
Panaetius in Athens, who taught at Rhodes and through whom
Stoicism continued to influence some of the best minds in Rome.
The greatest polymath since Aristotle, he was also the most
intelligent traveller since Herodotus. Though his own writings
are lost, extensive fragments are preserved in Strabo, Diodorus
Siculus, Cicero, Appian, Seneca and Plutarch. Modern scholars
have tried to identify these and to show how they may be used to
give at least an outline of the synthesis that Posidonius built up
on the nature of the world and of man. It is a task that has

generated much controversy and is far from finished. Some things
are clear. We can see how Posidonius' work was guided by his
belief that man's supreme object is 'to live in contemplation of
the truth and order of the whole (universe), participating therein
to the best of one's powers, and never acting under the influence
of the irrational part of the soul'. In the light of this, Posidonius'
works in the fields of astronomy, geography, ethnology, history
and ethics are seen to have a unifying purpose. They are an
attempt to understand the world of his time, the Mediterranean
world as unified by Rome, in its physical and human aspects.
Hence his study tours to the Western provinces which began in
96 B.C. and which took him to Massilia and Narbonensis, Spain,
Africa, the Balearic Islands and Sicily. He worked methodically,
studying the geology, climate, animals, plants, peoples and
customs of each region. Thus, in what is now southern Provence,
he notes the current of the Rhône, the limestone plain of the
Crau, the *mistral*, the city of Massilia and the customs of the
Gauls and Ligurians, including their predilection for exhibiting
the severed heads (*têtes coupées*) of their enemies. In Spain he
studied the Atlantic and its tides and wrote a monograph *On
the Ocean*. He was the first to suggest that the tides were due to
the pull of the moon, and that India might be reached by sailing
west across the Atlantic. Centuries later Columbus was to put this
theory to the test with surprising results. He notes the advanced
technology of the Roman mines in Spain—and the brutal treatment of the miners. He liked the native peoples of Spain. The
Celtiberians he called 'gentle and humane': he criticised Roman
brutality to the people of Numantia. To him is probably due the
favourable portrayal of Viriathus, the shepherd-general of the
Lusitani, in the pages of Appian, where he appears as the archetypal Heroic Barbarian.

Indeed, the relationship of Rome to the conquered peoples
seems to have been the central theme of Posidonius' monumental
History, which took up world history from Polybius' terminal
date of 146 B.C. and continued it to (probably) the death of Sulla.
His attitude to Roman world rule was not one of uncritical
admiration. On the one hand, Nature had constituted mankind
so as to form a human commonwealth or Great Society (*societas
humana*); Rome's world mission was to bring this society into
being. On the other, Roman history was full of disgraceful
episodes such as the Gracchan revolution, the Slave Wars in

Sicily and the wars between Marius and Sulla. Her mission could fail. It would succeed only if Roman statesmen were taught by philosophers 'to participate in the truth and order of the whole universe'. The hopes that Panaetius reposed in Scipio Aemilianus Posidonius directed to Pompey. When Pompey visited him at Rhodes on the way to fight Mithridates, he gave him the precept Peleus gave to Achilles, 'Ever excel, and be distinguished above others'. He seems to have written a monograph on the deeds of Pompey, whose lamentable end he did not know of for he died before the clash with Caesar. We can only adumbrate the mystic conception that lay at the heart of Posidonius' teaching—the link between Man the microcosm and the Cosmos itself, since our souls are a part of the Divine Fire into which they will return. No Greek of comparable intelligence studied the Roman world after his time, and his is the last great cosmology (in ancient times) to be built out of a synthesis of the sciences.

After Posidonius, the influence of Stoicism at Rome continued to be more powerful than that of any other Greek philosophy. But the political failure of Rutilius Rufus and the defeat of Pompey symbolise the failure, for a long time to come, of the high hopes once conceived by Panaetius. Stoicism was to become associated with idealists, like Cato of Utica, 'who thought he was living in Plato's Republic and not among the scum of Romulus', his son-in-law the tyrannicide, Marcus Junius Brutus, and with austere extremists like Marcus Favonius. Already there is a foretaste of its rôle under the early Empire, and especially under Nero when it taught men how to die well rather than how to live.

Epicureanism, the other missionary philosophy of the Hellenistic world, made fewer converts. Its beginnings in Rome are obscure, but we know that in 75 B.C. Calpurnius Piso presented a villa in Campania for an Epicurean academy, under the charge of Philodemus of Gadara. The writings of Philodemus (in a charred manuscript) were among the papyri discovered in Herculaneum: they set out the teachings of Epicurus in plain and undistinguished Greek. He was succeeded by Siron, one of whose pupils was the youthful Virgil. Cicero's friend Atticus, Horace and Maecenas were also attracted to Epicureanism. And indeed it had much to offer in the turbulent and competitive world of the late Republic. It preached the laying aside of ambition, withdrawal from politics, abandonment of the search for riches, in favour of a life of retirement devoted to simple pleasures in the company of friends and to the contemplation of the universe. Withdrawal in fact to a kind of Arcadia, a high fortress buttressed by philosophy, 'from which', as Lucretius wrote, 'you can look down, and see on all sides others far astray, desperately searching for the true road of life'. As such, it was directly opposed to the Roman tradition of the primacy of the life of politics and affairs. 'If', said Philodemus, 'a man were to undertake a systematic inquiry into what is most destructive of friendship and most productive of enmity, he would find it in the system of political life. Witness the envy roused by those who compete for the prizes, the rivalry that springs up between them, the animosities that accompany the introduction of new laws and the deliberate organisation of factions which set, not only individuals, but whole peoples by the ears.' Already in Rome there was a class of *otiosi*, men who devoted themselves to leisure in their country houses in Campania or near Tivoli. In the philosophy of Epicurus they could find a rationale.

Whether Lucretius was a pupil of Philodemus we do not know. Little is known of his life: to us he appears a lonely and gigantic figure—'I wander through pathless haunts of the Muses, untrodden by the foot of man'. We can say little more than that his six books *De Rerum Natura* (On the Nature of the Universe) were published not later than 55 B.C., and that his object was to convert his friend, the Roman noble Gaius Memmius. Farrington rightly says that it is a monologue of Lucretius to Memmius, which we overhear. (So too with the *Confessions* of Augustine, a monologue between the author and God.) Lucretius makes his own claim to originality in setting out the teachings of Epicurus in Latin verse—for the rest, he follows in the master's steps. Original it certainly was. Epicurus' own writings were dry and technical, his subject-matter might seem abstruse beyond the compass of a didactic poem. Lucretius succeeds because of his poetic gifts, especially in the use of imagery and metaphor, and his command of a sonorous and archaic diction admirably attuned to the high seriousness of his theme. His poem is the main source for what we know of Epicureanism as a philosophy, and of the atomic system which it refurbished to explain the nature of the physical world. Whether it converted Memmius we do not know. But it has fascinated or repelled men of many ages as a statement on the highest level of poetic intensity of the materialist view of the universe. As a work of art it challenges the *Aeneid* as the noblest achievement of Latin poetry.

Originality is also the mark of the New Poets, a group of young men whose values and tastes we can only judge from the poems of Catullus. They mostly came from the towns of Cisalpine Gaul—Verona, Brescia and Novum Comum—a romanised land, but as yet a province. Theirs is indeed the first major contribution made by provincial Romans and it was a revolutionary one. The poet, as they saw him, was not to concern himself with national themes or public figures. 'I'm not much concerned, Caesar', wrote Catullus, 'with seeking to please you —nor to know whether you're black or white.' The poet should live in a private world, whose delights should be love, the craft of verse and the refinements of Greek mythology. He should write for himself and his circle of friends.

These highly self-conscious young men had their own critical vocabulary, their own canons of taste and their own exemplars, notably the Alexandrian poets Callimachus, Philetas and Euphorion. They sought polish, urbanity and learning (*doctrina*) —the learning standing for versatility in metre and erudition in the handling of Greek legends, especially the more obscure. The formula helps understanding of the poems of Catullus. It does not explain why he is one of the world's greatest lyric poets, nor why his poems to Lesbia are among the finest ever written on the theme of love. Now that modern appraisals have swept away the old dichotomy between Lesbia's lover and the 'learned poet' we see Catullus in a clearer light. The key lies in his emotions, which were of unusual and perhaps unique intensity. Where they are not engaged his poems are what he calls them himself, *nugae* (trifles)—agreeable, satiric, light-hearted, the range of mood is wide—but no more. They were engaged when he wrote his version of the legend of Attis, making him a young Greek athlete caught up in the horrors of an orgiastic and savage cult. They went out to Ariadne deserted on Naxos and rescued by Bacchus—a symbol of redemption by divine love. They went out to his friend Manlius Torquatus and his bride Junia Aurunculeia as he wrote an epithalamium as their wedding gift. They went out, very naturally, to the pair of true lovers Acme and Septimius, who found all their delight and joy in each other. Like Donne's lovers they would have said:

> 'Let sea-discoverers to new worlds have gone,
> Let Maps to other, worlds on worlds have showne
> Let us possesse one world, each hath one, and is one.'

Catullus' emotions were engaged, all of them, in his violent and passionate love affair with 'Lesbia', who was almost certainly Clodia, the most notorious beauty of her day. It brought him ecstasy, humiliation and despair. She must have found him amusing but finally boring with his insistence on a faithfulness and tenderness quite beyond her range. His finest poems sprang from this unequal love. We should be grateful to Clodia.

Caesar, Sallust and Cornelius Nepos survive from the considerable historical writing of the late Republic, and it is known that they do not represent its full range. Cornelius Nepos, another author from Cisalpine Gaul, wrote biographies—*The Lives of Famous Men*—for a popular audience. They lack critical insight and grace of style and suggest that the loss of his *Universal History* is not a major one. But at least they show a freedom from national prejudice and political *parti pris* which cannot be credited to the more important works of Caesar and Sallust, both of whom wrote rather to defend themselves than out of concern for history. This is the more blatant with Sallust. A 'new man' from Amiternum in the Sabine country, he held his own for a while in the violence and corruption of late Republican politics; in 50 B.C. he was expelled from the Senate for immorality. Later Caesar made him governor of Numidia and he seems to have exploited his province with the zeal of a Verres. Caesar's death put a finish to his political career, but the famous Gardens of Sallust provided a luxurious retreat for his second career as historian of the degeneracy of the Republic. This is the theme that runs through his two monographs, the *Conspiracy of Catilina* and the *War against Jugurtha*. Both stress the venality and incompetence of conservative senators, both present great 'popular' figures, Caesar and Marius, in a good light. The *Histories* survive only in fragments, but are known to have covered the years 78–67 B.C. Sallust has been surprisingly highly praised, both by Tacitus who used him as a model, and by Quintilian who compared him with Thucydides. From the historical point of view the praise will hardly stand: on stylistic grounds it is not inept. Sallust went to great pains to evolve a terse, pointed, violent prose, well suited to the harsh and violent times. He saw history as determined by the character and morals of its protagonists and tried to penetrate the psychology of each. He understood the value of vivid descriptions of battles and other dramatic incidents, and the note of authenticity that comes from the inclusion of letters and speeches. With him for the first time in Latin history becomes literature. That it loses something in the process cannot be denied; what the gain might be is more amply shown by Sallust's greater successor Tacitus.

Bias and special pleading are more pervasive in the historical works of Caesar—and much more skilfully concealed. After all, the depredations of Sallust in Numidia were as nothing compared with those of Caesar in Gaul. The *Gallic Wars* are notable for a dry and factual style, a sober tone, a constant use of the third person singular, a preference for action rather than description, and for events rather than character. All this gives the subtle impression that Caesar had anticipated Ranke and was 'simply writing exactly what happened'. But these in fact are the memoirs of a victorious general who had a host of political enemies and are written from the self-centred viewpoint usual in the genre. This granted, one must not deny their very real merits. It is invaluable for the student of warfare to have the account of his most notable campaigns by one of the greatest commanders of antiquity. Moreover, the narrative moves between the Rhine and Brittany, from the Alps to the English Channel and the Thames. Here is the first substantial account of the lands, peoples and customs of northern and western Europe. The written history of Britain, France and Germany must always begin with Caesar's *Gallic Wars*. The *Civil War* is a tight-lipped account of the main struggle with Pompey. Less interest attaches to the narratives of the wars in Egypt, Africa, and Spain compiled by Caesar's lieutenants to round off the story of their commander's wars.

Quintilian wrote that the name of Cicero had come to be regarded as that not of a man but of eloquence itself. From the first public Professor of Oratory in Rome, this was the highest tribute he could pay. Today it falls flat. Many barriers stand between the modern reader and appreciation of Cicero's speeches. One is the habit of silent reading; Greek and Roman authors wrote to be read aloud. Another is the current distrust of oratory, which may be a healthy reaction against the demagogues of the Fascist powers—though Churchill and Roosevelt showed how to use oratory in a just cause. More important, perhaps, now that the English-speaking peoples are no longer brought up on the Authorised Version of the Bible, they seem to have lost all feeling for the grand style in prose. Who now can command the cadences of the Gettysburg Speech? Cicero's speeches are the fruits of a highly subtle and diligently practised art, firmly applied to the end of persuasion in the Senate House, Forum and law courts in competition with many other speakers of almost equal skill. It called for an expert knowledge of the art of elocution, the resources of the Latin language and the psychology of the audience to be addressed. Armed with these the orator could then turn to the facts of the case and the nature of the law. The voice of Cicero was an organ of ample register, and its nobler tones are heard in the great public speeches against Catiline, Verres, or in the series of Philippics (especially the Second) aimed at Mark Antony. Burke was entirely right when he said that Cicero left 'to the world and to the latest posterity a monument by which it might judge what course a great public accuser in a great public cause ought to pursue. . . .' Of his letters I have already spoken; they are still read and appreciated. But the philosophical writings are under something of a cloud; although up to the nineteenth century to read the dialogues such as *On Old Age, On Friendship, On Duties* were part of the education of a gentleman. The modern world has little use for his ethics and prefers to obtain its philosophy from Plato. Cicero would not grumble at that. None the less, it would do well to turn again to his political writings, especially *On the State (De Re Publica)* and *On the Laws (De Legibus)*. The titles acknowledge a debt to Plato but Cicero makes his own contribution. His political experience was wider and deeper than that of Plato, as the political life of Rome was on a grander scale than that of Athens.

The most lasting influence of Cicero, however, is that over the Latin language. It subsumes, of course, all the work of writers and orators of his own and the previous generation who made Latin prose a suitable vehicle for expressing a very wide range of ideas and emotions—a world language to match the world power of Rome. Cicero has survived because he was the most accomplished of them all: in oratory, supreme master of the periodic structure through which it achieved its most striking effects; in his letters, at once urbane and idiomatic; in his philosophical works, lucid and copious. He has been one of the two great normative influences in the history of Latin—the other being the *Vulgate*, the translation of the scriptures by St Jerome. Between them they have made Latin the most ubiquitous and enduring of the great world languages. Who can yet say that its day is done?

CHAPTER 23

The Augustan Principate

AFTER THE BATTLE OF ACTIUM Octavian did not return to Rome until August 29 B.C. Antony and Cleopatra had been dead for a year but the problems of the East, notably those of incorporating Egypt in the Empire, account for the delay. While in Alexandria, he had been at pains to visit the sepulchre of Alexander the Great, prompted perhaps by thoughts of the great tasks ahead rather than by historical curiosity. For when he was asked whether he would not also like to see the tombs of the Ptolemies, he replied sharply 'I came to see the King, not a row of corpses!' Only Alexander and Julius Caesar had been confronted as Octavian now was with the problems of ruling the world. Alexander had died young at about Octavian's age. Caesar had been murdered. A few days before his threefold triumph of August 13–15, 29 B.C., Octavian (it is said) heard a private reading of the *Georgics* of Virgil, as yet unpublished. At the end of the First Georgic he would have heard the famous prayer for his own preservation:

'Gods of our fathers, native gods, Romulus and our
mother Vesta,
You who guard the Tuscan Tiber and the Palatine of Rome,
At least do not prevent this young man from the rescue
of an age turned upside down.'

The passage is one in which Virgil voices the predominant feelings of the Roman world—revulsion from the horrors of

139

civil war, universal longing for peace and the recognition that peace depended on a man in his early thirties known to be of uncertain health. Of all the gifts which might have been asked for Octavian, that of long life must have seemed the most unlikely to be granted. But granted it was and in full measure: he was to reach the age of 77, and to enjoy a reign of 45 years. This gift of time made it possible for him to overhaul and reform almost every institution of the Roman state, and to establish the Empire on a sound and rational basis that endured for more than two centuries. Few men in the history of the world have accomplished so much and it is proper that the most creative period of Roman civilisation should be known as the Age of Augustus.

This universal longing for peace, expressed again and again by the writers of the decade 40–30 B.C., was one of his chief assets. He had won over Lepidus' troops, and those of Antony's after Actium. Unlike Julius Caesar, he would find few irreconcilable rebels and none who was to be a major menace. He kept intact much of Antony's settlement of the East and it has been noted that he took some of his most successful provincial governors from the former supporters of his rival. His own supporters and advisers, M. Vipsanius Agrippa and C. Maecenas, were among his best assets. Agrippa, a man of obscure family, had the military talents that Octavian lacked and he was ready to devote all his formidable powers of work and organisation to the loyal support of his friend. He might have made a good ruler in his own right, and at one point was designated by Augustus as his successor, but while Augustus lived he was content to be second-in-command. Maecenas, descended from Etruscan kings, was a man of a very different stamp—sophisticated, a connoisseur of the arts, the archetypal patron of literature, a sensualist and a *bon viveur*, he was yet a fine administrator and diplomat and his influence could reach into quarters where Agrippa was disliked.

Agrippa died in 12, Maecenas in 8 B.C.; both should have had many more years, but they had advised Augustus through the formative phase of the Principate and lived to see it firmly established. Later, in his step-sons Drusus and Tiberius, and especially in the latter, Augustus had two splendid generals who could carry great commands as worthy representatives of the imperial house. Hardest to evaluate is the influence of his wife, Livia Drusilla, whom he married when he was 25, and who outlived him by 15 years. It was a lasting and, to all appearances, a happy marriage. All that scandal could find to say against Livia's morals was that she tolerated her husband's infidelities. Baffled there, it has tried to make her the intriguer behind the scenes, ruthless in advancing the interests of her own sons, but it fails to convince. None the less, it is possible to regret that through her first marriage to Claudius Nero the eccentric qualities of the Claudian house were introduced into the first dynasty of Roman emperors, there to compound the *gens Julia*.

In the jungle of Roman power-politics survival depended on personal qualities. The political gifts of Octavian were of a very high order. He could appraise a political situation with the cool judgement that Caesar had brought to military affairs, and he showed a like tenacity of purpose. He was a good judge of men. Above all, he had what Caesar lacked, an acute sense of the emotive power of words, titles and slogans. It was this that made him such a master of propaganda—witness the blast that he turned on Antony in the year before Actium. This same quality was to be used in a subtler form in the constitutional settlement he devised for Rome.

Such a settlement needed careful preparation and staging. Meanwhile there were pressing problems and obligations. The need for demobilisation was acute with some 70 legions in arms. They were reduced to 28 and the men discharged were settled in a major programme of colonisation. Indeed, Augustus claims that in the course of his reign he settled 300,000 veterans, and as a founder of colonies he ranks second to none—witness his foundations in Africa, Sicily, Spain, Narbonensis, Macedonia, Achaea, Asia, Syria and Pisidia. 'Moreover', he adds, 'Italy has 28 colonies which I established, some of which have grown to be famous in my lifetime.' Many Augustan foundations are famous cities today, notably Emerida (Merida) and Saragossa (Caesar-augusta) in Spain, Nîmes (Nemausus) and Avignon (Avennio) in Gaul, Augusta Taurinorum (Turin) in Italy and Patrae (Patras) in Greece. The revenues of Egypt could be drawn upon to provide for his programmes of land grants, and in the *Res Gestae* Augustus is careful to stress that he paid fair prices for all the land so acquired in Italy and the provinces—'the first and only one to do so up to my time'. Some of his provincial colonies, such as those in Pisidia, were built primarily for defence, but all helped the spread of Romanisation in some degree.

Two debts were discharged by new buildings in Rome. On

the site of his cremation in the Roman Forum, a Temple of the
Deified Julius Caesar was consecrated on August 18th, 29 B.C.—
only three days after the triple triumph of Octavian. Its proximity
to the Temple of Vesta, the Regia, and the Temple of Castor and
Pollux associated it with some of the most venerable cults of
Rome. Enclosed in his temple Julius Caesar was quietly dropped
by Augustan propaganda. Apollo, for whom Augustus had a
personal veneration, was rewarded with a splendid Temple on
the Palatine Hill, in gratitude for the help he had given at Actium.
The first major building in Rome to use the marble of Luna
(Carrara), it was consecrated on 9th October 28 B.C. As God of
Prophecy Apollo was given custody of the Sibylline books, as
Patron of the Arts he presided over the Palatine Library which
offered all the treasures of Greek and Latin literature. The new
age was to be one of civilisation as well as peace. In this same year
Augustus carried out, by decree of the Senate, a comprehensive
restoration of 82 temples in Rome 'neglecting none which then
stood in need of repair'. This was, of course, more than mere
antiquarianism, it was part of a larger design of bringing the
Roman people back to a proper relationship with the gods.

It was not until 27 B.C. that Octavian felt ready to tackle the
constitutional issue. The operation was to be known as 'The
Restoration of the Republic'. Since the Republic had not functioned for some 20 years, it might not have seemed implausible.
On January 1st, Octavian proclaimed invalid all the illegal acts
he had committed as Triumvir; on January 13th he appeared
before the Senate and laid down his supreme powers. It was a
reconstituted Senate, purged of some of the dubious characters
who had been admitted in the Triumvirate, reduced to 800 (?)
members and solidly packed with Octavian's supporters. They
had rehearsed their lines. The reluctant Octavian was asked to
administer by special request of the Senate and People the
provinces he now governed. To do so, he would be granted
proconsular powers for ten years. The proposal was confirmed by
the People in Assembly. Octavian accepted. A few days later a
grateful Senate voted him new and striking honours. 'For this
service of mine', he wrote in the *Res Gestae*, 'I received the name
of Augustus by decree of the Senate, the doorposts of my house
were publicly bedecked with laurels, a civic crown was placed
over my doorway, and a golden shield was set up in the Senate
House, whose inscription testifies its award to me by the Roman

Senate and People because of my valour, clemency, justice and devotion to duty'. The house so honoured was (presumably) the modest house on the Palatine Hill now known as the Casa di Livia: its garland of oak-leaves (the civic crown) is mentioned in the Calendar of Praeneste as awarded QUOD REMPUBLICAM POPULO ROMANO RESTITUIT (because he restored the Republic to the Roman People). A marble replica of the golden shield has been found at Arles; presumably there were such in all the major cities. But the most important honour is the name Augustus, by which Octavian chose henceforth to be known. It belongs to the vocabulary of religion not of politics, a word of good auspices and sanguine expectation suggesting growth and fertility (*augere, auctor*, etc.). Its connection with Romulus who had founded Rome *augusto augurio* placed Augustus in the revered tradition of the Founder. Describing his position in his own terms Augustus used the word *Princeps*—familiar in many contexts and hence unalarming, conveying no more than a leader in the State. His unerring skill in the use of words led him to eschew such words as *Rex* or *Dictator* with all their hateful associations.

But what of the powers that lay behind this smooth façade? The provinces that Augustus governed gave him control of almost all the armed forces of the State, who took the oath of loyalty to him as *Imperator*. He held the consulship each year and could control the appointment of provincial governors; he held the personal sacrosanctity of a tribune. All these powers, in each case derived from good republican precedents, were fused together into the new amalgam which we know as the Principate of Augustus.

Like so many other great Roman projects the Principate did not at once assume its final form. There was a major revision in 23 B.C., when Augustus after giving up his near monopoly of the consulship was granted tribunician power (*tribunicia potestas*) for life, thus enabling him to veto the acts of all magistrates and to deal directly with the People. After his return from the East his position in Italy was strengthened by the grant of the consular power, and in 18 B.C. tribunician power was conferred on Agrippa, marking him out as Augustus' successor. After this Augustus neither needed nor received any further powers, though the honorary title of 'Father of his Country' (*pater patriae*) was conferred on him in 2 B.C. The concatenation of powers exercised by Augustus is well seen in the titles he used on inscriptions. Dedicating an obelisk to the Sun-god, he pro-claims: IMP. CAESAR DIVI F. AUGUSTUS PONTIFEX MAXIMUS IMP. XII. COS. XI. TRIB. POT. XIV. AEGUPTO IN POTESTATEM POPULI ROMANI REDACTA SOLI DONUM DEDIT. Here *Imperator* used as a title asserts his command over the army: *Caesar* and *divi filius* (son of the deified Julius) refer to his connection with Julius Caesar: *Augustus* is the name given to him by the Senate. As *Pontifex Maximus* (Chief Priest, a title acquired in 12 B.C.) he stands at the head of the state religion: *Imp. XII* refers to his own generalship which has been acclaimed 12 times by troops in the field: *Cos. XI* to the consulship which he has held 11 times: *Trib. Pot. XIV* to tribunician power held 14 times (this gives the date of 10–9 B.C.). The rest of the inscription proclaims that, having brought Egypt under the sway of the Roman People he dedicated the obelisk to the Sun-god.

'Augustus gradually concentrated in his own hands the functions of the Senate, the magistrates and the laws' was Tacitus' hostile comment. As for the Senate, under his new settlement it still enjoyed prestige and powers, administering Rome, Italy and the more highly civilised provinces, serving as a high court of justice and appeal, conferring, or in theory, with-holding grants of power to the *Princeps* himself. Yet in any real sense Augustus had complete control of its functions. He handled admission to the order and could purge it of an unworthy member. As *Princeps Senatus* he took part in its debates; his speech indicated the line he wished to be followed and it would be a bold man who did not adhere to it on an important occasion. Moreover, he controlled its agenda through a kind of Senate steering com-mittee which he used as a sounding board for legislation he had in mind. Small wonder that, as Dio Cassius remarked, 'nothing was actually done that did not please Augustus'. While the power of the Senate was thus closely confined, Augustus was careful to preserve the public standing of the order and its members. Reduced to 600 members by the middle of his reign, it still con-tained some Celts and Spaniards, but there was no flood of new recruits from the provinces. In this as in many other things, Augustus showed a conservatism which tended to camouflage even his radical reforms.

CHAPTER 24

Augustan art, architecture
and public works

AUGUSTUS EXCELLED IN THE USE of art and architecture in
the service of the Imperial idea. As *Princeps* he was content to live
in a modest house on the Palatine which once belonged to the
orator Hortensius: unremarkable in itself it stood near to the
Cottage of Romulus, the archaic round hut of sticks and reeds
maintained as a national monument and said to be that of the
Founder. To this spot the imagination of Virgil brought Aeneas
to spend his first night in Rome. Close, too, was another ancient
Palatine site, the Lupercal, where the Wolf suckled the twins—
the sacred site and its monuments were restored by Augustus
and they included a statue of Drusus the great conqueror of
Germany. Here the new régime is brought into close association
with the earliest legends of Rome. But as Founder of the first
dynasty of Roman Emperors Augustus could be more ostentatious, as he showed in the great mausoleum built in the Campus
Martius for himself and his family, which in scale and treatment
rivals the funeral monuments of Hellenistic and Oriental Kings.

The ideals of the Principate are expressed above all in the
Forum of Augustus and the *Ara Pacis* or Altar of Peace. Begun as
early as 37 B.C., the Forum was not completed until 2 B.C. It
follows in a more sophisticated form the pattern set by the Forum
of Caesar, that of a temple in a piazza with surrounding colonnades. The temple was dedicated to Mars the Avenger, to fulfil
a vow taken at the battle of Philippi. So much was due to Caesar's
memory. What is original is the use of the colonnades to form a
kind of Hall of Fame, filled with the statues of the great men of
the Roman past. Degrassi's study has shown that there were

145

rather more than 100 of these, each with an inscription (*elogia*)
recording his deeds. On the right facing the temple were the
Julio-Claudians headed by Aeneas, on the left the heroes of the
Republic. According to Suetonius, 'next to the gods, Augustus
honoured the memory of those great men who had raised the
Empire of the Roman People from obscurity to greatness. So it
was . . . that he dedicated statues to them all, in triumphal dress,
in the two colonnades of his Forum, issuing at the same time a
proclamation: 'This I have done to bind the Roman People to
require me while I am alive, and also the princes of ages yet to
come, to live by the standards set by these great men.' Here he
decreed that the Senate should discuss war and the granting of
triumphs: that thither those who were leaving to take up military
commands in the provinces should be ceremonially escorted, and
that to it the returning conquerors should bring the tokens of
their victories. The triumphal statues are known to have been
copied in other cities—notably at Pompeii and Arretium, another
linking together of Rome and Italy.

The Forum of Augustus stood for the arts of war that had
founded and defended the Empire. The *Ara Pacis Augustae*
symbolised the peace which Augustus brought to the Roman
world. It was decreed by the Senate to mark his return from
Spain and Gaul in 13 B.C., though its dedication was four years
later. It took the form of an altar enclosed in a precinct wall,
round whose outside ran a band of the most important sculptures.
In these, as in the Column of Trajan and other great Roman
monuments, there is a mixture of the symbolic and the factual.
The factual, on the two long sides, is a realistic treatment of the
procession of the Imperial family, the Senate, and the People of
Rome, with the Princeps and the great officers of the State cults
at their head on the day when they offered thanks for Augustus'
safe return. It is the high noon of the Principate: Augustus is
there with his friends Agrippa and Maecenas, the younger
members of the Imperial family and their children. The procession
moves with an easy dignity, serious but not solemn. Augustus
is not put in any central position, nor is the cynosure of the public
gaze. He walks at the head of the procession among the priests
and their attendants—the First Citizen, certainly, but not set
apart from the Senate and People. The symbolic scenes on four
short slabs form two pairs, first, the Sacrifice of Aeneas and the
Wolf and Twins, symbolising the Trojan and the Roman origins

of Rome, second, Dea Roma (the Goddess Rome) and Terra
Mater or Italia. Two only are well preserved. In the Sacrifice of
Aeneas the emphasis is on *pietas* and simplicity: the grave piety
of the founding hero, the rapt attention of his friend Achates,
the sacrifice of the White Sow as token that here he would have
an abiding city. On the other slab depicting Terra Mater or
Italia (I prefer the second), the emphasis is on fruitfulness and
peace: the serene young matron and her two babes, the cattle
and sheep and birds, the flowers and fruits and the kindly breezes
which sustain the richness of the land.

Two other features of Augustan Rome call for notice. First,
the kind of art centre created between the Capitol and the river,
where the Theatre of Marcellus and the Porticus of Livia with
their statues, libraries and colonnades commemorated members
of his family. Secondly the benefactions of Agrippa, himself a
great builder, especially the group in the Campus Martius which
included the Pantheon and the Thermae of Agrippa, the first of
the Thermae or public baths of Rome. The Greek geographer
Strabo who saw it in the early years of Tiberius has given a good
description of Augustan Rome. He begins with the Campus
Martius and the crowds of people playing games or wrestling.
'The many works of art that surround it, the ground covered
through the year with green grass, the ridges of the hills rising
above the river . . . all look like the painted backcloth to a stage,
and form a spectacle from which it is hard to tear yourself away.
. . . There too is the Mausoleum, a huge mound near the river on
a base of white marble, covered with evergreen trees to the
summit. It bears a statue of Augustus Caesar . . . behind it is an
enclosed precinct with superb walks. . . . Again, if one should
go to the Old Forum and see one Forum after another ranged
beside it, with their basilicas and temples, and then see the
Capitol and the great works of art on it and the Palatine and the
Porticus of Livia, it would be easy to forget the world outside.'
The last comment is just. Noble architecture has this power of
riveting attention on itself. Rome which has exercised such
magnetism over the centuries beyond all other cities did so first
in the days of Augustus. At last, in Suetonius' words, 'it was
adorned as the splendour of the Empire demanded'.

Care was devoted to the administration and public utilities of
the city. The Tiber was embanked, and its banks and channel
placed under the care of a senatorial commission—the *curatores*

alvei et riparum Tiberis. Despite their activities, the intransigent
river remained liable to flood—as it is to this day. The water
supply was overhauled and enlarged, a task which at first was
entrusted to the practical genius of Agrippa. As *aedile* in 33 B.C.
he repaired all the aqueducts, began the construction of the Aqua
Virgo, and constructed '700 basins, 500 fountains and 130
distribution points, many of which were finely decorated'. Later
the supervision of aqueducts was entrusted to another senatorial
commission, the *curatores aquarum.* At the end of his reign Augustus
himself doubled the Aqua Marcia and put through a thorough
programme of repairs. The corn supply, vital to the urban poor,
was an especial interest to Augustus. The acquisition of Egypt
had secured a new source of supply and at times in his reign
20,000,000 pecks were contributed annually. None the less there
were years of scarcity, calling for the intervention of the Princeps
himself. Eventually (A.D. 8?) a powerful commission was set up
under a *praefectus annonae* or Prefect of the Corn Supply, an
official of equestrian rank. His organisation controlled granaries
overseas and in Italy, supervised transport by sea and negotiated
with corn-growers in the provinces and with bakers in Italy. But
the distribution of the ration to persons entitled to receive it in
Rome seems to have been the duty of another body.

    Augustus entertained the Roman People as well as feeding
them. The *Res Gestae* records numerous *spectacula*—either gladiatorial shows or wild-beast hunts—which he provided; there
were also three world athletic festivals and a mock naval battle
in which 30 large ships and 3,000 combatants took part. All
Emperors after him had to undertake these expensive obligations,
which showed that the populace of Rome was in some sense the
clientela of the Emperor. A series of fires in A.D. 6 emphasised
the need for a public fire brigade and this was met by the *vigiles*
under the command of a *praefectus.* As night-watchmen as well as
firemen they had police duties to perform, each of their cohorts
being responsible for two of the 14 regions of Rome. Another
aspect of police duty, that of riot control, was in the hands of a
para-military formation known as the *cohortes urbanae,* a force of
3,000 men under the control of the City Prefect. This office
(*praefectus urbi*) was always entrusted to a senator and later became
of great importance. All this—though it probably fell short of
modern standards—was a great improvement in public security.
Finally we should mention the division of Rome into 14 regions

(*regiones*) and more than 200 wards (*vici*), each having magistrates of its own. Established in 7 B.C. these measures suggest some scheme for local administration, but it does not seem to have been allowed to develop very far.

Italy was divided into 11 administrative districts—primarily it would seem for purposes of the census, for of course local administration remained in the control of the various colonies and municipalities. Italian towns as we have seen copied the public monuments of Rome, and their calendars recorded Roman festivals—naturally enough, since their people were Roman citizens. Their aristocrats often became members of the Roman Senate. Augustus encouraged the *juventus*, a youth movement in which young Italians of good family could obtain pre-military training, especially in horsemanship. He carried out a major repair of the Italian road system: the *Res Gestae* records his reconstruction of Via Flaminia from Rome to Rimini in which he repaired all the bridges except two, one being the Pons Milvius just outside Rome. Later a body of *curatores viarum* was established for the maintenance of Italian roads, and it was responsible to the Senate.

The conquest of the Alps (see p. 158) led to some spectacular road building across the high mountain passes, such as the St Bernard Pass and Mt Genèvre. A journey from Ivrea to Aosta will show, even today, the engineering genius of Augustan road builders which followed the brutal suppression of the Salassi. At Ivrea (Eporedia) the Roman bridge still crosses the Dora Baltea. As we ascend the valley towards Aosta the Roman road runs parallel to the modern and many of its bridges across the mountain torrents are in position, notably at Pont St Martin. Aosta in its high mountain setting displays much of the Roman colony of Augusta Praetoria, founded in 25 B.C. Its street plan is, substantially, that of the *colonia*, the Roman walls with their monumental gateways are well preserved, there is an Arch of Augustus, an amphitheatre and a theatre of remarkable size. Beyond it the road led to the St Bernard Pass—whose dangers are eloquently described by Strabo—and down to Geneva. The same impression of Roman durability is made by the journey along the Dora Riparia to Susa (Segusio), the ancient capital of the client-king Cottius, commanding the passes over the Cottian Alps. Roman civilisation came surprisingly late to these Alpine lands, but its mark was strong and enduring.

CHAPTER 25

The organisation of the provinces

THE REPUBLIC HAD FAILED to set provincial administration on a sound footing. The Triumvirs, it seems, possessed themselves of the right to appoint provincial governors in their own spheres of influence, but had not attempted any general reform. Between 31 and 27 B.C. Octavian exercised this right as residuary legatee. The settlement of 27 B.C. dividing the provinces between the Princeps and the Senate did, therefore, include a measure of 'restoration' to republican practice. It could also be said that the Princeps, by taking over provinces on the frontiers, or exposed to internal disorders in the first instance (Spain, the Gallic provinces, Syria, Cilicia and Egypt) was shouldering the harder part of the assignment. The object was, of course, to bring all the great military commands under the direct control of the Princeps and to prevent the rise of any more war lords. But in the process the way was opened up for reform. For the Princeps governed his provinces through representatives (*legati*), senators whom he selected with much care and kept in office at his pleasure on a fixed but generous salary. The standard of administration maintained in the Imperial provinces would obviously be reflected in the *legati* of the Senate who could not allow themselves to fall too far behind in honesty and efficiency. The finances of an Imperial province were now made the responsibility of a *procurator*, a man of equestrian rank, who was the agent of the Princeps and could communicate directly with him. Through him if need be a check could be kept on the *legatus*. Other *procuratores* of lesser rank would be in charge of mines and Imperial estates, so that in an important province the Princeps would have a network of his own agents.

In the senatorial provinces the governors used the old title of *proconsul*; Africa and Asia were reserved for governors of consular rank. These *proconsules* were chosen by lot from qualified senators and usually held office for a year. There had to be an interval of five years between the holding of a city magistracy and a provincial governorship. The finances of a senatorial province were in the hands of a *quaestor*, who as the governor's second-in-command might have to undertake other duties. But there would, again, be *procuratores* in charge of Imperial property even in a senatorial province: through such men the Princeps could receive an early distant warning of trouble. If it came the Princeps would not hesitate to intervene. The famous Edicts of Cyrene (7–4 B.C.) show him doing so in that senatorial province, revising its judiciary system and limiting the privileges of Roman citizens who had been rigging the law courts against non-Romans. The intervention is done with tact and the joint control of Princeps and Senate in Cyrene is asserted. Thus procedure is laid down 'until the Senate makes a decision on the matter or I myself find some better system'; an edict is published 'so that it shall be evident to all inhabitants of the provinces how deeply both I and the Senate are concerned that none of our subjects suffer wrong or extortion'. Moreover on his provincial tours, such as that to Sicily in 22 B.C. and to Asia, Bithynia and Syria between 21 and 19 B.C., Augustus entered senatorial and Imperial provinces without distinction to settle their affairs. The same was done by Agrippa during the years when he held extraordinary powers in the East. Again if the Princeps could go to the provinces the provincials could go to him. The cities of Asia, especially, sent regular embassies to the Princeps in Rome, bringing petitions, complaints and congratulatory addresses. (Byzantium it was later found did so annually; a pleasant if expensive jaunt for local dignitaries.) Another and more weighty channel of communication came with the development of provincial councils, such as those of Asia and the Three Gauls (see p. 168). There was thus no lack of means for the voices of the provincials to make themselves heard directly by the Emperor.

The new system of provincial administration devised by Augustus worked well and lasted without major revisions through the first two centuries of the Empire. There were some transfers. In Augustus' reign Baetica, Gallia Narbonensis and Cyprus were transferred to the Senate, while Dalmatia was taken over by the Emperor. All new provinces acquired then or later—the Danube provinces, Britain, Mauretania—naturally became Imperial provinces. Men of ability served in both kinds of provinces as openings arose. There can be no doubt that it was an enormous improvement over the system of the Republic and that it was the chief reason for the stability of the Empire until the troubles of the third century A.D. It reduced the opportunity for misgovernment and provided the means for correcting it; it could not of course eliminate it completely. There were still venal and avaricious governors, as Agricola discovered when he went to Asia as *quaestor* to Salvius Titianus—a man 'very ready to arrange the mutual covering-up of malpractice'. Eighty years earlier the same province had suffered from the brutality of Valerius Messala Volesus. The famous pearls of Lollia Paulina probably reflect the greed of M. Lollius in Syria. The province of Bithynia prosecuted four of its governors in the first two centuries A.D. and won two convictions. In the notorious case of Marius Priscus early in the reign of Trajan, Africa pressed the charge with vigour and obtained a sentence of exile but still felt the defendant had come off lightly. Nor were all imperial *procuratores* honest men. In Britain, the rebellion of Boudicca was precipitated by the cruelty and greed of the *procurator* Catus Decianus, unchecked by a governor who cared more for military glory than civil administration. But the number of scandals recorded is not large and even such hostile witnesses as Tacitus have to admit that the provinces were content under the Principate.

CHAPTER 26

Frontiers and armies

BESIDES GOOD ADMINISTRATION the Empire needed firm
defence; this in its turn called for good internal communications
and a viable system of frontiers. This last need occupied Augustus
throughout his reign and is the reason for most of the wars he
undertook. In northern and central Europe, especially, his plans
were on the grand scale; if they did not come to full fruition, he
was so far satisfied that he could enjoin his successors not to
extend the Empire beyond the boundaries as he left them. In the
East as we have said he largely retained the structure established
by Pompey and Mark Antony. Client kings continued to rule
Pontus, Galatia, Cappadocia and Judaea. Augustus took particular
care over their treatment, regarding them as part of the Imperial
system, educating their children in Rome, interesting himself in
their marriages and defending them against their enemies if they
were worth it. For client-kingship was a status open to review on
the death of an incumbent, and sometimes it was expedient to
turn the country into a Roman province—as happened with
Galatia in 25 B.C., Judaea in A.D. 6 and Cappadocia in A.D. 17. A
client-king was judged by the services he rendered Rome,
whether in defending a dangerous frontier or promoting civilised
life among his people. Kings such as Archelaus of Cappadocia
and Herod of Judaea were promoters of Romanisation. They
built temples for the cult of Rome and Augustus, and they
founded new cities bearing the Emperor's name. Hence the
splendid port of Caesarea built by Herod on the Palestine coast
which became one of the chief cities of the East.

Towards Parthia, Augustus quietly withdrew from the forward policy favoured by Caesar and Antony. The Great Parthian
War was left to the imagination of Roman poets where it flourished

mightily for a few years. But in 20 B.C. the opportunity for a diplomatic settlement was welcomed on both sides. Tiberius went to Syria to recover from the Parthians the standards captured at Carrhae and those Roman prisoners who wished to return. It could be made a propaganda triumph and the coins bore the legend *Signis Receptis* (The Standards Recovered). But the posting of the four Syrian legions showed that Augustus had no intention of invading Parthia. The frontier post of Zeugma, at the crossing of the Euphrates, was strongly held, but the legions were quartered in the towns of Syria and the capital city of Antioch. The behaviour of the Roman troops in that most agreeable of postings must have shown the Parthians that there was little threat of aggression. Though there was occasional friction, there was no Parthian war in Augustus' time and both empires profited from the rapid growth of the caravan traffic.

Armenia was another matter. Augustus' wish was to see it ruled by a Parthian prince approved by Rome. But, as Tacitus remarked, 'Geography and the character of that people have long made it an unreliable country. . . . Placed between two world Empires, it has frequently been on bad terms with both, hating Rome, jealous of Parthia.' Pro-Roman nominees on the throne of Armenia invariably provoked a chauvinistic reaction: there was a series of rebellions in Augustus' reign, and Armenia continued to give trouble until the time of Trajan.

What counted for most in the East was the acquisition of Egypt, 'for the Roman People', as Augustus claimed, but in fact it could not be incorporated in the provincial system. It was a turbulent country with constant tension between Jews and Greeks, a native population allergic to Greco-Roman civilisation and the capital city Alexandria containing the most notorious of urban mobs. Its strategic position, the revenue from its taxes and its importance as a source of corn, made it essential to keep Egypt under the control of the Emperor. In any case, Egypt had always been treated as a royal possession and Augustus appeared as the natural successor of the Pharaohs and the Ptolemies. He governed Egypt through a *praefectus* of equestrian rank who held the highest post in the Empire open to a man from his order. The first Prefect of Egypt, Cornelius Gallus, failed to appreciate the limits within which he had to act. He seems to have embarked, without authority, on a war against Ethiopia and to have been injudicious in publicising his achievements. Pressure was brought upon him and he committed suicide. Henceforward no senator was allowed to visit Egypt without special permission from the Emperor. Germanicus aroused the suspicions of Tiberius when he did so in A.D. 19, though he proffered the excuse that he wanted to inspect its antiquities. (It is a plea that does not always disarm suspicion today.) Vespasian in the Civil Wars of A.D. 69 was careful to possess himself of Egypt before making his bid for power. It was the most sensitive point in the body of the Empire. So two legions were stationed in Egypt to defend the country and to put down disorder. They seem to have done more engineering than fighting, for Augustus set them at work on the repair of canals and irrigation channels and restoring the banks of the Nile. As a result much land was reclaimed for agriculture and there was an increase in fertility. Once the system of taxation had been revised and tightened, Egypt was in condition to play its part as the milch-cow of the Roman Empire.

In North Africa Nature provided a frontier, making the boundary of the Empire the division between the desert and the fertile land. Beyond it to the south was the land of the nomadic tribes—Garamantes, Musulamii, Gaetuli who were sometimes traders, sometimes raiders, according to the strength with which the settled lands were defended. What was needed was to have a network of military roads and blockhouses to keep their raids in check—and an occasional demonstration in force into their own grazing-grounds and oases, such as Cornelius Balbus led against the Garamantes in 19 B.C. We hear of minor wars, ill-recorded; in the reign of Tiberius the Musulamian prince Tacfarinas gave much trouble. Yet throughout this period the normal force maintained in the whole area from the western boundary of Egypt to Morocco seems to have been one legion, with auxiliaries. Mauretania was made a client-kingdom under King Juba II, a Numidian prince, a philhellene and an historian. Educated in Rome and married to Cleopatra's daughter, he is an outstanding example of Augustus' care for the personal lives of his client kings. He too built a Caesarea as his capital city: its dual name of Iol Caesarea (Chercel, in Algeria) represents the blend of Roman and North African culture that was developing along the seaboard as far as Tangier. Development was most rapid in the old province of Africa, now restored to the Senate and enlarged by the addition of Numidia. With the refounded Carthage once again the greatest city in Africa west of Alexandria and a strong demand for corn and oil, the staples of African agriculture, the province enjoyed an economic boom reflected alike in the growth of towns and exploitation of the countryside.

Once the mountain peoples of north-western Spain could be subdued, there was another splendid natural frontier—the ocean, protecting Spain and Gaul from the Straits of Gibraltar to the mouth of the Rhine. The wars fought by Augustus and his generals in north-western Spain were nasty, brutish and long. Field warfare lasted from 27 to 19 B.C. and was followed by nearly a decade of 'pacification' which needed the presence of five legions. It proceeded with the familiar methods—a network of military roads, the founding of cities such as Braga (Bracaraugusta) and Lugo (Lucus Asturum) and veteran colonies at Emerida and Saragossa. So well was the work done that these were the last wars Rome had to fight in Spain. The newly won lands provided a valuable source of manpower for the Roman army and a great access of economic strength from their mineral resources. The gold of Asturia and Lusitania, the copper of Rio Tinto, the iron of Cantabria, came to reinforce the silver mines of Sierra Morena already in production for more than two centuries. For the drainage and extraction of ore in these mines of north-western Spain the most elaborate hydraulic machinery of ancient times was evolved.

It was now possible to plan the administration and economic development of the Iberian peninsula as a whole. Three provinces were established, of which Baetica went to the Senate, Lusitania (roughly the modern Portugal) and the large amorphous province of Tarraconensis to the Emperor. A system of roads through the Meseta provided links with the principal ports and also with Gaul. Spanish agriculture flourished, notably its wines and olive oil: the famous *garum* or fish-sauce (perhaps a kind of anchovy relish) reached a world market. As in Africa, the growth of towns was stimulated by the boom in agriculture and it is in the age of Augustus that the tide of Romanisation in Spain is at its highest point.

No part of the Roman world stood more in need of Augustus' fostering care than Gaul. At the settlement of 27 B.C. he was in charge of the whole of it and he took his responsibility seriously. One of his earliest acts as Princeps was to take the census in Gaul: Agrippa was sent there in 20 B.C.: Augustus was present in person from 16 to 13 B.C.: he left Drusus in charge of Gallia

Comata. Gaul could not complain of lack of attention by the Imperial house, and its gratitude is attested by temples, monuments and inscriptions. In Narbonensis the attention was a further stimulus to an already flourishing urban and economic life. This has left its mark in such buildings as the Temple of Augustus and Livia at Vienna, the Maison Carrée at Nîmes, the theatres of Orange and Arles, the cenotaph for Gaius and Lucius Caesar at St Rémy (Glanum) (if indeed that is what it is). The Pont du Gard, the most impressive of all surviving Roman monuments in France, was built by Agrippa to supply water to Nîmes. Under Augustus, Narbonensis became a transalpine extension of Italy. In Gallia Comata things were very different. The scars of conquest had not healed a generation after Caesar left Gaul, and the substructure needed for Romanisation had yet to be supplied. A key-point in development was Lugdunum (Lyons), which had been founded as a colony by L. Munatius Plancus in 43 B.C. Agrippa made it the nodal point of a system of five military roads, leading respectively to the English Channel, the Rhineland, the Po Valley via the St Bernard Pass, the mouth of the Rhône, and Bordeaux on the Garonne. Standing as it does at the confluence of the Sâone and the Rhône, it also became a great river port. The city grew rapidly, and was made the capital of the largest and most central of the three new provinces created in Gaul—Gallia Belgica, Lugdunensis, and Aquitania. When they were established, Narbonensis was handed over to the Senate.

Augustus took care that this provincial organisation did not obliterate the tribal system of the Gauls. With some rationalisation, these Gallic tribes were organised into 64 *civitates*, each a unit of local self-government. Each *civitas* aspired to have a Romanised city as its capital and Augustus encouraged the growth of Latin schools. Archaeology has laid bare the growth of such cities as Augusta Treverorum (Trier), capital of Belgica, Augustodunum (Autun) the new centre for the Aedui replacing Mt Beauvray, Augustonemeton (Clermont Ferrand) for the Arverni, and Burdigala (Bordeaux) capital of Aquitania. Moreover, to this phase of urbanisation may be traced the origins of many of the most famous cities of France, among them Paris, Reims and Metz. The consummation of these plans was the dedication of an altar to Rome and Augustus at Lyons in 12 B.C. Here the Council of the Gauls would meet annually, on federal territory,

for a great festival that asserted at once the unity of the Gauls
and their devotion to Rome. Augustus was much exercised with
the question of finding a proper frontier providing for the
defence of Gaul against the Germans. Caesar had pointed to the
Rhine. But Augustus, viewing the problem in a larger context,
thought that a better solution might be found.

No ancient author paints on a wide canvas the story of the
wars fought by Augustus and his generals to establish a viable
northern frontier, to which was devoted the major military
effort of his reign. The story has to be put together piecemeal,
mainly from Velleius Paterculus (who took part in some of the
campaigns), Pliny, Tacitus, Suetonius and Dio Cassius, supplemented by inscriptions and other archaeological evidence. Many
details are lacking, but it is possible to appreciate the main
outlines of a grand design whose outcome was to be crucial alike
for the future of the Roman Empire and for the subsequent
history of Europe.

The first stage is the conquest of the Alpine lands and peoples,
part of which is recorded by the Trophy of Augustus at La
Turbie near Monaco. Once Gaul had become part of the Empire,
it was intolerable on strategic and economic grounds that the
major Alpine passes should not be under Roman control. This
was no less true in the Eastern Alps, where it was necessary to
prevent enemy inroads to the head of the Adriatic and to provide
land routes to Illyricum, Macedonia, Greece and Asia. The key
campaigns were those of 15 B.C. Tiberius advanced from the
west to Lake Constance. Drusus drove north over the Resen-
Scheidegg Pass and down the Inn Valley past the modern Inns-
bruck. Beyond the Alps their armies converged and did not halt
until they reached the Upper Danube. Perhaps in the same year
the old Celtic kingdom of Noricum was taken over as a Roman
province, bringing the Danube under control as far as Vienna.
Coordinated planning had been needed to conquer the large
tracts of mountain country with their formidable natural obstacles.
Their administration was organised piecemeal as local considerations required. The tribes in the southern valleys of the Alps
were mostly 'attached' to the territory of an important city; the
Salassi of the Val d'Aosta belonged to the new colony of Augusta
Praetoria (Aosta); two Alpine valleys were administered by
Brixia (Brescia). By these means Italy was extended to the water-
shed of the Alps. At the western end of the chain the small

Imperial province of the Alpes Maritimae was set up. It was flanked by a client kingdom ruled by the redoubtable King Cottius from his Romanised capital of Segusio (Susa). The northern slopes of the mountains and the tract as far as the Danube formed a new province—Raetia-Vindelicia—with a capital and military base at Augusta Vindelicorum (Augsburg).

The second stage develops from the new horizons thus opened. The Danube is cardinal: it was now possible to think of a Danube frontier the entire way to the Black Sea, for its lower stretches had already been reached in what is now Bulgaria. Such a frontier would arrest the menace of the Celtic, Illyrian and Dacian peoples to Dalmatia and Macedonia. It would outflank the mountains of Bosnia and provide an easy route down the valleys of the Save or Drave to Belgrade and then on to Nish and down the Vardar Valley to Salonica. In fact, it would bring under Roman control the route now followed by the Orient Express—Trieste (Tergeste), Ljubljana (Emona), Belgrade (Singi-dunum), Nish (Naissus), thence via Sofia (Serdica), Plovdiv (Philippopolis), Edirne (Adrianopolis) to Istanbul (Byzantium). The Roman names are some of them later than the age of Augustus.) The middle Danube, the missing part of this design, was secured by ill-recorded wars fought between 13 and 9 B.C. Illyricum was organised as a Roman province. A vast new imperial command in south-eastern Europe replaced the former proconsular command based on the Adriatic coast.

What of the Rhine, which Caesar had seen from Gaul to be the natural frontier for the Empire between the Alps and the Atlantic? From the new vantage of Raetia and the Upper Danube it did not look so attractive. It has an awkward re-entrant angle at Bâle: a Rhine-Danube frontier would be long. Moreover, it would leave unsubdued German tribes such as the Sugambri and Usipetes, who had been insolent enough to invade Gaul and to defeat the Roman general Lollius in 17 B.C. But north of the Danube and the highlands of the Bohemerwald was another great river system—the Elbe and its tributaries. A frontier might be organised on the Elbe to link with the Danube near Carnuntum (in modern terms Hamburg-Magdeburg-Prague-Vienna). It would be shorter by some 300 miles than the Rhine-Upper Danube limes; it would give Gaul defence in depth and it would add Germany as a new province to the Empire. This formidable task —whose problems seem to have been underestimated—was taken

up by Drusus in 12 B.C. In three successive campaigning seasons
his armies advanced from the bases on the Rhine up the strategic
valleys of the Lippe and the Main towards the Elbe. His fleets
explored the North Sea coast from the Zuyder Zee to the mouth
of the Elbe. No other Roman general achieved so much in
Germany. But in 9 B.C. his run of success was cut short by a fatal
accident. His body was brought back to be buried in the Mausoleum of Augustus. He was commemorated by a cenotaph at
Mainz and by a statue in the Forum of Augustus whose inscription
ended with the words EXSTINCTUS IN GERMANIA.

In truth, more than the life of Drusus was quenched in
Germany. From then on, it is hard to interpret the northern
campaigns of Augustus. Tiberius, who took up the German
command, did little more than pacify the tribes along the east
bank of the Rhine and show that a Roman army could still reach
the Elbe. But soon new problems arose in Bohemia. Drusus had
displaced the powerful people of the Marcomanni from the valley
of the Main; under the leadership of an able king called Maroboduus they had seized the strategic Bohemerwald and built up
a powerful empire, reaching into eastern Germany and Poland
and posing a threat to the entire Danube frontier and even to
the Rhine. In A.D. 6 Tiberius at the head of 12 legions was on the
point of crushing them, but at this critical moment there broke
out an alarming rebellion in Pannonia and Dalmatia. It was now
15 years since the Roman conquest of that area—a dangerous
period, in which grievances had had time to build up and a new
generation of warriors and leaders had arisen who knew Roman
methods of warfare. Tiberius needed all his forces and four years
in the field to stamp out a rebellion which caused hysteria in
Italy, broke the nerve of the ageing Augustus, and exposed in a
startling fashion the military weakness of the Empire.

Maroboduus kept quiet during those years and it was as well
he did. Not so another and younger German leader, Arminius,
prince of the Cherusci, who trapped and annihilated a Roman
army of three legions under Quinctilius Varus somewhere in the
Teutoberger Wald near the modern Osnabrück. Tacitus praises
Arminius highly and makes him the worthy foe of his hero, the
young Germanicus. He accords him the honour of an obituary,
saying. 'There can be no doubt that he was the liberator of
Germany. He fought against the Roman people not, as did other
kings and generals, in the early days of their power, but at the

height of their imperial glory. . . . To this day he lives in the songs
of the barbarians. Greek historians know nothing of him—their
admiration is for what is Greek. We Romans undervalue him;
while we belaud antiquity we take too little thought for the
history of modern times.' Our own age does not undervalue
Arminius. The site of his victory is a challenge to German
scholarship: its result a stimulus to German pride. And to this
day the name Hermann lives on in Germany

The sequel fell in the reign of Tiberius. That Emperor allowed
Germanicus to wage war beyond the Rhine to reassert Roman
prestige. In A.D. 15 he reached the site of Varus' disaster and
buried the bones of the dead; the next year he won what could be
built up as a victory over Arminius. But when he talked about
finishing the German business in another year, Tiberius recalled
him to Rome. 'I was sent into Germany by Augustus nine times',
Tacitus makes him say, 'and I achieved more by diplomacy than
by war. . . . As for the Cherusci and other warlike tribes, the
vengeance of Rome has been asserted. Now we can leave them
to quarrel among themselves.' Quarrel they did. Arminius was
killed by the treachery of his kinsfolk. Maroboduus, driven out
of his kingdom, died in exile in Italy. The dream of a German
province reaching to the Elbe died with Quinctilius Varus, and
Tiberius brought back the Roman frontier to the Rhine.

With the wisdom of hindsight, the Roman failure in Germany
seems calamitous—and never more so than in this century. But
this is to make the large assumption that Germany, with its
forests and swamps, warlike peoples and harsh climate, could
have been successfully organised as a Roman province. It is also
to neglect Augustus' achievement with the more important part
of his Northern policy—the establishment of a Danube frontier.
Illyricum was to be a bastion of strength for the Empire, a source
of valiant soldiers and fighting emperors. Romanisation made
good headway in the valleys of the Save and Drave. East and
West were linked by great strategic highways. Viewed as a
whole, the frontier policy of Augustus well deserved the tribute
allowed by Tacitus. 'The Empire was protected by the Ocean,
or by distant rivers: legions, fleets, provinces, formed a single
interconnecting system.'

The legions and fleets were the object of some of Augustus'
most important reforms. They date in the main from 13 B.C.,
when he returned to Rome from the Western provinces and it

seemed possible to put the armed forces of the State on a permanent footing. The number of legions was established at 28, each
consisting of a nominal strength of 5,000 men divided into 10
cohorts of six centuries (80–100 men) each. A legion had its own
force of specialists—armourers, blacksmiths, medical orderlies,
etc.—and included a small troop of cavalry used for scouting.
The combat-soldier was the infantryman, equipped with throw-
ing-spear (*pilum*), stabbing-sword (*gladius*) and wearing carefully
designed body armour which protected the vital points while
allowing maximum mobility. The legionary soldier was a Roman
citizen, usually in Augustus' day from Italy or the Roman
colonies in the provinces, though the Eastern legions recruited
heavily in Galatia and Cappadocia. He served normally for 16
(later for 25) years, though he could be kept longer with the
colours and received a bounty on discharge. His pay was 225
*denarii** a year. The commander of a legion bore the title *legatus
legionis*, indicating that he was the personal representative of the
Emperor, and was always a senator. Its senior officers, the *tribuni
militum*, were young men of senatorial and equestrian class
starting out on a public career. There is a distinct note of amateur-
ishness about the higher personnel of the legion, but it was offset
by the professional efficiency of the 60 centurions (six to each
cohort), who provided the hard core of experience and toughness
that any fighting unit must have. Some were recruited from the
ranks, others were of equestrian rank on entry, hoping that their
military service would qualify them for a number of well paid
posts after they left the army.

There were thus about 150,000 legionary soldiers in Augustus'
army and it was never easy to recruit to that level. To man the
frontiers as he had designed them he was forced to take the bold
measure of raising another army of equal size (the *auxilia*)
recruited entirely from the provinces. There had of course been
provincial units, especially Gallic, Spanish, and Galatian troops,
in the armies of the late Republic, largely to meet the need for
cavalry. But to raise an army of this size—again about 150,000
men—is a tribute to the confidence Augustus felt in provincial
loyalty. It did not invariably pay off: occasionally an auxiliary
unit would put nationalist feelings before loyalty to Rome: the
list of rebels and enemies who had served in the auxiliary forces
was to include the German Arminius, the Batavian rebel Civilis

* Nominally about $37 or £15, but this does not allow for inflation.

and the African guerrilla leader, Tacfarinas. But through service in the *auxilia* many thousands of Celts, Spaniards, Thracians, Illyrians and Germans came to think of themselves as Romans and indeed received Roman citizenship for themselves and children on discharge. It has been calculated that in normal times some 15,000 new citizens would be added to the list each year in this way. The auxiliary units were kept small and mobile—the cavalry *alae* of 500 or 1,000 men; the infantry *cohortes* of 500. Their commanding officers were *praefecti*, sometimes of Roman some-times of native origins. For garrison duty and in battle the *auxilia* supported the legions: on a campaign it was usual to send out a balanced force containing units of both kinds.

The famous Praetorian Guard owed its origin to Augustus, though it did not exert any political influence until the reign of Tiberius when it was given permanent barracks in Rome—the Castra Praetoria. Recruited in Augustus' time from Italians only, the nine cohorts of the Praetorian Guard formed a kind of Household Brigade, receiving a daily pay three times that of the legionary soldier, enjoying better terms of service and seeing battle only when the Emperor took the field in person. Cordially disliked by the fighting troops as parade-ground soldiers who slept too soft, they were later to prove a menace as the makers and breakers of Emperors.

The Roman navy was always a secondary service. There were no rival naval powers and its duties were to put down piracy and to provide for the transport of troops and their supplies as required. None the less, Augustus organised two Mediterranean squadrons, one for the Western basin based on Misenum in the Bay of Naples, the other for the Adriatic based on Ravenna. There were also squadrons operating from Alex-andria, the Syrian ports, and in the Black Sea. River flotillas patrolled the Rhine and the Danube. However, there was no uniform naval training or tactics (so far as we know); a naval career was not thought important and professional efficiency seems to have been low.

The prime duty of the Augustan army was to defend the frontiers of the Empire, its second, to put down rebellion in the provinces, as it did in Pannonia in A.D. 6–9. We have no army posting list earlier than the reign of Tiberius, when Tacitus, provides one for A.D. 23. By this time the idea of a German province had been abandoned and the policy of keeping within

the Augustan frontiers prevailed. At that time then the legions
were posted as follows: eight on the Rhine, the main concentration of force; three in Spain; two in Africa; two in Egypt; four
in Syria; along the Danube, there were two in Pannonia, two in
Moesia and two in reserve in Dalmatia where they could move
quickly if an emergency arose in Italy. The role of client-kings is
acknowledged—Juba in Mauretania, Rhoemetalces in Thrace,
eastern client-kings such as those of Albania and Iberia in the
Caucasus. As for the *auxilia*, Tacitus says that their strength
almost equalled that of the legions, but he will not give a list of
stations because their numbers varied and their postings changed
rapidly. In fact, groups of *auxilia* were often deployed in association with legions. Including the forces kept in Rome—nine
cohorts of the Praetorian Guard and three urban cohorts—the
total figure will have been some 300,000 men. For the armed
forces of an Empire whose total population must have been at
least 60 and perhaps 70 millions, this figure is low. Ludicrously
so by modern standards, when Sweden with a total population
of only 8,000,000 can provide 600,000 men for the services. Let
us consider, first, the problem of manpower, then that of
economics.

The starting-point must be the consideration that, for many
reasons, it would have been unwise to have a larger body of men
in the *auxilia* than in the legions. The 150,000 legionaries were
Roman citizens, of whom there were 4,063,000 at the beginning and 4,937,000 at the end of Augustus' reign. Here is one
limiting factor. Finance provided another. According to Tenney
Frank's estimate, the total of expenses met from the public
treasury (*aerarium*) was about 450 million sesterces, of which the
armed forces took about 240 million, say between 50 and 55 per
cent. Comparison with the budget of a modern state breaks down
because the Emperor also had a treasury, the imperial *fiscus*, out
of which he would disburse money for *ad hoc* expenditure. For
example when discharge bounties were introduced for the
troops a special fund was created, the *aerarium militare*; it received
a float of 170 million sesterces from the *fiscus* and special taxes
were introduced to maintain it.

These considerations suggest that Augustus had to maintain
an army on the lowest level consistent with security, and that his
grand strategy had to be shaped accordingly. What can that
strategy have been? The fact that there was no central reserve

indicates that it did not provide for wars of aggression: the small force of four legions stationed in Syria shows that aggression from Parthia was not expected. The Northern frontiers are much the most important. They demand 14 of the 25 legions (the three destroyed by Arminius were not replaced). The Rhine was more important than the Danube, with eight legions and *auxilia*, perhaps 80,000 men altogether, guarding some 200 miles of the river from Vetera (Xanten) north of Cologne to Strasbourg. The huge Danube line of more than 1,600 miles was guarded by six legions and *auxilia*, some 60,000 men, together with the the forces of the Kings of Thrace. This explains why it was found necessary to transplant friendly barbarians to the Roman bank of the river. It is clear that only tribal warfare was expected. Any large grouping of enemy strength (such as Maroboduus had assembled, and such as was to arise later in the first century in Dacia) would at once call for a new appraisal—unless it could first be nipped in the bud. There was no precedent for maintaining a static military frontier over such great distances. But one thing had been foreseen by Augustus and Tiberius—that such a posture called for an active diplomacy. And during the first century A.D. we find Roman diplomacy at work cultivating friendship for Rome, stirring up discord between the tribes, preventing any strong power arising on the frontiers, over the entire world of the free Northern peoples, from Scotland and even Ireland to the Ukraine and the Caucasus. Some of the fruits of this diplomacy are mentioned in the *Res Gestae* of Augustus.

CHAPTER 27

Administrative and social reforms

WHILE THE ARMED FORCES required reform, a Civil Service had to be improvised. There is no firm evidence for its establishment and cost under Augustus and in any case it does not seem to have been organised on a systematic basis until the reign of Claudius. It is however possible to show where Augustus recruited his Civil Servants from, and some at least of the duties they undertook. For senior posts he had a ready-made source of recruitment in members of the equestrian order, men who had already shown a talent for business and affairs. Such men existed in large numbers in all the Romanised parts of the Empire. There were 500 men qualified for the equestrian *census* at Gades, and the same number at Patavium. Augustus revised the equestrian rolls and expelled unworthy members of the order: at the same time he exercised the right to make individual grants of equestrian status. Under him the *equites* found a wide range of employment in collecting provincial taxes, serving as Imperial procurators or providing the senior officers in auxiliary units. Senior centurions who left the army with good characters often received Civil Service posts—a natural promotion, for they had shown loyalty and ability to handle men. The top posts accessible to the *equites*, such as that of Prefect of Egypt and Prefect of the Annona, were among the most important in the Empire. Members of the senatorial order might be inhibited from giving full support to the Principate because of a nostalgic loyalty to the Republic: the *equites* had no such historical associations and were enthusiastic in working for the new order.

Another useful reservoir of talent was to be found among the freedmen, especially those employed in large numbers in the management of the vast estates owned by Augustus and other members of the Imperial family. Such *liberti Caesaris* were found in many responsible positions and often became very wealthy. The staffs under their supervision were usually made up of slaves. We hear of C. Julius Hyginus, a freedman of Augustus, a Spaniard by birth, who was Librarian of the Palatine Library (*praepositus bibliothecae*) and 'taught many pupils'; clearly a scholar who had time for research and teaching. A successor, Tiberius Julius Pappus, extended the scope of the post and proclaims himself in his epitaph as 'superintendent of all the Imperial libraries from the times of the Emperor Tiberius to that of the Emperor Claudius'. Other inscriptions preserve the names of two of his library clerks, 'Alexander, slave of Germanicus, a Paphlagonian, clerk in the Greek Library in the Temple of Apollo', and Antiochus, slave of Tiberius Claudius Caesar, clerk in the Latin Library'. Such slaves might of course become freedmen themselves. As a general feature of the social order under Augustus it has been pointed out that although the various classes were sharply differentiated, they were not organised in water-tight compartments. For each was devised an appropriate means of contributing to the new order of Augustus.

In the provinces were other loyalties to be won—those of the political leaders of local communities. Whether they were Gallic chieftains in the Romanised *civitates* or magistrates in historic cities of Greece or Asia, self-interest alone would attach most of these men to Rome. But a more personal link with the Emperor was devised in the Imperial cult. If it strikes us today as incongruous or absurd that Augustus should have been widely honoured as a god during his lifetime, that is because we have been brought up in the monotheism of Judaeo-Christian tradition. Polytheism was the rule in the Roman world and in its Eastern parts the practice of ruler worship was familiar. Such worship had been accorded to many Hellenistic kings from Alexander onwards; even Roman officials had been honoured in this way. So when the provinces of Asia, Galatia, or Bithynia proposed to establish temples and priesthoods to Augustus—or to Rome and Augustus —it was no startling innovation for them, except perhaps in the scale of magnificence felt to be appropriate. (The massive portal of the Temple of Rome and Augustus at Ancyra, a replica of which is in the Museo Nazionale Romano, will illustrate this point.) And what the provinces did was imitated widely by individual cities, kings and petty rulers in the East. Augustus did not refuse such honours, though he was careful not to seem to encourage them in Rome and Italy. But they provided a useful precedent for the Western provinces and it was official policy that encouraged the Imperial cult in Tres Galliae, Germany and Spain. The altar established by Drusus at Lyons in 12 B.C. appears to be the first in Tres Galliae: at the annual meeting of the *concilium Galliarum* the rites of the Imperial cult provided a focus for Gallic loyalty to Rome. Ara Ubiorum (Cologne) was to have been such a centre for Germany had there been a German province; Tarraco did become one for its own part of Spain.

Individual cities established cults of their own accord. Thus the people of Narbo set up an altar to the spirit (*numen*) of Augustus in 11 B.C., providing for sacrifices on five days in the year, one being the anniversary of a dispute which he settled between the town council and the local residents. As for Rome and Italy, they gave him all honours short of deification. The month *Sextilis* was renamed in his honour and preserves the name August to this day. In the calendar of Praeneste, at least 16 festal days in the year commemorated important events in his life, or those of his heirs. The poets likened him constantly to Hercules, Bacchus, Mercury, or Apollo and to other benefactors of the human race, heroic or divine. His 'father' Julius Caesar had been deified: he was *Divi filius* in his life: only a few days after his funeral the Senate accorded him divine honours in his turn, with a college of priests and a temple in the Forum Romanum. But such honours were not automatic. Of his Julio-Claudian successors only Claudius attained them. They were denied to Tiberius, Gaius, and Nero.

The problem of succession was crucial to the Principate. Circumstances—his own ill health and the fact that he had no son—forced Augustus to contemplate the problem from the outset of his reign: his efforts to solve it were dogged by fantastic ill fortune. Augustus' only child was Julia, his daughter by his first wife Scribonia. Livia had two sons by an earlier marriage, Tiberius and Drusus. There was also Augustus' nephew, Marcellus, son of his much loved sister Octavia, and on this young man Augustus' hopes were fixed at first. Marcellus was married to his cousin Julia; children of this marriage would have carried the blood of Augustus in a third generation. But in 23 B.C. Marcellus died childless. The young widow of 16 was now married to Agrippa, a man of 40. This was a fruitful marriage,

1   Cosa was founded in 273 B.C., on the Etrurian coast. Excavations
have revealed the Forum and Basilica. The harbour, now a partly
drained lagoon, is in the background (*top left*).

2. Alba Fucens was founded in 303 B.C. as a strong point against the
Marsi. It controls the junction of three mountain passes on the Via
Valeria between Rome and the Adriatic.

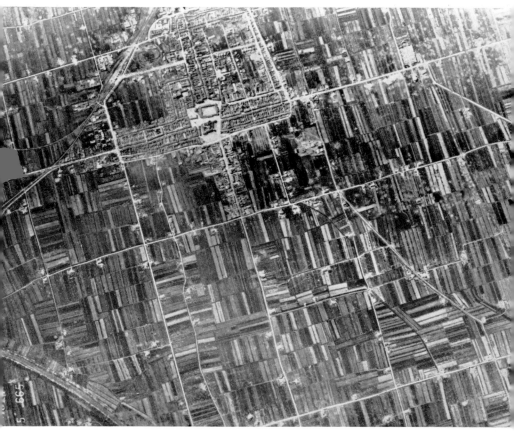

3 Lugo, near Ravenna. Air photography shows an extensive pattern of Roman centuriation, as used to divide the land for settlers, or for the assignment of public land to individual settlers. There are many such centuriation systems in northern Italy and along the east coast of the Adriatic.

4 The tracing of the ritual furrow to delimit the boundary of the new colony. The founder drives a bronze plough, drawn by a bull and a cow.

5 Founder's inscription.
L. MANLIVS L.F. ACIDINVS
TRIVMVIR AQVILEIAE
COLONIAE DEDVCVNDÁE—
'Lucius Manlius Acidinus
son of Lucius, member of
the College of Three for the
founding of the colony at
Aquileia' (189 B.C.).

6 Verona on the Adige (Athesis) commanded the route to the
Brenner Pass. The air view shows the site of the Roman Theatre (*top
right, E of river*), and the Amphitheatre, to the right of which the grid-
plan of the Roman streets is well preserved.

7   Brescia (Brixia), in the territory of the Cenomani, became a *Colonia*
in the time of Augustus. The Capitolium is Flavian.

8   Turin (Augusta Taurinorum, 27 B.C.) was a key Augustan foundation in north-western Cisalpine Gaul, commanding the route that
led past Susa (Segusio) to the Mt Genèvre. The colony is dignified
by the monumental Porta Augusta.

9　Aosta (Augusta Praetoria), in the territory of the Salassi, commanded the route up the Dora Baltea Valley to the St Bernard Pass. The settlers (25 B.C.) were from the Praetorian Guard, and have left their mark in the lay out of the city. The air view shows part of the Roman street-plan, the theatre, amphitheatre, and part of the Roman baths.

10 The *Tropaeum* at Adamklissi commemorated Trajan's northern
wars, especially, it seems, the victories over the Roxolani. Other such
monuments were at La Turbie, for Augustus' Alpine campaigns, and
(probably) the Tetrapylon at Rochester, Kent, where only the foundations survive.

11   This reconstruction shows one span of Apollodorus' great bridge across the Danube at Turnu Severin (Drobetae) below the Iron Gates. Pier foundations still survive on the Yugoslav bank of the river.

12   Trajan's Forum was designed by Apollodorus. Its principal monument was the great column dedicated on May 12th, A.D. 113. The spiral column rests on a base decorated with trophies of Dacian arms. Above a laurel wreath rise the reliefs which record the two wars. In the first of these the Roman Army marches from its base at Viminacium to cross the Danube by a pontoon bridge. Father Danuvius rises in a great spout of water to watch.

13   Trajan's Column. A *contio*, or Address to the Troops, on campaign. Standard-bearers and soldiers surround a *tribunal*, on which the Emperor will present decorations and deliver a speech. The emphasis throughout is on the intelligence and discipline which bring victory to Rome.

14   The Arch of Constantine was adorned with sculpture from earlier
triumphal monuments, including some of the time of Trajan. The
noble figure of a Dacian chieftain finely conveys the proud spirit and
martial vigour of Rome's northern enemies.

15 The Column of Marcus Aurelius, commemorating his victories in wars on the Danube, was erected after his death in A.D. 180. In contrast to those of Trajan's Column, the sculptures emphasise the misery and disasters of war. The Rain Miracle, which brought an unexpected Roman victory, occurred in a battle against the Quadi, perhaps in A.D. 173.

16 Hadrian himself surveyed the line of the Wall during his visit to Britain in A.D. 122 The picture shows its most impressive stretch, between Housesteads and Winshields (1230 ft above sea-level).

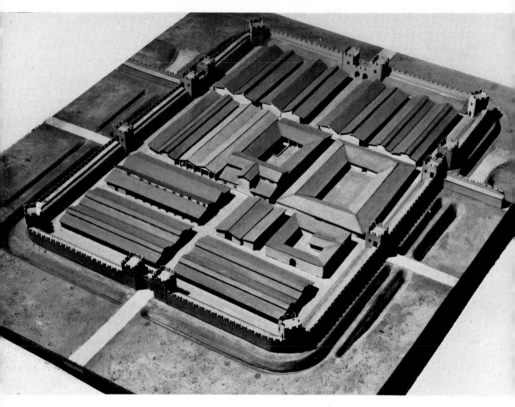

17 Hadrian's Wall. Reconstruction of the third-century cavalry fort at Benwell (Condercum), two miles west of Newcastle upon Tyne. The fort shown is that rebuilt by Septimius Severus, and seems itself to have been damaged in the rising of A.D. 296

producing five children, the two oldest of whom were boys, Gaius and Lucius. For a number of years the position looked secure. The trusty Agrippa was there to step into Augustus' place should he suddenly die and to protect his two grandsons. Augustus' stepsons, Tiberius and Drusus, were winning laurels in the field. Agrippa's death in 12 B.C., aged only 50, changed the whole picture. Poor Julia was forced into a third dynastic marriage, this time to Tiberius, who had to divorce a wife he loved. Their marriage was childless and unhappy and Tiberius became embittered by the premature honours Augustus designed for Gaius and Lucius, thus clearly marking them out for the succession. In 6 B.C. Tiberius withdrew to Rhodes, a soured and lonely man. In 2 B.C. Julia's immoralities, notorious (it was said) throughout Rome, became known to her father also and she was sent into exile. Gaius and Lucius were now coming to manhood, only to fall victims to the same evil destiny that had struck down the young Marcellus. Lucius died of illness at Massilia in A.D. 2; Gaius of wounds in Lycia in A.D. 4 Only Tiberius was left. In that same year Augustus invested him with tribunician powers for ten years, using words that made it clear that he did so in the absence of any other choice. In A.D. 13 the grant was renewed with additional powers. All had been arranged for a smooth transfer of power when Augustus died in A.D. 14—except that Tiberius could not bring himself to accept it with good heart and grace. No one had done the State more splendid service nor received less thanks for it and no one knew better the nature of the burden he was asked to bear. Only the intellect of Augustus could, in Tiberius' view, sustain the burden of Empire. The scenes in the Senate so dramatically described by Tacitus, who makes him appear to decline what he feign would have, could have been more genuine than the historian would allow.

Julia should have a further word. The women of the Roman aristocracy were accustomed to being pawns in the game of political marriage. To be so used thrice, as Julia was, went perhaps beyond the call of duty and might be thought to excuse a measure of indulgence. That Julia received no indulgence whatsoever from her father was not solely due to her flagrant behaviour and the eminence of her lovers. She had become a political liability, bringing into contempt her father's attempts at social and moral reform and now making the Princeps himself an object of ridicule.

T.R.—N

These moral reforms had been embodied in a carefully framed programme of legislation, notably the *Leges Juliae* which belong to the year 18 B.C. It made adultery a crime visited by severe penalty, penalised celibacy and childless marriages, and gave privileges to the parents of three or more children. A code of sumptuary laws tried to curb various forms of extravagance and luxury. Admirable in intent, they were unsuccesful like all attempts to make people virtuous by legislation. Tacitus, who might have sympathised with their purpose, says that their chief result was to raise a crop of spies and informers. Augustus had conceived them as the final stage in his programme of reform, bringing a purged and rejuvenated Roman People into a proper relationship with the gods.

The revival of the ancient ceremony of the Secular Games in 17 B.C. was intended as a signal manifestation of the new order that had been achieved. The long inscription set up by the Board of Fifteen responsible for the ceremonies makes clear its unique character—no one living would see its like again. The gods invoked, the prayers offered and the sacrifices paid are duly recorded, the archaic ritual and the spectacles provided briefly noted. The central roles throughout were played by the Emperor and Agrippa, and by a group of 110 Roman matrons of proved fertility and spotless reputation. 'When the rites were over, a choir of 27 boys whose fathers and mothers were certified as being alive and an equal number of girls sang the Hymn. The Hymn was composed by Q. Horatius Flaccus.' The Hymn—known as the *Carmen Saeculare*—is felicitous for an official piece. It concludes with an appeal to Apollo, patron of the new order that 'if he looks with favour on his altars on the Palatine, may he prolong Rome's Empire and Latium, new and better, into another age'. So the whole Roman People were brought together in a solemn mood of thanks for the past and hope for the future. Such ceremonies, as at a Coronation, can raise a people for a little while above the reality of a workaday world.

No long reign maintains an even tenor. That of Augustus divided fairly sharply into two phases, the second much more sombre than the first. The year 8 B.C. which saw the deaths of Maecenas and Horace is a convenient divide. We are just into the second half of the reign and already many of the greatest Augustans are gone—in politics and war, Agrippa, Maecenas and Drusus; in literature Virgil, Horace, Tibullus, Propertius.

To the second half of the reign belong the disasters in Pannonia and Germany, the deaths of Gaius and Lucius Caesar and the scandals of Julia and her daughter. In its last decade the ageing Emperor and Empress live on, out of an Imperial family stricken in two younger generations. There was one surviving grandson— Agrippa Postumus, a boorish lout. For political support there was Tiberius—unwanted, unwilling and indispensable. In the field of literature there was Ovid, but in A.D. 8 he too was banished into lasting exile at Tomi (Constanza) on the far Black Sea fringe of the Empire. Livy lived on to teach history to the future Emperor Claudius. There was the didactic poet Manilius. But Augustus had the quality the Romans so much admired— *constantia*. He endured misfortune and disaster and came in the end (like Queen Victoria) to win that strange affection sometimes accorded to aged sovereigns when they come to be seen as the embodiment of their people's experience.

CHAPTER 28

Augustan literature

IT IS TO THE LAST YEARS of the Triumvirate and the first part of the reign of Augustus that we must look for the best of Augustan literature. In this period there appears a group of poets whose work alike in epic, lyric, satire, pastoral, amatory and didactic poetry is of the first rank and has been of cardinal importance for the literature of Europe. They were men of original talent even when, like the three elegists, they wrote in the same genre: there was no school of Augustan poetry. But they came to flower from a common seed bed whose features should be noted before turning to the writers themselves. The older men—Virgil, Horace, Propertius and Tibullus—had suffered in one way or another from the Civil Wars. The coming of the Augustan peace brought a new life, new hopes and a phase of creative energy. They were eager to support Augustus' plans for the revival of Italian agriculture, the new emphasis on the dignity of Rome and Italy, the new concept of Rome's mission in the world. When Virgil wrote on lines like these he was also helping to shape events, for he did so as the *vates,* the inspired poet who discloses to the people the revelation he has learned from a higher power. All the great Augustans it should be said were Italians. Virgil came from Mantua, Livy from Patavium (Padua) in Cisalpine Gaul, Propertius from Umbria, Ovid from Sulmo, Tibullus from Pedum near Tibur and Horace from Apulia. They found enlightened patronage, in which Augustus and Maecenas played the leading parts, and worked for a while in Rome. All could command that style that belongs only to the classical masterpieces in any field of art— such as King's College Chapel at Cambridge, or the Parthenon at Athens, or certain of the works of Mozart.

Virgil (70–19 B.C.) first made a name with the *Eclogues*—a collection of ten short pastoral poems which appeared about 37 B.C. The genre had been founded some two centuries earlier by Theocritus, who gave literary form to the shepherds' songs of the mountain pastures in his native Sicily—an authentic folk art that survives today. Theocritus wrote in Alexandria, and to the Greeks who had come from all parts of the Aegean to this crowded and cosmopolitan city his poems brought nostalgic memories of a lost countryside. The *Eclogues* were similarly evocative and won the same success in the Rome of the Civil War. They are deceptively simple. Their aim, says the poet, is to bring rest and refreshment—'as sleep in soft grass brings to the weary, or as a drink of pure water from a running stream quenches thirst in the heat of summer'. But there are hidden depths. Modern scholarship has only recently taught us to appreciate the arrangement of the book as a whole, with its subtle balance of harmony and contrast. And, while the poems are set in the limpid summer air of some landscape by Claude Lorraine, one is never quite sure where that landscape is. It may be Sicily or Arcadia, it may be the north Italian landscape of Virgil's childhood. Time too is as flexible as space. The dead shepherd of the lament in the Fifth Eclogue somehow becomes Julius Caesar—acceptably while the spell lasts, incongruously when we come out of it. For the Arcady of Virgil is really a state of mind, of associations which can be aroused by poetry or by some old country air. It is a limited magic and it does not give complete protection against the realities of life. The miseries of the evicted peasants sound harshly in the First and Ninth Eclogues: Virgil may have his farm restored, but the others go to exile in strange lands and a brutal soldiery possess their fields. The Fourth Eclogue, with its prophetic vision of the Golden Age come again, the Reign of Saturn restored throughout the world, voices a theme to which Virgil will return many times. It is the basis, too, of the medieval tradition of Virgil the magician, Prophet of the Gentiles who foretold the birth of Christ, and who dispensed prophecies to his consultants, if they would follow the formula for divining the future through the *sortes Virgilianae*.

Over his next poem, the *Georgics*, Virgil, as was his habit, worked long and slowly: he was engaged for more than seven years on its 2,000 lines. It was launched at a reading to Octavian, a few days before his triumph in 29 B.C. The time was apt, for the theme of the *Georgics* was how to make best use of the peace that the victor of Actium had won. Addressed to the farmers of Italy, of whom Virgil could count himself one, it showed that the moral regeneration of the country rested with them. It could come only if they realised the true values of a farmer's life and eschewed all others, understood the various branches of agriculture, accepted the need for hard work, respected the gods of the countryside and its ancient pieties, and dealt fairly by the land and the crops and beasts to which it gave life. Here too a debt is acknowledged to a Greek poet, in this case Hesiod of Ascra in Boeotia, whose *Works and Days* is sometimes dated to 800 B.C. But this debt is little more than formal, a tribute to the first poet to take farming for his theme. There is more than a gap of time between the earthy voice of the Balkan peasant in Hesiod and the deeper insight and consummate art of the Augustan poet.

The *Georgics* form a poetic symphony, to be understood as a whole. The First deals with corn-growing, the hard work it entails and the hazards to which it is exposed—pests and mildew, lightning and flood, winds and storms. As we hear of signs of foul weather the mood darkens with the sky to recall the prodigies that preceded the assassination of Caesar—'the graves stood open, and the sheeted dead did squeak and gibber in the Roman streets'. The poem closes with an apocalyptic vision of the evil times thus launched and a prayer to heaven to spare Octavian for the rescue of a world turned upside down. The Second on vines, olives, and orchard trees, under the patronage of Bacchus, is written in a happy vein proper to that kindly god. It contains the famous Praises of Italy (*laudes Italiae*), a passage of 40 lines (136–176) which is a superb evocation of the landscape of Italy in all its richness and variety, its fine cattle and horses, its noble cities and towns and its hardy breed of men. Here truly are the *Saturnia regna*, the realms of Saturn, which once were in Italy and could be brought back. Later comes a passage on the origins of life on earth, symbolised by the Marriage of Heaven and Earth in the cosmic springtime. The mood of joy is sustained in the description of the Happy Farmers who live 'as once did the ancient Sabines and Remus and his brother; that was how Etruria grew strong, how Rome became the fairest city in the world . . . that indeed was the life that Saturn led in the Golden Age, long before the trumpet had sounded for war, or swords groaned as they were

sharpened on the anvil'. The Third Book deals with animals—
horses, cattle, goats, sheep and dogs. These creatures like man
know the pangs of love and the assault of disease; again the mood
darkens and the poem ends with a description of an outbreak of
pestilence among the herds of Noricum in Virgil's day. Death,
silence and the stench of rotting corpses grip the countryside,
as they did over much of the Marches of Wales through some
stark months of 1968. Book Four is happier, dealing with bees
and their polities, a tiny version of our own and a model for their
loyalty and devotion to duty. Bees have their diseases too—what
is worse for a beekeeper than that all his bees should die? This
happened to Aristaeus, the archetypal beekeeper, but he knew
where to go for help to bring his swarms back to life. So halfway
through the Fourth Georgic Virgil launches into the 280 lines
that serve as a finale. Outwardly, here is an *epyllion*—a miniature
epic with a story set within a frame. The frame is Aristaeus and
the renewal of his bees; the story is Orpheus and Eurydice in the
most moving of all versions of that legend. Is this no more than
a pretty piece of mythology, substituted for a passage on Cornelius
Gallus that was expunged when that poet fell out of favour with
Augustus? So commentators once thought, but surely it cannot
be. The passage is no appendix but occupies the most important
position in the *Georgics*. It should contain a clue, perhaps a revelation. There are two underworld journeys with two opposite
endings. In one Aristaeus, the archetypal beekeeper, goes down to
meet his mother, the water goddess Cyrene. He sees her palace
beneath the sea and the beautiful water nymphs that live in it and
is told to consult the sea god Proteus, to force him to give a
recipe to revive the bees. He follows the recipe faithfully: it
works and his swarms are revived, bigger and better than before.
In the other journey Orpheus, the archetypal poet, goes down to
the kingdom of the dead. His songs move the powers of Hell, as
they move all creatures on earth. He wins permission to bring
back his lost Eurydice on one condition—that he does not turn
to look back at her. They have almost regained the light when
he turns: there is a crash of thunder in Hell: she is gone forever.
Maddened by grief and loneliness, Orpheus wanders the cold
mountains of Thrace; at last he is torn to death by Maenads. In
the mystery religions, bees symbolise the souls of the dead
as they wait for reincarnation. They are there in the Sixth
Aeneid, crowding the banks of Lethe 'like bees in the meadows

on a sunny day in summer, settling on flowers of many kinds
and clustering round the white lilies'. Perhaps, then, Virgil means
that the magic art of the poet may not in the end prevail against
the powers of Hell and may only bring agony and loneliness.
But the initiate of the mystery cults, if he follows the instruction,
is assured of eternal life. Perhaps.

The last decade of Virgil's life was spent on the *Aeneid*, an
epic poem whose real subject is the origin and destiny of Rome.
The narrative begins with the sack of Troy, followed by the
wanderings of Aeneas in search of a home for the Trojan refugees
in a western land, and his stay in Carthage, which almost wrecked
the divine plan for Rome. Forced to sail on, he reaches Italy
where the Sibyl of Cumae escorts him to the Underworld to
receive from his father Anchises a revelation of the real nature
of his mission. The second and in Virgil's view more important
part of the poem deals with his arrival at the site of Rome, the
wars he had to fight in Italy, his projected marriage with the
Italian princess Lavinia, and his final triumph in personal combat
with Turnus, the great champion of the Italian cause. The
project was gigantic and Virgil later said he had been mad to
undertake it. At his death in 19 B.C. the poem was unfinished and
in his will he asked for it to be destroyed. It was Augustus who
rescued it and had it published unaltered. At once it won a place
among the very few great epics of the world.

It is easy to see the reasons for Virgil's doubts. Epic was an
archaic form of poetry: it was uncertain whether it could be
revived. The last major attempts to do so in Latin, the *Bellum
Punicum* of Naevius and the *Annals* of Ennius, had shown that
success could be won by the treatment of an historical theme,
and more recently chroniclers had tried their hands at the Gallic
wars of Julius Caesar. Virgil himself once thought of something
of the kind, but finally undertook the much bolder challenge of
the *Aeneid*. For this was a full-scale Homeric epic, in an Homeric
context, making ample use of material from the *Odyssey* and the
Iliad. The comparison with Homer was inescapable: indeed, it
was being freely made even before the *Aeneid* appeared. But
there were gains as well as risks. The old legends of the Italian
peoples could be brought in and vested with an heroic dignity.
Although Aeneas appears in the *Iliad* he is not a major character:
Virgil was thus free to develop him as he wished. With Dido and
Turnus he had a free hand. And some of the conventions of

epics—speeches of the gods, underworld journeys and prophecies
—enabled the poet to look beyond the context of the narrative to
the Rome of his own day, or to the common destiny of man.
Thus the shield of Aeneas in Book Eight carries a picture of the
Battle of Actium; in Book Six, Anchises expounds the doctrines of
the reincarnation of the soul, and of the indwelling of the Divine
Spirit throughout the physical universe and in all living creatures.

Aeneas is cardinal to the poem. An unsatisfactory hero, many
think. He lacks the simplicity of an Achilles or a Hector. He is
complex: a modern man. He is in part the Wanderer, like
Odysseus—but all Odysseus wants to do is to get back home.
Aeneas does not want to go to Italy: he wants to found a new
Troy; but he accepts it as a burden. He is also a Man of Sorrows.
He lost the wife he loved, Creusa, at Troy, though he would have
died to save her. When Dido Queen of Carthage offers him her
love and half her kingdom, he has to leave her. A betrayal, say
modern critics. The Romans, who knew Antony and Cleopatra,
Queen of Egypt, will have thought it less heinous. Badly cast as
the Romantic Lover, Aeneas will not do as the Heroic Warrior.
He is a good fighter, but by the time of the wars in Italy he has
come to hate war—he would rather make peace instead ('They
would have it so,' said Caesar, gazing on the Pompeian dead
after Pharsalus). Perhaps Aeneas is best understood as the
Pilgrim, for he might have said with another pilgrim at the end—
'though with great difficulty I am got hither, yet now I do not
repent me of all the trouble I have been at to arrive where I am'.
But whereas Christian had won the reward of Heaven, Aeneas'
reward was the consciousness of duty done and the hope of
fame. These were, of course, all that could be looked for by the
Roman who had done service to the State.

In the Roman view, history and poetry were close associates
and it would have seemed natural to set Livy beside Virgil. Livy
worked at the enormous task throughout the whole of his professional life of narrating the history of Rome from its foundation
to the death of Drusus in 9 B.C. His work ran in the end to more
than 130 books, of which some 35 survive complete, the rest
being known only through epitomes. Certainly Virgil would have
commended the precept which Livy enjoins upon his readers,
'that they should give serious consideration to the kind of lives
lived by our ancestors, and to see who were the men and what
were the means both in peace and war by which the Empire of

the Roman People was first acquired and later expanded. . . . In history, fortunately, you can find a record of the ample range of human experience clearly set up for everyone to see; in that record, you may discover for yourself and for your own country examples and warnings.' It is a formula that would serve for historical epic as it would for the *Aeneid*.

In some ways, Livy was not so well equipped for the writing of history as Polybius or Posidonius. He did not conduct scientific investigations, nor pay personal visits to battlefields. He was not a man of action or politics like the other great Roman historians, Sallust, Julius Caesar and Tacitus. Nor was he a senator, which meant he lacked a knowledge of Roman politics at first hand. He came from Patavium in northern Italy and there was always about his outlook something of the provincial, as the acute critic Asinius Pollio did not fail to note. His great asset lies in his narrative style, copious and ample for the wide panorama which he has to present, and capable of rising to the dignity of great themes, such as those of the Second Punic War. In the portrayal of character he cannot rival Tacitus, but some of his characters are memorable and his Hannibal is possessed of a demonic energy. It has been noted that he has an eye for economic detail uncommon in an ancient historian, and he does give a number of valuable statistics, though far fewer than a modern historian would feel bound to provide. In politics he was a moderate republican and it seems that Augustus had good reason to call him a Pompeian. He took a gloomy view of his own times as being an age when 'we can neither endure our vices nor the remedies necessary to cure them'. So much for the Principate!

Virgil's friend and contemporary, the poet Horace, was on much the same terms with Maecenas and Augustus as himself, and shared the same hopes and fears in the Triumvirate and the early phase of the Principate. Their poetic achievements are as distinct as their temperaments. Virgil was introspective and melancholy, brooding on distant or receding horizons. Horace lived on the surface of life and for the pleasures of the moment; he was acutely perceptive within a limited range of feeling. He is sometimes presented, wrongly, as a poet of two sides—the *Odes* on the one hand, the *Epodes, Satires* and *Epistles* on the other. In fact, there is a logical progression about his works, the seeds of which are all visible in the *Epodes*. These 18 neglected poems deal with patriotic themes relating to the Civil War and the Battle of Actium, nostalgia for life in the country, social problems and also erotic themes. The title of the *Satires* suggests social commentary in the manner of Lucilius but the tone is very different. The acerbity shown in the *Epodes* has now mellowed and Horace shows a wide tolerance of human beings that only stops short at bad or incompetent poets. In the *Odes*, the first three books of which appeared in 23 B.C., Horace set out to win himself a place among the lyric poets of the world. In the opinion of most good critics he succeeded. But it is lyric poetry of a very individual kind—formal, elaborate, highly finished. When it touches on love there is none of the intense personal feeling of Catullus. The tone is rather one of reminiscence, of the old master retired from the game, the sailor home from the sea. The first six Odes of Book Three constitute a special group, to which the name of 'Roman Odes' is commonly applied. They deal with public themes, teaching faith and morals to a new generation. Here Horace's model was Pindar, but his own achievement enlarged the scope of lyric poetry. The *Epistles* deal with questions of manners or conduct and of literature. The so-called *Ars Poetica* is one of the most important pieces of ancient literary criticism. It failed in its object—to revive drama on the grand scale in the age of Augustus—but it has had a profound and not always beneficial influence on later drama, especially in France. As early as 37 B.C., Maecenas had presented Horace with a small country estate near the modern Tivoli. The home farm was worked by a bailiff and eight slaves, and five tenant farmers leased the outer lands. It gave Horace the independence that all poets long to have and increasingly he spent his time there rather than at Rome. He even refused the offer of a private secretaryship from Augustus. The well-known words '*Satis beatus unicis Sabinis*' could be prosaically translated: 'I derive an adequate income from my one Sabine farm'.

The influence of the *poetae novi* and their Alexandrian models persisted in the age of Augustus. It is strong in the *Eclogues* of Virgil and is seen in the *Georgics*, especially in the miniature epic of Orpheus and Eurydice. In the *Aeneid* it finds no place. But in one form, the love elegy, it was handled by a succession of poets until the time of Ovid, by whom it was worked with such assiduity that the vein ran out. Most of these poets were members of the literary circle of Messalla Corvinus—Sulpicia, Lygdamus and the greater talents of Tibullus, Propertius and Ovid. Their themes are the conventional ones of Hellenistic love poetry—the jealous husband, the lover locked out, the intrigue with the maid, the night of ecstasy, the jealous mistress and so on. These are of course the stock situations of the lover's world, limited but intense. It is one of the attractions of Latin love elegy that each of its three major poets treats them in a highly individual style. The poetry of Tibullus is simple and sparse, its tone that of romantic longing for a lost happiness. His mistress, Delia, seems less a woman of flesh and blood than an ideal companion in the Arcadia of the *Eclogues*. The poetry of Propertius is subtle, complex and passionate; his first book is obsessed with his mistress Cynthia, as real as the Lesbia of Catullus. He is an urban man, finding pleasure in works of art and architecture rather than in the sights of the countryside. There is something Jacobean about his insistence on the twin themes of love and death, and the comparison with John Donne is sound on other points than wit, passion and obscurity.

The earliest love poetry of Ovid is in the light bantering tone of the amused recorder of love's absurdities. The *Heroides* are a series of letters addressed by the heroines of romance to their betrayers. Ovid manipulates his puppets with skill but their gestures are those of contemporary rhetoric. Sometimes however he shows feeling and insight—as for Hermione, daughter of Helen, her whole life overshadowed by her mother's beauty and her childhood blighted by her mother's absence in Troy. His description of the early dawn when Ariadne awoke to find herself deserted on Naxos has the freshness of the best of ancient landscape painting. The *Amores* are a series of love adventures in contemporary Rome. Many fashionable ladies are said to have claimed to be Ovid's Corinna, but she is really no more than an amalgam. The *Ars Amatoria* professes to be a didactic poem: its theme that most delectable of human technologies, the art of love. The *Remedium Amoris* or 'Cure for Love' was written as a necessary postscript. About halfway through it the impetus falters and the parody begins to wear thin. Ovid by now was the favourite poet of fashionable society in Rome and all but the Emperor were amused. Ovid had taken love poetry as far as it was safe or wise to go, and he now embarked on patriotic and mythological themes. The *Fasti* dealt with the festivals of the Roman calendar and the legends associated with them. To the

loss of anthropologists and students of Roman religion, it breaks
off at the end of June.

The *Metamorphoses*, a vast baroque epic, was Ovid's bid for
eminence in yet another field. Its theme—legends involving a
change of shape—gave him access to practically the whole of
classical mythology. Also to Roman history both ancient and
modern: Romulus had mysteriously disappeared to reappear in
heaven as Quirinus; a vote of the Senate had metamorphosed the
dead Julius Caesar into Divus Julius. Ovid's poetic gifts ran
best in the short or middle distance events. Each legend selected
was treated as a miniature epic and the transitions are usually
made with skill. But a metamorphosis of Ovid himself into the
official poet of the late Augustan era was not to be. In A.D. 8
he became implicated in some scandal—perhaps concerning the
younger Julia. Augustus' resentment brought a sentence of
exile. So began the last phase—Ovid the Black Sea poet com-
posing poems in the Getic language which have not survived,
and in Latin the *Tristia* and *Letters from Pontus,* which failed
to earn him a recall to Rome. Augustus did not relent and
Tiberius followed his example. The poet of high Roman society
died (? A.D. 17) in exile among some of the most backward
peoples of the Empire. They came to like each other in the end.

Their own merits and the long dominance of Latin in education
have given the great Augustan writers a deep and wide influence.
Virgil is central for the whole literary tradition of Europe.
Theocritus may have founded the pastoral; Virgil diffused it—
how widely, the mention of Spenser, the sheep-shearing scene in
A Winter's Tale, Milton's *Lycidas*, Matthew Arnold's *Thyrsis* and
The Scholar Gipsy, Adonais, certain poems of W. B. Yeats and
Dylan Thomas, will attest for English literature alone. The
Georgics have a progeny in all the literatures of Europe from
Poland to Ireland—in English, a less distinguished one, perhaps,
than the *Eclogues*, among which Thompson's *The Seasons* is
outstanding. But it is in epic that he has counted for most. If he
had not revived the epic in the *Aeneid* we should in all probability
have had no Dante, no Tasso, no Milton, no Camoens. Here
Virgil has indeed been what Dante called him—the *largo fiume*
whose copious waters have irrigated many fields. His influence
has been felt in art as well as literature. It is to be seen in some of
the best works of Rubens, Claude Lorraine and Turner, the
sculptures of Bernini and especially the wonderful frescoes of

Pietro da Cortona in Palazzo Doria-Pamfili. Ovid has been perhaps the most widely read of any Latin poet. Through the *Metamorphoses* the Middle Ages learned what they knew of classical mythology: poets who knew nothing of the Greek lyric and not much of Catullus took as their model in love poetry 'Venus' clerke, Ovid'. The *Odes* of Horace have influenced all European lyric and his *Ars Poetica* has, with Aristotle's *Poetics*, been one of the standard works of literary criticism. Livy stood first among historians until the rediscovery of Tacitus in the fifteenth century and indeed it is only in the present century that Tacitus' claims have generally rated higher. Nor must we omit the influence of the technical treatise on architecture written by Vitruvius. The *De Architectura* went through numerous editions in the Renaissance and served as the standard guide to the architectural practice of the ancient world. Vitruvius and the visible remains of Roman antiquity were the twin sources of inspiration for Bramante, Michelangelo and Palladio. They in turn have diffused his influence widely throughout Europe and also to Russia, South Africa and North and South America. Whether they wrote on serious or light topics, the Augustans proclaimed the belief that their writing would bring them immortality. That hope has not been belied.

CHAPTER 29

Emperors and administration

ACCORDING TO SUETONIUS, Augustus published in an edict his hopes for the future of the Principate in these words: 'May I be privileged to establish sound and durable foundations for the Commonwealth of Rome. May I also achieve the reward for which I aim: that of being recognised as the author of the best possible constitution, so that when I die I may take with me the hope that those foundations will long endure.' Endure they did. The great political machine he had constructed worked effectively and on the whole smoothly until at least the death of Commodus in A.D. 192. Only once was there a challenge to the office of Emperor, as distinct from plots against the lives of individual Emperors of which there were many. After the assassination of Gaius in A.D. 41, there was a debate in the Senate on a proposal to restore the Republic. It did not get very far. Already the new Emperor, Claudius, had been proclaimed in the barracks of the Praetorian Guard. He had many disabilities— Augustus had even pronounced him as unfit to appear on any public occasion—but he was the next in succession in the Julio– Claudian line and that was enough for the troops. And in the year 69 after the murder of Nero the only question was which of four candidates could make good his claim to the throne. In that year, as Tacitus says, a secret of Empire was disclosed—that an Emperor could be made elsewhere than at Rome. The German armies put forward Vitellius, those of the East, Vespasian. Force of arms decided the issue, which was an evil precedent.

There was of course a good deal of sentimental republicanism in the Senate, fostered by the cult of the tyrannicides Brutus and Cassius and of the republican martyr Cato of Utica. This attitude is seen in the *Pharsalia*, Lucan's epic poem on the Civil War between Caesar and Pompey. When relations between an Emperor and the Senate became strained beyond a certain point, the Emperor might be called a tyrant and an attempt made on his life. Assassination, as Domitian once remarked, was the occupational risk of a Roman Emperor. But the general view is probably voiced in the words Tacitus gives to the *parvenu* senator Eprius Marcellus: 'I hope for good Emperors, but I take them as they come'. The problem of the Empire was to ensure that bad Emperors were not too frequent. Two of the five Julio-Claudians, Gaius and Nero, deserved the adjective 'bad', so did Domitian, the third of the Flavians and in the popular view by far the worst. The dynastic principle had failed, and after Domitian's death it was resolved to try something else. We have seen how the method of adoption had been used in the great republican families when there was no suitable heir: adoption of the 'best man' might solve the problem of succession to the Principate. And indeed it worked brilliantly in the sequence of five 'Good Emperors' from Nerva to Marcus Aurelius; their reigns which stretched from A.D. 96 to 180 were traditionally the best years of the Empire. When Marcus Aurelius, the first of the five to have a son of his body, reverted to the dynastic principle in the choice of Commodus, the fortunes of Rome changed sharply for the worse.

The Emperors of the first two centuries A.D. came from a wide range of social backgrounds. The Julio-Claudians were Roman aristocrats: their share of the traditional arrogance of the *gens Claudia* and the uninhibited power they enjoyed drove Nero almost and Gaius completely mad. Vespasian, first of the Flavians, was of good Sabine municipal stock; he brought with him into the Senate a number of provincials of the same modest tastes and bourgeois outlook. Nerva was a rich elderly senator of an old but not distinguished family. Then come Emperors of provincial descent or, to be more accurate, from Italian families long settled in the provinces—Trajan, Hadrian and Marcus Aurelius from Spain and Antoninus Pius from Gaul. Even in its rulers the Roman world was ceasing to be *imperium populi Romani*.

Thanks largely to Tacitus and Suetonius we know a good deal about the Emperors from Tiberius to Domitian. At one time Tacitus entertained the project of a history of the reigns of Nerva and Trajan. Unfortunately he never carried it out. The sources for Hadrian are wretchedly inadequate: what we know of him suggests that he was the most versatile and intelligent of all these Emperors, but it is hard to see him as he really was. The lack of good narrative histories for Trajan and Hadrian, whose times saw the Empire reach its zenith, must always impair judgement of the two Emperors. When the Senate conferred on Trajan the title *Optimus Princeps* (Best of Emperors) it knew what it was doing, but we could not complete the case for the citation. The sources for Antoninus Pius are not much better but this is a less serious matter. Marcus Aurelius we know well as a man through his *Meditations*; less well as Emperor. But the history of the Empire is not to be written in terms of the personalities of Emperors, either edifying or the reverse. Their sexual excesses and aberrations belong indeed to the field of the historical novel. What matters is their reaction to the enormous burden of duty they had to bear—comparable to that of a President of the United States. Some retreated from it into a private world of sensuality, like the youthful Nero, leaving administration to Seneca and Burrus. Some wrestled with it throughout their reigns, as did Trajan, Hadrian and Marcus Aurelius who wrote: 'Let the divinity within you guide a being that is manly, ripe in years, a statesman, a Roman, a ruler—a man who has taken up his post.' Vespasian in his dying moments of weakness and physical indignity tried to stand up, saying that a Roman Emperor should die on his feet. By the end of the first century A.D., the Stoic philosophers had formulated the high concept of kingship as being in the service of mankind, performed by the Emperor as the vicegerent of God on earth. The Emperors from Nerva to Marcus Aurelius, in their different ways, at least tried to rule by this precept.

While the administrative system devised by Augustus was retained in broad outline, Claudius brought in reforms to strengthen and rationalise the Civil Service. He established four great bureaux: for laws and edicts (*ab epistulis*), for finance (*a rationibus*), for records and archives (*a studiis*), and lastly for judicial matters (*a libellis*). Each was in the charge of a freedman who was the Emperor's nominee. Under Claudius these freedmen

—Narcissus, Pallas, Callistus, Polybius—the names show their Greek origins—dominated more than their departments. They dispensed official patronage and enriched themselves on a fantastic scale; even the choice of an Empress was determined by their rivalries. The Senate hated them and this attitude is preserved in the historical tradition. There is no reason to suppose that they were not efficient administrators and, on occasion, as in the aftermath of the Boudicca rebellion in Britain, they could take the part of trouble-shooters. Nero's freedmen were not so prominent as those of Claudius but they still made rich pickings, as did those of the Year of the Four Emperors. With the Flavians their influence was greatly curtailed, and Trajan used men of the equestrian order to fill the great posts in the bureaucracy. From the same class he recruited the finance inspectors (*correctores*) employed to examine and report on the financial problems of the municipalities. There was ample need for their services, especially among the cities of Asia, but they mark a further stage in the encroachment of the central government on the powers of local authorities.

CHAPTER 30

The Senate

ANTAGONISM BETWEEN THE EMPEROR and Senate was latent in the Augustan Principate, but it was kept within bounds by the prestige and tact of the Princeps. Under the Julio-Claudians, from Tiberius onwards, the Senate underwent a traumatic experience. Tiberius was uncongenial from the first. Malignant and implacable (such is the picture according to Tacitus) the only refuge for the Senate was flattery. The rise of Sejanus to the position of favourite was deeply resented. But the worst feature of the reign was the persecution of senators on the vaguely defined charge of treason (*maiestas*) which gave scope for a new and loathed class of *delatores* or informers. The treason trials ceased with Claudius but the senators resented the influence of his wives, Messalina and Agrippina, and above all of the Imperial freedmen. Another source of alarm was the Emperor's liberal outlook on the admission of provincials to the Senate. (Claudius' admirable speech on the recruitment of men from Tres Galliae is preserved on a bronze inscription at Lyons: it roused the xenophobia of the Senate and there were wild rumours of indiscriminate admission.) Nero's reign started well—a modest young prince guided by the wisdom of Seneca and Burrus would, it was thought, respect the Senate's prerogatives and return to the pattern of Augustus. This did not come about. Once the young man came into his own and contrived the murder of Agrippina, the Senate had to plumb new depths of abasement. A few men only stood out—Thrasea Paetus and his Stoic followers, Gaius Cassius, descendant of the tyrannicide. Yet, after so many eminent senators had been killed, the last word lay with the Senate. They denounced Nero as a public enemy, drove him to suicide and damned his memory.

With Vespasian a change began and a good relationship between the Emperor and the Senate was achieved. With the conspicuous exception of the reign of Domitian, it was to last for more than a century. The old Roman aristocratic families with their memories of the Republic were almost extinct. The new men recruited to the Senate by Vespasian were, like himself, of Italian municipal stock, or men of good standing from the provinces, especially Narbonensis and Spain. These men were content with a career in the public service, rather than as political figures in their own right. Confronted with the overbearing autocracy of Domitian which finally brought back all the worst features of the Julio-Claudian informers, treason trials and persecution, the Senate was reduced to panic and silence. A famous passage of the *Agricola* of Tacitus described the whole reign as a period of servitude, but the picture is painted with the colours of the last years of terror (88–96). Under Nerva who was an elderly senator, confidence began to revive: under Trajan it was clear (even to Tacitus) that 'freedom and the Principate' could be reconciled. In fact, the Senate of Trajan, Hadrian and the Antonines was very unlike the Senate of the first century.

CHAPTER 31

Local government

PROVINCIALS MADE UP ALMOST HALF the Senate's number, with the Eastern provinces well represented at last. Trajan ordered that they should invest a third of their money in lands in Italy, but this was rather as a stimulus to Italy's lagging economy than in the hope that they would replace provincial with Italian loyalties. Antoninus Pius and Marcus Aurelius were careful to consult the Senate on public policy and were friendly with its members: not until the reign of Commodus did good relations break down. Emperor and Senate had for most of the second century A.D. come to terms as partners in the service of the Commonwealth. It is a pity that no major literary source gives an account of this period, to set off against Tacitus' overpowering picture of the bitter years under Tiberius, Nero and Domitian. Whatever the nature of the Imperial administration, the politics of the Roman world continued to be important at a local level. In the provinces most people thought of themselves as citizens of a local community rather than of a universal state. The Roman Empire, it has been said, was a confederation of municipalities— the description is not wholly true, but it will serve. Certainly Greco-Roman civilisation depended, as the word shows, on the city as the milieu in which it could find full expression. In the Western provinces the growth of such cities was the surest index of Romanisation. In the cities the individual could lead a genuine political life though restricted within certain limits. Through the cities he was brought into contact with the general cultural life of the Roman world. The municipal aristocracy were at once the chief agents of Romanisation and its chief beneficiaries. They administered the affairs of the local community, collected its taxes, made contact with the governor of the province, and if

189

necessary, went on embassies to Rome. They were generous benefactors—remarkably so, by the standards of modern Britain. Thousands of inscriptions from all parts of the Empire attest their public spirit in donations for such things as the upkeep of poor children, a public banquet, a water supply, baths, a school, the setting up of statues, the repair of public buildings. Pliny for example was generous to his native Comum. In his will he left money for the construction, decoration and upkeep of public baths, a further sum for the use of his freedmen during their lifetime and thereafter for an annual public banquet. Another benefaction provided funds for poor boys and girls, yet another for the building and upkeep of a library. He also promised to contribute one-third above any sum raised for the building of a municipal school and wrote to Tacitus in Rome for a list of possible teachers. The benefactions of the multi-millionaire Herodes Atticus to the cities of Greece were on a truly princely scale—the Stadium and the Odeon at Athens being the most notable.

The cities developed in the Western provinces had certain physical features in common. Their streets were usually laid out on the grid pattern, with a generous area reserved in the centre for public buildings. There would be a forum, a basilica for the conduct of legal business and for large public meetings, a *curia* for the local council, administrative offices and shops whose rent went to the municipality. Colonnades would provide protection against rain or sun. There would be temples for both Roman and native cults. Those dedicated to the Capitoline Triad, the Emperor, or Dea Roma, would usually be part of the civic centre. There would be schools giving instruction in Latin and also providing the standard classical education. The larger cities had public professors of rhetoric and philosophy and sometimes a doctor who gave free treatment to the poor. There might be a library, perhaps as a result of private benefaction. The range of public amenities depended on the size of the city. At the very least there would be an amphitheatre for gladiatorial shows. Theatres were common in Gaul, rare in Britain. An *Odeon* for concerts would be a refinement. A very large city might have a circus for chariot racing, and some half-dozen cities in Gaul ran to this expensive form of amusement. There would be public baths, perhaps more than one and of different degrees of elaboration. An aqueduct would bring a supply of public water to a high point in the town, from which it would be distributed by means of lead pipes. Walls and monumental gateways would impress the traveller entering the town; there might also be triumphal arches, elaborate funeral monuments and public statues. But such cities were not built to a standard layout, as with a Roman fort, imposed upon the landscape like some gigantic rubber stamp. Due regard was taken of local topography and of existing settlements and buildings, especially temples. In Gaul, where urbanisation has been closely studied, it has been shown that the Gallo-Roman architects felt free to introduce ideas of their own, although they had a good knowledge of standard classical practice. These new cities of the Western provinces must have had a common likeness, but local rivalry and individuality redeemed them from the dull monotony common to the towns of our industrial civilisaton.

The provinces in the second century A.D.

- - - - - Provincial boundaries
———— Frontiers

Miles
100 0 100 200 300 400

5. The Roman Empire during the lifetime of Marcus Aurelius

COSTOBOCI

DACIAE
Apulum
A.D. 106
Sarmizegetusa
idunum R.Danubi INFERIOR
MOESIA
INFERIOR
Sardica Philippopolis
THRACIA
CEDONIA
MACEDONIA

Byzantium
Chalcedon
Nicomedia
Cyzicus
Pergamum ASIA
Smyrna Laodicea
Ephesus
Corinth Athens
ACHAEA

CRETA

PONTUS ET BITHYNIA

GALATIA
Tarsus
LYCIA
ET
PAMPHYLIA
CILICIA

CYPRUS

Satala
CAPPADOCIA
Melitene

Antioch
SYRIA
Orontes
Cyrrhus

R.Phasis
HIBERI
Artaxata
Elegeia
ARMENIA
R.Tigris
Edessa Nisibis
Carrhae
PARTHIA
R.Euphrates
Ctesiphon
Seleuceia

Palmyra

SYRIA
PALAESTINA
ARABIA
Petra

Cyrene
Alexandria

CYRENE
AEGYPTUS

R.Nile

CHAPTER 32

Frontiers

THE MAINTENANCE OF the *pax Romana* is the grand theme of
the period—unbroken save for the Civil Wars of A.D. 69 and
sporadic rebellions in Gaul. But the armies on the frontiers were
not allowed to stand idle.

Tiberius, who had no interest in the expansion of the Empire,
made no alteration in the Augustan frontiers. Gaius, son of
Germanicus, and brought up in the army camps along the Rhine,
planned expeditions in Britain and Germany. Both ended in
fiasco (the details are obscure). Under Claudius new territories
were acquired at opposite ends of the Empire and provinces
established in Thrace and Judaea in the East, in Mauretania and
Britain in the West. In the first two instances, it was a case of
converting troublesome client kingdoms into provinces at a
convenient opportunity. In Mauretania the civilising work done
by King Juba was in danger through a nationalist rebellion. A
series of brilliant campaigns won for Rome the entire African
coastline as far west as Tangier, and beyond the Atlas Mountains
to Volubilis near the modern Fez.

The reasons which prompted the invasion of Britain in A.D. 43
seem less than cogent. It is true that the political state of the
island was disturbed after the death of the powerful Cunobelinus
ruler of the Belgic Kingdom whose capital was at Camulodunum
(Colchester). Claudius needed a military triumph: the conquest of
Britain had in a sense been on the agenda since the time of Julius
Caesar and it would round off Roman conquest in north-western
Europe. The mineral wealth of the island was thought to offer a
rich prize. All this may be so. But in the light of the immense
efforts Rome had to put into the conquest of Britain for the next
80 years, and thereafter to the defence of its northern frontier for
nearly three centuries, and furthermore, of the meagre returns she

would seem to have got from the province, the whole venture looks very dubious. At the least, the difficulties of conquest seem to have been underestimated. The original plan—achieved fairly rapidly—seems to have been to make a province out of the old Belgic Kingdom and its dependencies, with a military frontier on the line of the Fosse Way (Lincoln to Exeter), and flanked by the client-kingdoms of the Brigantes (northern England), Iceni (roughly Norfolk) and of the Regnenses (roughly Sussex). The plan broke down because of the prolonged resistance of the tribes in Wales led by Caratacus and the uncertain loyalty of the people of Brigantia to their amorous queen, Cartimandua. Caratacus was defeated in A.D. 51, brought to Rome, paraded in a solemn spectacle and formally pardoned by Claudius. Resistance in Wales, now led by the Silures and inspired by the Druids of Anglesey, was fiercer than ever. Early in Nero's reign the abandonment of Britain seems to have been seriously considered. In the end, it was decided to make the efforts required for the conquest of Wales and Brigantia. The first seemed well in hand when Suetonius Paulinus in A.D. 60 invaded North Wales and reached Anglesey, but then there was a terrible rising in his rear, led by Boudicca, queen of the Iceni. The Romanised cities of Colchester, London and St Albans were captured by the rebels and their inhabitants massacred. Suetonius Paulinus and his army were Rome's only hold on the province, and they eventually defeated Boudicca's forces somewhere in the Midlands. The restoration of control was a slow business, hampered by Nero's death and the civil wars of 69. Early in Vespasian's reign the advance was resumed: his generals conquered Brigantia and then Wales which was organised as a military zone. A landmark in the history of Britain was the governorship of Gn. Julius Agricola, a long term of seven years (78–85). Thanks to the *Life* by his son-in-law Tacitus and to archaeological discovery we know his policy in some detail. He fostered Romanisation in the civilian part of the province. In the north he built roads and forts to extend Roman control to the Forth–Clyde line. The final stage was to have been the conquest of Caledonia and he did defeat the Highland tribes in a great battle near Inverness. But now that the geography of Scotland was better understood, it was decided in Rome that it would be unwise to incorporate it into the province. Agricola was recalled. 'The conquest of Britain was completed', in Tacitus' bitter words, 'and immediately thrown away.' The next phase is obscure, but the problem of finding a northern frontier for the Roman province was not solved for another 40 years, when Hadrian came to visit Britain.

The fact that the conquest of Britain is fairly well known must not lead us to exaggerate its importance. The more important problems were, as ever, on the Rhine and the Danube, as was very clearly shown when danger in that quarter in 85 led to the recall of Agricola and the abandonment of plans for the conquest of Caledonia. Once Tiberius had called off the aggressive plans of Germanicus and placed his trust in diplomacy there was no serious trouble along the Rhine until 69. The eight legions of the Rhine army settled down in their bases, stretched along the river from Vetera (Xanten) to Vindonissa (Windisch). These bases took on a permanent aspect and attracted civilians to the *canabae* or extra-mural settlements. In A.D. 51 a colony had been founded in the territory of the Ubii on the west bank of the river and named Colonia Claudia Agrippinensis—the modern Cologne. Here German tribesmen and Roman colonists lived in a happy symbiosis for a while. But in 69 the whole Roman position in Gallia Belgica and along the lower Rhine was shattered by the alarming rebellion led by the Batavian chieftain, Julius Civilis. The legions in Lower Germany had an incompetent commander. The civil wars of 69, and especially the burning of the Capitol, were interpreted by German and Gallic nationalists as a sign that the supremacy of Rome was coming to an end and that the Empire of the world was passing to the northern peoples. Civilis was joined by many of the free German peoples, and notably by the states of the Treveri and the Lingones from Gallia Belgica. The coalition won some sweeping military successes, and there was talk of an 'Empire of the Gauls'. But the victory of Vespasian and the despatch of a first rate general, Petilius Cerialis, against the rebels put an end to such flights of fancy. None the less, the whole position of the Rhine frontier had to be reviewed. Vespasian extended the system of roads and forts into what is now Holland and as far as the mouth of the Rhine. To improve communications between the military zones of the Rhine and the Danube, it was decided to pinch out the salient of Germanic territory enclosed by the bend of the Rhine at Bâle. The work of the Flavian Emperors added a new sub-province in the Black Forest area—the Agri Decumates—which was protected by a line of forts and a stockade. Vespasian also established the two provinces of Upper and Lower Germany out of what had been military commands. The work of the Flavians along the Rhine was solid and enduring. The more so, because judicious Roman expeditions across the river and their own endemic tribal warfare had greatly reduced the strength of some of the more bellicose of the western German tribes. On the Danube, however, new and far graver perils were beginning to make themselves felt.

The arrangements made after the crushing of the rebellion in Pannonia and Illyricum (A.D. 6–9) lasted until the reign of Claudius. In his reign the client kingdom of Thrace became a Roman province and a second province of Moesia was established to control the whole Danube line from its estuary to the junction with the Theiss, north of the modern Belgrade. The Governor of Moesia now held one of the most important posts in the Empire since he had charge of Roman policy from the Middle Danube to the Crimea. Plautius Silvanus Aelianus, governor under Nero, has left a summary of his activities in his epitaph. He settled more than 100,000 trans-Danubian tribesmen on the south bank of the river and made them pay tribute. He staged a ceremony on the Danube at which kings previously hostile or unknown to Rome honoured the Roman standards. He strengthened the peace of the province. He sent an expedition to the Crimea to dislodge the king of the Scythians (South Russia) from the siege of the Greek city of Chersonesus. He was the first to send great quantities of wheat from Moesia to Rome. But soon the position changed to Rome's disadvantage. In the year A.D. 69 the Dacians and Roxolani started raiding across the river. At the same time the Marcomanni and Quadi on the Upper Danube became more aggressive and a nomadic people, the Iazyges, won the Hungarian plain. The great change, however, was the appearance of a new and powerful kingdom in Dacia, exploiting the rich mineral, forest and agricultural resources of Transylvania and the Carpathians. There had been a short-lived Dacian Empire in the time of Julius Caesar ruled over by Burebista: now in the 80's appeared a yet more powerful Dacian High King, Decebalus. The Dacians were skilled engineers and metal workers, redoubtable fighters and sturdy patriots. They had religious ties with the trans-Caucasian peoples and the nightmare possibility appeared of a huge confederacy of barbarian peoples, under Dacian leadership, assaulting the entire Danube frontiers, with perhaps Parthia involved as well.

The wars between Rome and Dacia broke out in A.D. 85 and lasted, intermittently, for more than 20 years. They were the greatest Rome ever fought in continental Europe, not forgetting Caesar's campaigns in Gaul. The region of the Iron Gates saw most of the fighting. Rome suffered some fearful defeats: two commanding generals were killed in battle with heavy losses of troops. There were great feats of engineering, notably the strategic highway hewn along the south bank through the Danube gorges (first begun by Claudius, completed by Trajan, and now about to be submerged), and the famous bridge thrown across the river at Drobetae near the modern Turnu Severin. Trajan mustered 13 legions for his two Dacian campaigns, the second of which ended in the capture of the fortress capital of Sarmizegethusa and the suicide of Decebalus in 106. Thousands of Dacians fled north to freedom. Dacia became a Roman province and was opened up for settlement. These momentous events left two memorials which have lasted to the present time— the first, the records of Trajan's northern wars on the sculptured scroll of his Column in Rome and on the Tropaeum Trajani in the Dobrudja; the second, and more important, the name, the language and the Latin civilisation of Romania.

The Danube frontier became seriously disturbed again in the reign of Marcus Aurelius. Its garrison had been thinned for the wars against Parthia and further decimated by the plague. The barbarians did not fail to take advantage of this—Marcomanni, Quadi, Iazyges, Sarmatians, Buri, Cotini, Costoboci, some of them old enemies, some new—and in 166 they swamped the defences and raided as far as Aquileia. The series of wars commemorated on the Column of Marcus Aurelius were fought to restore the situation. They brought triumph and disaster. At one point it looked as if Rome would have two new provinces— Marcomannia and Sarmatia, and a new northern frontier running from the Carpathians to the Bohemerwald—a grander version of Augustus' frustrated schemes. But a rebellion in the East diverted Marcus at the crucial time: although he was able to return to the Danube to take up the unfinished task, he died in camp at Vindobona (Vienna) with the bitter knowledge that all his efforts in central Europe had failed to give Rome a durable frontier. Once again, as at the death of Drusus, fate had intervened against Rome. Henceforward she was on the defensive against the northern peoples.

In the East the Augustan settlement lasted well. There were indeed rumblings in the last years of Tiberius, when King Artabanus III talked ominously about recovering the empire of Darius. In fact, the danger of a confrontation between the two Great Powers was not very real. Parthia had her own frontier troubles on the north and east: the monarchy was insecure and rebellions frequent, and the mustering of a Parthian army for a serious invasion of Rome's eastern provinces could be ruled out. The demoralisation of the Roman troops serving on the eastern frontier was also a factor for peace. But in the year 54, under Nero, Rome found it necessary to reassert her prestige after her nominee had been driven from the throne of Armenia. There followed nine years of campaigning, of which Tacitus gives a lively account in the *Annals*. His hero is the great Roman general Domitius Corbulo. He put the troops of the eastern army through a vigorous programme of toughening on the Armenian plateau and then led them to a series of brilliant victories. For a time there was the prospect of a Roman province of Armenia, but it came to nothing through the incompetence of Caesennius Paetus, another Roman general in that theatre of war. A diplomatic settlement crowned nine years of campaigns. It was agreed that Tiridates, the Parthian nominee for the Armenian throne, should come to Rome to receive the crown from Nero in person. His reception there was the most brilliant public spectacle of Nero's reign and passed down into history as 'the Golden Day'. The account of Dio Cassius suggests that in these ceremonies Nero symbolised the god Mithras presenting a crown to the Sun god. This orientalised ceremony was followed by a thoroughly Roman one—the closing of the temple of Janus as a sign of the establishment of peace.

The peace did not last long, for in the closing year of Nero's reign a great rebellion broke out among the Jews of Palestine who were the most intransigent of all the peoples in Rome's eastern provinces. This was the war described by Josephus which ended in the capture of Jerusalem by Titus in A.D. 70. The dynasty of the Herods had stood for a pro-Roman and philhellene policy which maddened the orthodox Jews. When Judaea became a Roman province, its Roman rulers were baffled by the complexities of Jewish religious and political life. That is why at the trial of Jesus Pontius Pilate was concerned with appeasement rather than strict justice. The greed of Roman procurators rendered an explosion inevitable and it came at last. Josephus was at first a commander on the Jewish side; later he made his peace with the Romans and wrote the story of the war. That war has left two famous memorials—the arch of Titus in the Roman Forum and the great fortress of Masada. At Masada, as at few other sites of the ancient world, history, literature and archaeology came together. In the setting of one of the most remarkable landscapes in the world, it is possible to appreciate the desperate resistance of the Jewish extremists, the methodical siege tactics of the Roman army and the precision of modern archaeology. This place of heroism and disaster has become a source of inspiration for the new nation of Israel. Although the capture of Jerusalem and the destruction of the Temple brought an end to Jewish resistance for a time, it engendered a hatred of Rome in the Jewish communities scattered through most of the large cities of the Roman east and in the western provinces of Parthia.

The consequences of Rome's victory were to be seen in the wars against Parthia fought by Trajan. Outwardly, Trajan's Parthian wars were the most successful fought by Rome in the East, as his designs appear to have been the most grandiose. He contemplated and achieved the annexation of Armenia and turned Mesopotamia and Arabia into Roman provinces. He reached the head of the Persian Gulf at Spasinu Charax, near the modern Abadan. But success was not for long. A widespread rebellion broke out among the Jewish communities of the eastern provinces, suppressed only with the utmost difficulty. Rome had won her Parthian victories at a heavy price, including the life of Trajan. Hadrian wisely restored to the king of Parthia the lands he had lost. His own plan for the establishment of a Roman *colonia* (Aelia Capitolina) at Jerusalem sparked off another fierce nationalist rebellion some 20 years later, in which Jewish resistance was led by Bar Cochbar. After its suppression, there was an uneasy truce between the Jews and Rome during which a new centre of Jewish learning developed at Safed in Galilee. Under Marcus Aurelius there was another Parthian war marked again by Roman military triumphs, but culminating in two disasters, both of them at Seleuceia. It was folly for a Roman army to destroy that city, the centre of hellenism in western Parthia. In so doing they were punished beyond their deserts, for at Seleuceia Roman troops came in contact with a fearful outbreak of the plague which spread throughout the Roman world with terrible loss of life. This visitation, in the year 167, is one of the worst epidemics recorded and some scholars have supposed that the Roman Empire never recovered from the mortality thus inflicted.

A contemporary strategist has said that there are only two general maxims of war. One is 'never invade Russia'. In view of the history of Parthian wars since the time of Crassus, the maxim 'never invade Parthia' could well have been directed to those in charge of Roman policy in the East. Rome had won many victories and the title *Parthicus* had been bestowed on many commanders. But Parthia remained and in the next century the balance of military advantage was to swing decisively to her.

CHAPTER 33

The concept of a limes

AUGUSTUS HAD THOUGHT in terms of natural features for the frontiers of the Empire. Inevitably, the posting of the army along these barriers meant the evolution of a frontier of a different type. For this the Romans employed the term *limes*—originally used for the boundaries of farms, but, in its later sense, a military zone. A *limes* would imply, at the least, bases for the legions, forts for other units, a signalling system and a network of strategic roads, including a transverse road for movements of troops and supplies. The *limes* system first developed along the Rhine in the days of Tiberius and another such was established to protect the strategic stretches of the Danube. In the reign of Domitian a refinement appears—the construction of permanent barriers of turf, timber or stone. Domitian built an economy version *limes* with earth forts and signal towers in south-western Germany and a continuous earthwork in the Dobrudja between the marshes and the sea, later rebuilt on a more massive scale.

The most spectacular—and the best known to archaeologists—are the frontier systems developed in northern Britain. The military zone may be said to begin with the legionary bases at Chester and York: north of these the hill-country of the Pennines was controlled by roads and forts as in Wales. But when Hadrian visited Britain in 122 he surveyed in person a line to provide a continuous barrier over the 73 miles from the Tyne to the Solway. After eight years of construction and several changes of plan, this resulted in the completion of Hadrian's Wall—in essence, a kind of elevated sentry-walk linking sixteen forts and the intermediate fortlets and watchtowers. A further system of towers and forts guarded the Solway crossing as far as Maryport. The Wall will be misunderstood if regarded as a kind of Maginot

Line protecting a peaceful province. It was rather a means of
separating two groups of people potentially hostile to Rome—
the Brigantes of northern England and the Selgovae and Novantae
of the Central Lowlands and Galloway. Diplomacy played its
part for the Otadini of the Lothians were steadfastly loyal to
Rome. Within a decade the frontier moved north and a second
Wall was built from the Forth to the Clyde—the Wall of Antoninus, 37 miles long, whose forts were connected by a turf wall. In
the almost complete absence of historical sources, it is not
possible to be sure why this was done. Nor are we able to detail
the many wars fought on the turbulent frontier over the next
250 years—in which the Wall of Antoninus was abandoned and
reoccupied twice and that of Hadrian three times at least. This
northern military zone must in the second century have absorbed
some 30,000 Roman troops, half of whom were on the frontier
itself.

Nothing quite like the northern defences of Britain exists
elsewhere in the Empire. But, besides the *limites* already mentioned, a series of barriers was built against hostile mountain or
desert tribes in Numidia and Mauretania. The story of the eastern
frontiers is complicated and not yet well understood. Eventually,
it is clear, at least a military road and signal stations led from the
Euphrates to the Red Sea: its main features are known where it
crosses the Negev Desert. Further north lay stretches of a
continuous barrier which show up in air photographs of the
Syrian Desert. The purpose of this eastern *limes* was rather to
protect the great caravan routes than for military defence against
Parthia. In general, the *limites* of the Empire are a complex
phenomenon, conforming to local conditions rather than to any
general plan. Their elucidation is one of the major problems
studied by historians and archaeologists.

CHAPTER 34

Rome and Italy

THE AUGUSTAN CONCEPT OF the Empire was of a world ruled from Rome, with Italy as her partner filling the Senate and supplying the legions. We have seen how the propagandists of the time, Virgil among them, saw this as part of the divine plan for the world, indicated alike by the superior fertility of Italy and the quality of the men she bred. Rome retained her predominance throughout this period and there was no thought of another world capital. But the very success of her work in opening up the West posed a challenge to Italy, for it showed that Roman civilisation could thrive just as well in Narbonensis or Baetica. It would take time, of course, for the full implications to be understood. None the less by the reign of Hadrian Imperial propaganda was couched in terms of Rome at the centre of a sisterhood of provinces.

The population of Rome continued to increase throughout the first century A.D. and reached its maximum (perhaps one and a half million) in the reign of Trajan. It was a microcosm of the whole Empire, with Greeks and Orientals preponderant among the newcomers. Inevitably there were strains and tensions. There was latent anti-Semitism. In the hysterical atmosphere after the Great Fire of 64 members of the small Christian community were persecuted in the belief that they represented an extremist sect of Jews.

A certain xenophobia may be traced, at all levels of society, to newcomers who made a success at Rome. Many of the native born may have followed the example of Umbricius, in Juvenal's *Third Satire*, who left Rome because he could not bear 'a Greek City'. But on the whole tolerance prevailed, and there were no serious problems of racialism. Indeed, a recent study has shown that in general the record of the Empire in this respect was much to its credit.

To feed, clothe, house and amuse this vast population was a constant strain on resources. Under Augustus the arrangements for the *Annona*, or free corn supply, had been set on a sound footing as had those for the city's water supply. Both were to need supplementing. While the bulk of the corn continued to come from Egypt, Africa, Sicily and Sardinia, new sources became available in Moesia and in southern Gaul. The increased traffic made it necessary to provide better harbour facilities at Ostia, a task taken in hand first by Claudius and later by Trajan. Ostia, as the port of Rome, grew to a population of perhaps 100,000 and formed part of the same urban area as the capital. The water supply was augmented by the Aqua Claudia and the Anio Novus. Pliny's remark seems well justified that, 'if we take careful account of all the abundant supply of water for public buildings, baths, settling tanks, pools, private mansions, gardens and country estates close to the city, and of the distance the water travels before entering the city, the height of the arches, the tunnelling of mountains, the levelling of routes across deep valleys, one must rate all this as the most remarkable achievement anywhere in the world'. Frontinus, who was in charge of the water supply in the days of Nerva, states that the nine major aqueducts had a total length of about 264 English miles, with a capacity of more than 220,000,000 gallons every 24 hours.

But while Roman technology could provide water on a lavish scale, it failed to prevent fires. A large force of firemen could be sent to the scene of an outbreak, but all they had to work with were buckets and a few primitive siphons. If these failed, the best way of containing the fire was to pull down all buildings in its path. This explains the astonishing extent of the damage caused by the Great Fire in 64, one of the most terrible of such disasters in history and a landmark in the story of urbanisation in Rome. This conflagration raged for six days and affected 10 out of the 14 districts of the city. In three destruction was to ground level, in the other seven only a few houses survived. Nero was presented with a grand opportunity for the rebuilding of the city, for which he had the means, the architects and the will. Tacitus, whose description of the Great Fire is one of his most splendid passages, also gives a succinct account of Nero's work in rebuilding the city. 'Regulations prescribed the alignment of roads, the width of streets and the height of houses. They stood in spacious building plots and colonnades were added to the blocks of apartments so as to protect their street frontages. Nero undertook to construct these colonnades at his own expense and to clear up all building sites before restoring them to their owners.' The corn ships coming up the river were used to carry rubble on the return journey to a designated dumping ground in Ostia. A portion of all new buildings had to be made of fire resisting stone. Each house had to provide its own fire-fighting apparatus. Tacitus' final remark is of great interest. 'Necessity caused these measures to be accepted and they certainly added to the city's amenities. Some, however, thought the old city had been a healthier place to live in, arguing that the narrow streets and tall buildings offered protection against the intense heat of the sun, while now the open spaces, devoid of shade, reflect the sun's rays much more intensely.' Such was the *Nova Urbs* or new city of Nero, which determined in its main outlines the aspect of Rome until the end of the Empire.

The period from Nero to Hadrian is, indeed, the Golden Age of architecture in Rome. Freed from the trammels of Augustan neo-classicism, a series of great architects—Severus, Celer, Rabirius and Apollodorus of Damascus—exploited to the full the resources of new building techniques. Much of their efforts was directed to two continuing needs, which were to meet the appetite of the Roman people for spectacular entertainments and to house the Emperors on a scale suited to their dignity. Augustus' successors were not content to live in a modest house on the Palatine. Tiberius began and Gaius continued the first of the Imperial palaces; Domitian added a new and more spectacular complex of palace buildings, until finally the whole Palatine hill had been transformed into a palace quarter. Its inhabitants, the Palatini, numbered many thousands and served all the needs of the Imperial court and bureaucracy. But the most interesting design was never completed—that for the *Domus Aurea* or Golden House of Nero. Taking advantage of the Great Fire (as rumour had it, having caused it for that very purpose) Nero planned to build an immense luxury villa in the very heart of the city. 'He built himself a palace', wrote Tacitus, 'remarkable not so much for its gold and jewels—these are the usual trappings of luxury and have become commonplace—as for its meadows, lakes, artificial wilderness, now of woods and now of open spaces, and vistas.

Severus and Celer were its architects and engineers.' The details are amplified in a passage of Suetonius. Although [after Nero's death the Golden House was not completed and some of its features were turned to the use of the Roman people, it is clear that it was a landmark in the history of Roman architecture.

The engineers who built the huge places of popular entertainment had to face problems of housing and controlling very large and potentially disorderly crowds. Their methods are best observed in the design of the Flavian amphitheatre, later known as the Colosseum. Used principally for gladiatorial shows and animal hunts, the amphitheatre could seat about 50,000 spectators and was designed to control most features of the crowd—except their bestiality. The capacity of the Circus Maximus was increased to perhaps 350,000 spectators, or about a third of the population of Rome. Chariot racing rapidly became the favourite entertainment of the Roman People; the highly trained professional charioteers earned vast sums of money. Betting was on an enormous scale and there was much fixing of races. The maligned Emperor Domitian tried to provide more civilised entertainment in the Stadium for athletics and Odeon for music, which he built in the Campus Martius. The Stadium has been important in the later building history of Rome because it determines the outlines of Piazza Navona. The two surviving examples of Imperial Thermae (Baths) belong to a later period.

Additions were made to the sequence of Imperial *fora*. There is little archaeological trace of the Forum Pacis built by Vespasian, but contemporary descriptions show that it was one of the most splendid pieces of city planning in Rome, comprising a temple set in formal gardens and surrounded by colonnades and libraries. Hard by was the Arch of Titus, with its sculptures representing the capture of Jerusalem. The Flavian amphitheatre was not far away. This part of Rome constituted a kind of memorial to the achievements of the Flavian dynasty, matching the works of Augustus in the Campus Martius. The Forum of Nerva followed the earlier plan of a temple surrounded by colonnades. In the Forum of Trajan the architects set out to surpass all the achievements of the past. It provided Rome with virtually a new city centre, containing as it did buildings serving administration, law, commerce and the arts. The dimensions of its great basilica are reproduced exactly in the Church of St. Paul-without-the-walls which thus provides a unique impression of the grandeur of an ancient building.

When he visited Rome in 357 the Emperor Constantius II was overwhelmed by its magnificence and by the Forum of Trajan above all. According to the historian Ammianus Marcellinus, 'He stood still in amazement, turning his attention upon the vast complex around him, which is far beyond any description and not again to be rivalled by mortal men'. Archaeology has laid bare almost all of the vast complex, but its magnificence survives only in Trajan's Column and its sculptures. Hadrian was himself an architect of bold and original ideas and he embellished Rome with the Temple of Venus and Rome and the Mausoleum of Hadrian, now the Castel Sant'Angelo. His most remarkable work in Rome was the rebuilding of the Pantheon after its destruction by fire. The superb *rotunda* was entirely the work of his period: it has been called the first building designed as an interior. Its dimensions are those of a circle within a circle, and it is capped by the first of the world's great domes, ancestor of those of Hagia Sophia at Constantinople, the Duomo in Florence, St Peter's in Rome and St Paul's in London. Shelley divined its purpose—'It is, as it were, the visible image of the universe'. It presents a microcosm linked to the macrocosm of the universe by the huge *oculus* or eye in the roof, the sole source of light. Here are the concepts of Posidonius expressed in architecture.

Architecture, rather than literature, is the characteristic medium of the post-Augustan Empire. The term Silver Age indicates both the intrinsic merits of the literature and its standing vis-à-vis that of the age of Augustus. Augustan models, especially in epic, had a great appeal for the Silver Age poets. Lucan, Statius, Valerius Flaccus, Silius Italicus, all felt that they owed it to the memory of Virgil and to themselves to write epic poems inspired by the *Aeneid*. In general posterity has not been grateful, though the *Pharsalia* of Lucan may be said to stand in its own right. Seneca has been widely read at various times, both as philosopher and poet. His philosophical works are at a discount nowadays, their brilliant style insufficient counter to a lack of original thought and to the known gap between Seneca's conduct and his precepts. His tragedies, written for play readings rather than the theatre, were a powerful stimulus to the growth of Elizabethan tragedy. Until recently, they were regarded as literary fossils, but now it seems they are read by some of the revolutionary young people, who find congenial their empty rhetoric and charade of violence. Quintilian, holder of the first public Professorship of Rhetoric in Rome, wrote 12 books on the training of an orator, a useful guide to Roman views on education. Martial carried the art of the epigram to perfection, though he usually turned it to trivial themes. Pliny's *Natural History* shows more industry than learning: unreadable as a whole, it contains much valuable material. The works of Columella on agriculture and Frontinus on aqueducts are valuable technical treatises.

Three writers of the Silver Age stand in the first rank of Latin authors. Petronius, probably but not certainly the Arbiter of Elegance at the court of Nero, wrote the *Satyricon*, a work of unique quality, much of which is lamentably missing to us. What survives is the torso of a novel of low life, combining social satire, humour and bawdry in a most acceptable blend. The main part, the *Cena Trimalchionis*, is a brilliant description of a banquet given by a vulgar multi-millionaire. The host, his guests, their ideas, hopes, *faux-pas* and accents, are mercilessly portrayed. Some scholars have seen them as a low life parody of Nero's court. But Trimalchio is surely an original being: everything about him is larger than life, compelling liking without respect.

The 16 satires of Juvenal are the finest examples of that truly Roman *genre*. The driving motive he tells us is *saeva indignatio*—savage anger. Swift saw in him a kindred spirit and chose these words for his own epitaph. Juvenal's full powers of sarcasm, irony, innuendo and invective are most fully displayed in the first six satires which give a new dimension to the *genre* in Latin. Satires Three on Rome as the Megalopolis or Jungle City, Six, a huge biased intolerable outburst of misogyny, and Ten which was imitated by Johnson in *The Vanity of Human Wishes*, are the masterpieces.

Juvenal's contemporary, Tacitus, is on many counts the greatest of Roman historians. The larger works, the *Annals* and the *Histories*, formed a single great historical design of (probably) 30 books, which would have covered the period from the death of Augustus to that of Domitian—the Julio-Claudian and Flavian dynasties. There are large gaps as we have them—10 books of the *Annals* and parts of three others; of the *Histories*, only the books which deal with the year 69 and part of 70 survive. Thus we lack Tacitus on Gaius, the early years of Claudius, the end of Nero and on all but the prelude to the Flavians. What remains is beyond price both as literature and history. For Tacitus had evolved a unique personal style—the high point of imperial Latin prose. His political insight was acute and based on personal experience, though he always wrote from the viewpoint of the senatorial class. No one has excelled him in portrayal of character, and the formulae he used were his own. All his gifts were devoted to a high concept of the historian's duty, 'to see that virtue is placed on record, and that evil men and evil deeds have cause to fear judgement at the bar of posterity'. If there is more vice than virtue in his pages, that is the Roman world as he saw it. His two monographs—the biography of his father-in-law Agricola and the description of the lands and the peoples of northern Europe comprised in the *Germania*, were written before he turned to the larger themes. Since the rediscovery of the manuscripts of Tacitus in the Renaissance he has served again and again as a guide to political wisdom, valued alike by the sovereigns and political thinkers of Renaissance Europe, the Founding Fathers of the United States of America and the leaders of the French Revolution. Napoleon paid him the compliment of hatred and he has always been a foe to tyrants.

There is a good deal of evidence for Italy during this period though it is patchy. Archaeology and literary sources contribute. For example, the great eruption of Vesuvius on August 24th 79 preserved in lava or in ash the two towns of Pompeii and Herculaneum—arrested at a single moment in time—for a distant posterity. The bread is in the ovens, the meals on the tables, the municipal election notices on the walls. 'The petty thieves support Vatia for aedile'—but the election never took place. Archaeologists have been at work on them for more than two centuries and the task is very far from completion. The discoveries made there present the most detailed picture of everyday life from any classical site, though we now know better than to generalise from them about the life of the Roman world as a whole. The two letters which the younger Pliny composed for Tacitus to insert in his histories are an authentic contemporary record of the disaster, which made as great an impression on the world of its time as did the Lisbon earthquake in the eighteenth century.

Ostia came to an end through slow decline rather than sudden disaster. Excavations there were later and consequently more scientific; they revealed almost in its entirety the life of a great port. There are the warehouses and flour mills by which Ostia lived; in the *piazza* behind the municipal theatre stood the temple of Ceres, goddess of corn, and round it the offices of the ship owners from all parts of the Mediterranean who traded regularly with Ostia, and the local ship chandlers who supplied them. The domestic life of the town is known in great detail, unlike that of Rome. The people of Ostia lived in solid brick-built apartment houses of four or five storeys, sometimes set around a courtyard, with the best rooms on the first floor, the *piano nobile*. Some of them had first floor balconies to afford fresh air in the heat which bears so oppressively on the Ostia flatland. There too are the *popinae* or snack bars, offering shellfish, vegetables, hot snacks and drinks in a shady garden. It is possible to trace the full history of urban development in Ostia, and to see how, after the building of Claudius' harbour, Ostia gradually lost its shipping to its rival Portus. There has as yet been no opportunity to explore the Trajanic harbour at Ostia, but when this has been done it could give a very complete picture of harbour works and dock facilities. Aquileia, the chief port at the head of the Adriatic, is also known in some detail and its museum documents the trade with northern and central Europe.

In northern Italy, Roman antiquities of this period are prominent at Verona and Brescia. Patavium was one of the wealthiest cities of the Po Valley, its people priding themselves rather self-consciously on an old-ashioned austerity, as indeed did the peoples of Cisalpine Gaul in general. Thrasea Paetus, who led the stoic opposition to Nero came from Patavium. Cremona was virtually blotted out in 69 by the victorious Flavian troops in a siege whose horrors are described by Tacitus. It was restored by public subscription from all over Italy, and its surviving Roman antiquities are of this later period. The amenities of even a small city in northern Italy are impressively shown at Velia, in the Apennine foothills near Parma. From this site came the famous inscription which is one of the chief sources for the working of the *alimenta*, the maintenance grants for poor children instituted by Trajan.

The intensive Roman agriculture of the Po Valley still shows up in air photographs and reveals a man-made landscape on a scale unusual in antiquity. In the letters of Pliny we see the life of the northern municipal aristocracy. They have their town houses and their villas on the shores of the Italian lakes; the

wealthier, like Pliny himself, may have other villas in the neighbourhood of Rome. They move away, sometimes for years, to
follow a public career. But they remain rather tiresomely aloof
from the fast life of the capital and retire to lead a life of good
works and mutual admiration on their own estates.

In Campania and especially around the Bay of Naples things
were very different, as they always have been. This was Campania
Felix, the land of luxurious villas, smart resorts, natural beauty
and Greek culture. Neapolis and its hellenised life delighted
Nero—here was Greek civilisation within easy reach of Rome.
Some of these Campanian villas are described in the *Silvae* of
Statius, himself a native of Neapolis. Many of their owners are
wealthy freedmen employed in the Imperial Civil Service. They
live in the style of Roman nobles of the late republic, pouring
out money on elaborate buildings and landscaped grounds,
and filling them with (usually) replicas of the masterpieces
of Greek art. One wonders what was the effect of all this
villeggiatura. Not always dissipation and idleness; one of the poems
speaks of contemplation and poetry in the same tone that
Thompson used of Lord Lyttleton in Hagley Park. But, as with
the eighteenth century in England, it is uncertain how far the
tone is sincere. It is hard to believe that Priscilla, wife of Domitian's
minister of finance, 'waited for her husband's return from work
and served his supper as modestly as some Sabine woman waiting
for the farmer to come home from the fields'.

For Italian agriculture there are the writings of Columella,
the most systematic account of that subject from the classical
world. Columella's family was of Spanish origin and his uncle
Marcus Columella was one of the best farmers in Baetica. Columella himself who owned estates in Latium and Etruria finds
Italian practice deficient in many respects. Landowners, he says,
lament a falling off in the fertility of the soil; in fact, they are
ignorant of the proper farming technique. He finds it astonishing
that agricultural education has been neglected; the only way to
advance is by contact with an experienced farmer, or from the
reading of such handbooks as Columella proceeds to supply.
Besides being more systematic, his treatment is in many ways
more advanced than that of Varro. There is a notable increase in
humanity in his attitude to slaves. The farmer should speak to
them in familiar terms and consult them on the work to be done.
They do better when they are allowed to develop specialist skills

—tall men make the best ploughmen, short sturdy men should be sent to the vineyard. There will still remain the general farm worker, the *mediastinus*, who can be turned to any task. The oxen for the plough are also considered. The ploughman should not hurry or goad them, the furrow should not be too long, he should carefully massage the skin on their necks after ploughing, see that they do not catch cold from sweating and give them a rest before they are fed in their stalls. Since the whole of ancient civilisation depended on the ploughman and his oxen, it is pleasant to think that their lot may have improved.

Columella also stresses the importance of the owner's presence, however good the bailiff may be. The *colonus* or tenant farmer is becoming more important, and there are instructions on how to deal with him, getting one's rights, but without standing on the full letter of the law. The best tenants will be those who are natives of the place and have held their farms by long association.

During this period Italy lost the economic supremacy she enjoyed under Augustus. This was partly due to the opening up of new lands, especially in Gaul and Spain, whose resources were superior to hers. Wines from Spain and olive oil from Spain and Africa were produced in bulk and undercut those of Italy in the medium and cheap grades. Again, the growth of population in Gallia Belgica and Lugdunensis made it cheaper to produce food and other consumer goods locally rather than pay the transport charge from Italy. It is possible, too, that the population of Italy actually declined after the reign of Trajan, whether through emigration or the decline in peasant farming owing to the increase of large estates. If so, the Po Valley and Campania must be excluded from this recession. Whatever the reasons, Italy no longer stood on a markedly higher level of prosperity than the rest of the Empire. In all aspects of life both public and private the provinces were asserting their claims for equality.

CHAPTER 35

The provinces

IT WAS SAID EARLIER that Claudius tried to widen the circle of recruitment to the Senate. By the time of Trajan, 40 per cent of that Order were provincials, though the Italians never quite lost their majority until early in the third century. But during the second century men from Greece, Asia and Africa came to join the well-entrenched Gauls and Spaniards. They came, of course, as the Emperor's nominees, but they brought with them the outlook of their own lands, so that in some measure the Senate represented the upper classes of the whole Empire rather than of Rome and Italy only. There were extensive grants of Roman citizenship to favoured communities or individuals—discharged auxiliaries, municipal magistrates, or those who had rendered personal service to the Emperor and his legates. Aelius Aristides singles out this generosity in his address in praise of Rome, delivered perhaps in A.D. 143 'People are no more Greeks and barbarians, but Romans and non-Romans . . . There are many in each city who are no less your fellow-citizens than they are of their own people, though some may never have seen Rome.' Provincials held important military commands, as did the Moor Lusius Quietus under Trajan and the Syrian Avidius Cassius under Marcus Aurelius, though neither it should be added reflected much credit on the system.

This trend in favour of the provinces may have been inevitable, but it was advanced and intensified as an act of deliberate policy by Hadrian. He saw his rôle as that of the peripatetic Emperor, continually on the move throughout the provinces, acquainting himself at first hand with their problems, testing the efficiency of the army and the Imperial administration—above all, trying to deepen his own understanding of the Roman world. It was an impossible task, even for a man of his restless intellect and abounding physical energy. It has been pointed out that these provincial journeys took up 12 out of his 23 years on the throne, of which four years were spent in the West and eight in the East. New cities, improved roads and frontier defences, temples, harbours and public works, some of them designed by the team of architects who accompanied him on his travels, attest his presence in almost every province. His journeys are symbolised by the remarkable series of 'provincial' issues—coins portraying 25 provinces or cities. The same spirit is shown in the statues of provinces which adorned the *Hadrianeum* in Rome, which are attempts to portray each province in its individuality and as a member of the Roman commonwealth.

CHAPTER 36

Public careers

AN ECUMENICAL VIEW like Hadrian's could perhaps be held by none but the Emperor. But their public careers took many men of all levels, from senator to private soldier, to every part of the Empire. At Aquileia there is a dedication in honour of T. Caesernius Statius, who went in Hadrian's suite on two journeys, one through the East and Illyricum, a second through Sicily, Africa and Mauretania. This man had served as tribune in the XXXth and as commander of the Xth Legion, his civilian offices included that of commissioner of the Mint, supervisor of the Via Appia, *quaestor, praetor,* consul. At Aquileia he was a member of the Town Council and patron of the colony. At Minturnae an inscription commemorates L. Burbuleius Optatus Ligarianus, who died in office as Governor of Syria under Antoninus Pius. Earlier, he had governed Cappadocia and Syria, held the prefectship of the Treasury of Saturn, served as *curator* of Via Cassia, Clodia, and Ciminia, investigated the finances of Narbo, Ancona, and Tarracina, had served in the IXth and had commanded the XVIth legion. An inscription from Nedinum in Dalmatia commemorates L. Iaolenus Priscus, who had commanded the IIIrd and IVth Legions, served as Law Officer in Britain, and had governed the provinces of Germania Superior, Syria and Africa. At Camerinum in Umbria a section of the community records its gratitude for privileges received from Antoninus Pius through the good offices of M. Maenius Agrippa, a British specialist, whose military career included service in three auxiliary regiments, the command of the Classis Britannica and who was selected by Hadrian for a campaign in Britain. The Town Council of Aquileia honours a prominent equestrian, C. Minicius Italus, who served in the VIth Legion and four auxiliary regiments,

was decorated for valour by Vespasian, held Imperial procurator-
ships in the Hellespont, Asia, Gallia Lugdunensis and Aquitania,
and who finally became Prefect of Egypt. Inscriptions at Chester
give details of soldiers who served in the IInd and XXth Legions;
they include two men from Syria, one from Asia, three from Thrace,
seven from the Danube provinces, four from Cisalpine Gaul,
four from Narbonensis, five from Spain and one from Germany.

CHAPTER 37

Travel

MEN TRAVELLED THE EMPIRE, of course, on their own occasions. There is a well known passage of Plutarch who in the winter of 83–4 met at Delphi two learned Greeks, travellers, literally, from the ends of the Empire. One of them, Cleombrotus of Sparta, had spent a good deal of time 'wandering about Egypt and around the country of the Troglodytes'. He had sailed 'far down the Red Sea' (perhaps as far as Aden?) 'not for trade but because he loved seeing things and learning about them'. The other was the grammarian, Demetrius of Tarsus, returning home after an eventful visit to Britain. Agricola's policy of Romanisation was in full swing in the province: no doubt Demetrius had gone there to explore the educational possibilities of that under-developed country. At the command of the Emperor, he under-took exploration of a more literal kind, for he joined an expedition which sailed far to the north-west, apparently to the Hebrides, about which he brought back some remarkable occult information. This same Demetrius is also known from a dedication he made at York (discovered in 1860) to the god of the Atlantic, Oceanus, and his consort Tethys. Delphi was indeed 'the navel of the world' for the meeting of these far travellers.

Throughout the Empire the roads must have been full of travellers—Cynic philosophers, begging their way from town to town to preach basic philosophy in the market-place; wealthy Greek Sophists, travelling in style to lecture to fashionable audiences; members of the Guild of Travelling Athletes on their way from pitch to pitch; oculists, doctors, astrologers, thauma-turges and missionaries of many religions, including Christianity. Many, too, shared the taste of Cleombrotus for seeing things, and a flourishing tourist industry grew up to cater for them. It took them mainly to classical and historic sites rather than to the picturesque—to Greece, Asia, Rhodes, Sicily, Syria and for the wealthy to Egypt for a trip on the Nile and the dissipations of Alexandria. Pausanias' *Description of Greece*, a work of ten books and published about 150, is the best guide-book of classical times. The western provinces had less to offer the cultivated tourist, but there, too, were fairs, religious festivals and the cures offered at spas and health resorts kept people on the move.

It is commonly said that travel was easier in the Roman world in the second century A.D. than at any time until the invention of the stage-coach. None the less, it was arduous and slow by modern standards. We are apt to forget how the invention of the steam locomotive transformed speed of travel: a second transformation has taken place with the aeroplane. Tiberius made the best 24 hours' mileage by carriage (160 miles) known to Pliny and there is an instance of 332 miles being covered by relays of horses at an average of 10 m.p.h. But no one in the ancient world ever travelled faster than a horse's gallop or covered 30 miles in an hour. At sea, a fair wind might take a ship 100–120 miles in a single day, but there were long periods of adverse winds or calm. The longest regular sea voyage, from the Arabian Gulf to the west coast of India, took about 40 days when the trade winds were blowing. On land, the *cursus publicus* or Imperial travel service was well organised, with posting-stations and relays of horses at regular intervals. But it was open to official travellers only and permits were sparingly issued. (It was supplied by requisitions made on the districts through which it passed—a constant source of complaint.) For the private traveller there were carriers from whom it was possible to hire a horse or a carriage. But frequently the Roman traveller walked, carrying his things in a *mantica* (a kind of duffle-bag), putting up at uncomfortable inns, many of which ranged, to judge from descriptions, from the uncomfortable to the vile.

CHAPTER 38

The Western lands

A BASIC FACTOR IN THE LIFE of the Roman Empire was the linguistic-cultural divide between the Latin-speaking West and the Greek-speaking East. So far as the Mediterranean lands are concerned, it is neatly marked by a line drawn from Dyrrhachium (Durazzo), at the north-west corner of Macedonia, due south to the boundaries between Africa and Cyrenaica—a little short of 20° E. In continental Europe the situation was more complicated, for the Danubian provinces and Dacia must go with the Latin-speaking West, apart from the scanty Greek settlements near the Danube delta. The whole African littoral west of Cyrenaica belongs to the Latin part of the Empire. Thus weighted with the addition of the Danube lands the Latin half of the Roman world is considerably the larger in area, though less wealthy and populous than the East. This vast area was never again to be united under a single government, and if one looks at it on a large-scale map the first impression is one of an almost infinite diversity. What can there be in common between the mountains of Wales and the Sahara Desert, the Hungarian grainlands and the Alps, the central plateau of Spain and the Netherlands, the rich valley of the Garonne and the kaerst limestone of the Dinaric Alps? In race and language, too, the diversity is manifest—its peoples include Libyans, Berbers, Iberians, Celts, Germans, Illyrians, Pannonians and Dacians.

None the less, in Roman times it is possible to point to certain factors which applied throughout the West. Over the whole area, Rome appeared first as conqueror and then as coloniser and bringer of civilisation. She was not always the first coloniser—witness the Greek settlements at the mouth of the Rhône and in north-eastern Spain, or the Carthaginians in Africa. But these examples only emphasise the difference between Roman colonisation, deep and enduring, and the less effective work of her precursors. Only the Carthaginian settlements in Spain between the First and Second Punic Wars might have grown into something resembling the stability of a Roman province—but this development was cut short by Rome herself. Rome appears in these western lands as the advocate of an urban civilisation. She provides the modes, institutions and material substructure on which such a civilisation can be based—a common code of law, a common language, a network of communications, including roads, waterways, harbours, and a common currency. She develops their material resources, not so much by the use of a superior technology as by superior organisation, especially in the intensive use of capital and labour. The economic products of the West now have access to a world market and the profits benefit the material standard of life in the West. The Syrian merchants, the shippers of Gades and the Asian trader whose epitaph proclaims that he made 72 voyages between Asia and Italy—all contribute to this process. Culturally, we discern in all these lands a conflict between Roman and Barbarian, to use Roman terminology, or as we might put it, between a metropolitan and a native culture. Such a conflict may of course end in a synthesis; while the odds were inevitably weighted in favour of the more advanced Roman way of life, it is rare to find it swamping the native culture completely.

It is important to see the process from the native side. First, it is to be noted how much of the substratum of the population was Celtic. This was the dominant element in Gaul, Britain and Noricum: it left its mark in northern and north-western Spain, and there was a Celtic element also in the population of the Danube lands. Theirs was a world of tribal societies, whose nobles would not resist Romanisation when they could see where its advantage lay. After a few generations the nobles could be enlisted in the public service of the Empire and the peasantry would provide excellent fighting material. The same broad pattern is also to be seen in Mauretania and in the Balkan provinces. The general trend towards Romanisation none the less allows for local self-government, for the survival of the native tongue, though commonly not as a literary language and the continuation of the local cults. Indeed, it was usually in religion that the native culture continued and often found support from

Roman officials and settlers. In the *interpretatio Romana* the local divinity might acquire as it were a Roman personality—a temple, a cult statue, identification with an established god in the Roman pantheon. Just as the goddess of the hot springs at Bath became Sulis-Minerva, so did Nemausus, presiding divinity over the healing fountain at Nîmes, become equated with Apollo. Some gods it is true were hard to Romanise. The Celtic Cernunnos, with his stag's antlers and the nether limbs of a snake, is a case in point. But it was very rare for a cult to be suppressed or perse-cuted. In all the western lands, we can only point to the attempts to suppress Druidism in Britain and Gaul, ostensibly on the grounds of human sacrifice, in fact because of its anti-Roman political stance. It should also be said that while native cults remained strong in their own localities they seldom extended their territory. The native cultures were thus local and regional; where a world religion won adherents, as did Christianity from the second century onwards, it did so in the wake of the influence of Rome.

The concept of zones of Romanisation will be found helpful. Within the Latin West there were areas where Romanisation was as intensive as in Italy itself and others where its influence was minimal. Regions where Italian agriculture could flourish would attract settlers from Italy, and naturally it was there that Romani-sation was most successful. Such were Narbonensis in Gaul and Baetica in Spain. By the middle of the first century A.D. both these areas were as prosperous and as Romanised as Italy itself. Hardly less Romanised were the valley of the Garonne from Tolosa (Toulouse) to Burdigala (Bordeaux), the valley of the Moselle and the Rhine from Trier to Cologne, and the country round Lugdunum (Lyons), Augustodunum (Autun) and the territory of the Remi around the modern Reims. In the Iberian peninsula there were highly Romanised districts around Tarraco in modern Catalonia and the lower Tagus Valley in what is now Portugal. East of the Adriatic such districts grew up round Salonae and the adjacent islands. By contrast, Romanisation was sparse or minimal in north-western Spain, in Brittany and on the limestone plateau of what is now Bosnia.

The process of Romanisation in the West is best understood from examples: the pattern and tempo varied from province to province. First then the Allobroges, one of the wealthiest and most populous of the Gallic states, exploiting the rich and various resources of the lands between the Alpine summits and the

Rhône. 'Formerly', according to Strabo, 'the Allobroges used to be at war, but now they farm the plains and the Alpine glens, living in villages, except for their notables, who live in Vienna (Vienne). This itself was once a village, although called the metropolis of that people. But now they have built it up into a city.' In political terms, their history was more complicated. They had been included in Narbonensis in 121 B.C. and the urbanisation of Vienne had gone far enough by 70 B.C. to attract numerous Italian settlers. In 61 B.C. came a native rebellion led by a chief called Catugnatus. The Italian settlers were expelled. But the rebellion was suppressed and a pro-Roman party was in control after the war. They would have nothing to do with the rebellion of Vercingetorix and received their reward when Vienne was given the status of a colony in 43 B.C. Under Gaius Roman citizenship was granted and the leaders of a wealthy and Romanised community could aspire to be senators at Rome. So the grandsons of men who fought with Catugnatus could have sat in the Senate with the grandsons of those who suppressed him. Historical memories were not forgotten on either side. Vienne, in the words of Jullian, the great historian of Roman Gaul, 'called and felt itself Celtic'. And nothing was more Celtic than the *élan* with which its wealthier citizens embraced the delights of Roman civilisation. Valerius Asiaticus, for example, who was consul in 35 and again in A.D. 46, became one of the richest men in the whole Empire. He bought the gardens of Lucullus in Rome and was the lover of the elder Poppaea Sabina. On both counts he earned the jealousy of the empress Messalina and was put to death through her intrigues. He used to keep a private troupe of actors and was lavish in staging spectacles in Vienne. The Emperor Claudius described him as 'that monster of the wrestling ring'. But for Vienne itself the Emperor has the highest praise—it is *ornatissima et valentissima colonia*, 'a splendid and flourishing colony'. Even so it was not the most splendid in the middle valley of the Rhône. That position was held by its rival Lugdunum; in Tacitus' phrase, the two cities were 'separated by a single river, but united by a long enmity'. In the Flavian period their rivalry became one of a contest in ostentation. Archaeology attests this today. The theatre of Lugdunum with its 11,000 seats and the Odeon with 3,000 seats for an élite audience are matched by a similar theatre and Odeon at Vienne. Both in the second century built splendid temples dedicated to Cybele.

Vienne was, in Martial's phrase, *'bella Vienna'*, its buildings rising on the terraced slopes above the Rhône. Nothing yet discovered at Lugdunum rivals the elegance of the Greek statues from the baths in Vienne's residential quarter of St. Colombe. Greek culture indeed, disseminated from Massilia, found a new home in Vienne. The Roman Senate professed itself shocked at the immorality of the Greek festivals held in that city.

The second instance of Romanisation in the West might be the Treveri of Gallia Belgica. This powerful people supplied auxiliary troops to Julius Caesar, but abandoned him when he attacked their kinsfolk the Nervii. Thereafter they were anti-Roman until the time of Augustus, who founded a city and perhaps a colony at Trier in 15 B.C. The city of Augusta Treverorum very rapidly became the most important in Gallia Belgica. At the same time, nationalist feeling was by no means extinct amongst the Treveri and they joined in anti-Roman uprisings in A.D. 21 and again in 70, the latter being in the great rebellion of Civilis. The fanaticism of their nationalist leaders is vividly portrayed by Tacitus, as is their defeat at the hands of Petilius Cerialis at the hill of Rigodulum (Riol).

After his victory Petilius Cerialis, according to Tacitus, addressed the senators of the Treveri on the benefits of Roman imperialism. Very rapidly thereafter they realised those benefits on the material plane. The entire area became heavily Romanised and Trier itself was a notable centre of industry, banking and glassware. The famous ship of Neumegen graphically illustrates the wine growing which developed along the Moselle. A notable school of local sculpture developed, represented by such works as the funeral monument at Igel. The remarkable temple quarter at Trier, which dates from the pre-Roman period, now found room for Greek and Oriental cults while maintaining its devotion to those of Gaul and Germany. When the German peril grew more dangerous along the Rhine the pace of economic activity languished and Trier itself was captured by the Alamanni in 275. Once Roman control was firmly re-established, Trier entered on its most brilliant period as an Imperial capital. The court of Constantius Chlorus and his son Constantine the Great was in residence there, and this period produced a series of splendid buildings such as the Porta Nigra, the audience hall of the Imperial palace (now a Protestant church) and the famous baths. Two noble basilicas were built side by side by Constantine

—one was probably the metropolitan seat of the bishop, the other the *capella* for the Imperial court. Much of the former survives in the present cathedral of Trier, while the great medieval church of the Liebfrauenkirche is built on the foundations of the Imperial basilica. The brilliant life of the region is described in its late Imperial splendour in Ausonius' fine poem, *Mosella*. It came to an abrupt end when on 31st December 406 the invading barbarian hordes swamped the Roman defences along the Rhine. In the Frankish period the history of Trier is not well known and the royal capital was established at Aachen. But even now the memory of Rome permeates the land of the Treveri, to be felt by the most casual traveller. Along the banks of the Moselle the terraced slopes of the vineyards looked exactly like the tiered seats of a lofty theatre—just as Ausonius described them in his poem.

The last example of Romanisation comes from Britain. An observer on the western scarp of Cotswold—say on Birdlip Hill above Gloucester—has within his view a good cross-section of the zones of Romanisation in Britain. On the high limestone plateau the *civitas* of the Dobunni developed one of the most prosperous and Romanised cultures in the province. The notables lived on their estates in comfortable country houses, like the well-known villa at Chedworth, with central heating, private baths, good mosaics and elaborate dining-rooms. More than thirty villas are known within 15 miles radius of Cirencester. Their wealth came from agriculture, especially from wool, though cereals were also grown.

Corinium (Cirencester), the capital and market-town, seems to have grown out of a Roman auxiliary fort sited some three miles from the former tribal centre at Bagendon. Later it became the second largest city in the province (240 acres) and may have had some 10,000–12,000 inhabitants with a full share of civic amenities, as these were understood in Roman Britain. There were some fine town houses which produced the mosaic pavements now to be seen in the Corinium museum. As for its religious life, most of the known dedications are to the gods of the Greco-Roman world, but native British cults, especially the Mother Goddesses, are by no means lacking. In the late Empire, when Britannia was divided into four provinces, Cirencester was probably the capital of Britannia Prima.

Some 35 miles to the south-west was the spa town of Aquae Sulis (Bath). The hot springs—one of the marvels of Britain—

had been known to the Celtic peoples and were associated with the goddess Sul or Sulis: in the Roman period the goddess was equated with Minerva and provided with a temple of classical design, while the taking of the waters was facilitated by the most elaborate bath buildings in the province. They attracted visitors from all parts of Britain and also from Gaul and the Rhineland. The area round Bath was also notable for its villas and for the lead mining of the Mendips.

Below in the Severn Valley the *colonia* of Glevum (Gloucester) was founded by Nerva (A.D. 96–98) for veterans from the Second Legion at Caerleon. It was sited at a strategic point, where the Severn could first be bridged by a road going into South Wales and where sea-going vessels could (and still do) bring their cargoes. Around it lies some of the best land of the fertile vale of Severn. While no traces of Roman centuriation have been found, it is likely that the territory of the *colonia* stretched from the Cotswold slopes to the river. It was of course a self-governing unit—the *Res Publica Glevensis*—and its inhabitants were Roman citizens. Tiles stamped R.P.G. are found over the area. Up the Severn Valley and beyond Worcester was heavily forested land. Little of this large tract was cleared in Roman times, but in the Severn and lower Avon valleys at least, it is becoming clear that there were more farms than have yet found their way on to the map of Roman Britain. There are no signs, however, that we shall have to modify the picture of very thin settlement in Roman times on the heath and scrubland of the Midland plateau, now the setting for the heavy industry of Birmingham and the Black Country.

Indeed, to find Romanisation on a scale at all comparable to that of the Cotswolds our observer would have to look more than 60 miles to where the hogsback of the Wrekin shows on the far horizon, a little west of north, overlooking the large city of Viroconium (170 acres), which was the tribal capital of the Cornovii. The westward view looks beyond the bold ridge of the Malvern Hills to Herefordshire and Wales—the long ridge of the Black Mountains (2,600 ft.), the stronghold of the Silures, the high moors of Radnor Forest (2,200 ft.) and Clun (1,800 ft.). There was Romanisation in the marchlands of Wales but it was patchy and discontinuous. The better soils of the Herefordshire plain were farmed; there are four or five known Roman villas and no doubt more to be found. Just west of Hereford was the small town of Magnae (Kenchester, 17 acres) which may have been the centre of an administrative area. There were also small settlements along the roads such as Epocessa (?Stretton Grandison) and Bravonium (Leintwardine). At Ariconium (Weston-under-Penyard) was an industrial settlement—hardly explored by archaeology—which was clearly connected with the iron workings of the Forest of Dean. And at the eastern edge of the forest at Lydney by the Severn stood the remarkable shrine of Nodens, hunter-god of the Forest, who became equated first with Silvanus and, later, with the healer-god Aesculapius. But all this indicated no more than a thin veneer of Romanisation and the evidence of native hill forts such as Sutton Walls suggests continued occupation by a people only superficially influenced by Roman ways of life. Further west, in the Black Mountains and beyond, was the military area of the highland zone controlled from the legionary base at Isca (Caerleon), home of the Legion II Augusta for almost three centuries. Here Rome is represented only by strategic roads and forts or occasionally by the exploitation of minerals. The Silures, it is true, did develop a Romanised district in the plain of Gwent around the tribal capital of Venta Silurum (Caerwent). But those who chose to stay British could do so undisturbed in the mountain lands, so long as nothing was done to disturb the *pax Romana*. This seems to have been breached more often than was once supposed.

While certain general tendencies can be seen at work throughout the Western provinces, they must not be overstressed. Variety within a common framework was a mark of the *orbis Romanus*. By the end of this period Africa, from Carthage to Morocco, had become one of the most important areas of Latin culture. Italian settlement continued on a large scale, especially in the province of Africa Proconsularis, and the growing of cereals, first applied scientifically by the Carthaginians, favoured the growth of very large estates. It is said that in the time of Nero six landowners owned practically all the corn land of the province of Africa. If that Emperor confiscated their estates and killed the owners, it was because they were dangerously placed to interrupt the flow of African grain to Rome. The confiscated lands were the origin of the vast Imperial estates in Africa, of whose workings a good deal is known through the evidence of inscriptions, most of which date from the reign of Hadrian. In the second century A.D. the intensive cultivation of the olive in Africa introduced a different type of farming. It pushed the boundaries of cultivation into lands of lower rainfall and gave an opportunity for thousands of small farmers, many of them of native stock who were formerly at least semi-nomadic. The olive tree does not yield until 10 years after it has been planted; its owners must remain settled around their *oliveta*. In supplying water for the growth of olives in these parched lands the Roman knowledge of hydraulics came into its own. Where the terrain allowed it, reservoirs were constructed by the building of dams, and the water led off in irrigation channels to the olive plantations. Elsewhere the system of 'dry farming' would be used, which has been so brilliantly expounded by the recent work of Israeli archaeologists in the Negev Desert. By catching and conserving every drop of water that falls—and it may be as little as five inches in the course of a year—it has been shown to be possible to farm about one-twentieth of the catchment area. This made possible the growth in the Negev Desert of towns like Oboda (Avdat) on the great trade routes, which contained a few thousand inhabitants and whose middlemen's profits enabled the provision of urban amenities. It was the neglect of Roman irrigation by the Arabs which led to the great decline in population in all the North African lands and caused the desert to advance towards the sea.

The 500 or so cities of Roman Africa were mostly set in the old republican province, thinning out rapidly as one travelled west through the newly won lands of Numidia and Mauretania. In general they were small: the bulk of them country towns serving the surrounding district. Geography and economics dictated that Roman Africa was not organised laterally, east-west, but rather north-south, from the coast to its hinterland as far as the northern edge of the desert. Hence the largest and oldest cities were usually on the coast—Leptis Magna, Sabratha, Hadrumetum, Carthage, Hippo, Iol Caesarea, Tingis. The most notable inland were Cirta, Madauros, the military colonies of Timgad and Djemila and King Juba's foundation of Volubilis (near Fez). All these were fine cities with a full range of urban amenities. Carthage alone could rank as a world city—she was the intellectual and commercial capital of Africa, with a population of perhaps 250,000. In all the cities of Africa both large and small was a municipal aristocracy, eager to get on in local politics and ready to pay the price as benefactors. In all of them were schoolmasters, flogging a Latin culture into their pupils as they flogged it into the young Augustine. Roman Africa was fertile in lawyers, writers and later in Christian martyrs, apologists and heretics. In Imperial politics and entry to the Senate Africans got away to a late start, after Narbonensis and Spain had made the running. But the second century brought African senators forward and it ended with the African dynasty of the Severi.

Yet the Berber language remained vigorous and in the country-side the Berber culture did not succumb to Romanisation. These were the people from whom the Donatist Church drew its congregations in the fourth century. The experiment of settling nomadic peoples on the land, which went on along the desert frontiers, was not uniformly successful. Where for some reason control was weakened there was a tendency to slip back to the old desert ways. And there can be little doubt that the Atlas Mountains were a bastion for the native culture. The cultural achievement of Roman Africa was impressive, as its material remains attest. But it was confined to no more than a coastal strip of the huge continent that bears the name of Africa.

Classical sources stress the importance of Spain in the economic and cultural life of the Roman world; later history proves how enduring was the creative work of Rome in the Iberian peninsula. Unfortunately, the material side of Roman Spain is poorly documented because of the comparative backwardness of Spanish archaeology. The cities of Baetica, for example, were no less splendid than those of Narbonensis, but only Italica near Seville has been adequately explored. The province had attracted Italian colonists ever since the Late Republic and many of them prospered in their new lands. Economic prosperity reached a high level under Augustus when Gades was said to be the second city of the West. In the first century A.D. the descendants of these Italian colonists were prominent in the Senate and the Imperial service; in the second century the three great emperors, Trajan, Hadrian and Marcus Aurelius were of this stock. In Tarraconensis there is a similar development on a lesser scale in the Ebro Valley, but the cities (Bilbilis, Ilerda, Calagurris) were not so large as those in the south. For some 50 years Latin literature was dominated by men of Spanish origin—the two Senecas, the poets Lucan and Martial, Columella and the great educator, Quintilian—a tribute to the Latin authors of Spain and the excellence of its schools. In the north and west the native political organisation and the Iberian language long persisted. By the time of Vespasian pacification had gone so far that it was possible to reduce the number of legions from three to one and to encourage urban life by numerous grants of municipal privileges.

The natural resources of Spain were exploited on an impressive scale—above all its minerals. Production seems to have reached a peak under the Flavians and to have remained high throughout the second century. As well as gold, silver, copper, tin, lead and iron, Spain produced rarer minerals, such as the cinnabar of Sisapo which was a world monopoly carefully regulated by the State. The development of Spanish agriculture was no less notable. Its wines and olive oil were successfully directed at a mass market: Spanish cereals were of high repute: flax and esparto grass were specialist crops. The rich farmers of Spain could regard those of Italy as rather backward. The fisheries were on a par with those of the Black Sea and more varied since they used Atlantic as well as Mediterranean fishing-grounds. The famous *garum*, a relish made from salted fish entrails, was the Worcester Sauce or Tabasco of the Roman world.

In Gaul, the cities of Narbonensis were at their most prosperous under the Antonines and present a picture as varied as it is brilliant. Massilia had lost its commercial importance to Narbo and Arelate, but was still a centre of Greek culture and the seat of a famous university and medical school. Roman and Greek culture were blended in the elegant little city of Glanum (St Remy-en-Provence) in its enchanting setting. The Roman colony of Arelate (Arles) was a great commercial centre where the goods carried down the Rhône were transferred to sea-going vessels. What New Orleans once was to the whole Mississipi Valley, so was Arelate to that of the Rhône and Saône. The remains of the theatre, amphitheatre, circus, temples, baths and the ancient cemetery of the Aliscamps attest to a wholly Roman life. Nemausus (Nîmes) remained the high sanctuary of the Gallic water god whose name it bore, though his cult was Romanised and provided with fine classical buildings. The city developed as an attractive and fashionable spa with close links with the Imperial house, eventually producing an Emperor of its own in Antoninus Pius. Vasio (Vaison-la-Romaine), chief city of the Vocontii, lay off the main traffic routes in the fertile valley of the Ouvèze. Though not of more than local importance, it was a beautiful city some of whose opulent town houses have been excavated. Its most distinguished citizen was Sextus Afranius Burrus, appointed

Prefect of the Praetorian Guard by Claudius and one of Nero's chief advisers in the first years of his reign. Vienne has already been described. These are only some of the 30 or so cities of Narbonensis, a province that was indeed a kind of transalpine extension of Italy.

Of the Three Gauls, Belgica had at least an ethnic unity. Lugdunensis and Aquitania were large amorphous territories carved out for administrative purposes only. Lugdunum (Lyons) the federal capital and seat of the Provincial Council and of the Imperial cult was much the largest city and may have had 250,000 inhabitants. Such a figure seems high but is accepted by French scholars who make large claims for the population of Gaul and its cities. They estimate 15–20,000,000 for the whole country: the latter figure would be about that of France under Louis XIV. They also claim at least six cities of 80–100,000, among them Tolosa and Burdigala (Toulouse and Bordeaux) in the south and Trier in the north. But urbanisation in the Three Gauls followed a pattern of its own. Apart from Lugdunum which was founded as a Roman colony, most of the larger cities developed as tribal capitals or more accurately, capitals of the *civitates* or cantons, the Roman administrative units which replaced the tribal community of free Gaul (a useful means of linking tribal loyalty to Roman political forms). There were more than 60 such *civitates*, large and small, and often the tribal name is preserved in that of a modern French city (the Atrebates survive in Arras, the Remi in Rheims, the Suessiones in Soissons). Such cities might be well provided with the amenities of Roman life— as for example Autun (Augustodunum) with its famous school— but not on the same scale as Narbonensis. The magnates of these Gallic *civitates* were by no means ready to abandon life on their country estates for the urban delights introduced from the south.

The economic prosperity of Gaul came from agriculture. The famous regions of French viticulture—Burgundy, Bordeaux, the Rhône Valley, Alsace, the Moselle—derive from those of Roman Gaul. Gallic hams, cheeses and sausages were famous. Cereals were grown extensively, especially in the north. There linen and textiles were also important, ancestors of the woollen industry of Flanders. Iron was extensively worked in the north-east, though this is no more than a feeble anticipation of the great steelworks of Lorraine and Luxembourg. Pottery and glass were important industries, to be described later. A network of Roman roads and the wonderful system of navigable rivers with which Nature has endowed France made for the easy flow of goods and commerce. But the Three Gauls did not lose their native heritage. The Gallic language continued to be widely spoken and could be used for giving evidence in the courts in the second century. The Gallic cults continued, except for Druidism, which was driven underground. The native costume, better suited for the climate, remained the workaday habit though the *curiales* might wear the toga in the local Senate house. Finally, the major Gallic *civitates* never lost their identity, so that up to the end of the Empire a man would think of himself as belonging to the Remi, the Arverni, or the Treveri.

A similar Romano-Celtic synthesis is seen in Britain. Romanisation of any significant kind was confined to the Lowland zone in the south and east of the province; the Highland zone with its mainly pastoral economy was controlled by the Roman army. The most recent estimate of the population is about two million, a figure not reached again until the fifteenth century. In spite of official encouragement urbanisation made only intermittent progress. There were three Roman colonies (Colchester, Lincoln and Gloucester—a fourth developed later at York), about a dozen *civitas* capitals and the same number of country towns which were not administrative centres. The status of London (*Londinium*) is not defined in any ancient source, but there can be no real doubt that it was the capital of the province, at least after the rebellion of Boudicca. Rome made London what it still remains—the biggest port, the centre of communications and the most populous city in Britain. Roman London in the second century may have had 30,000 people. There might have been three or four other cities of 15–20,000, but most towns had perhaps no more than 5,000. The public buildings of these Romano-British cities seem out of scale with their modest population: the basilica in London was bigger than all but one of those in Rome, nor is this the only example of its kind. Was this ostentation, or deliberate policy to show the native Britons what urban life might be? The native aristocracy were slow to introduce Roman amenities on their country estates; of the 700 or so Roman villas known in Britain, none attained much sophistication before the second century. The elaborate house or rather palace recently found at Fishbourne near Chichester, undoubtedly of the first century, may prove to have belonged to the British

18 Reconstruction of the *Castellum* at Deutz, founded in A.D. 310 as a bridgehead for the protection of the Rhine frontier at Cologne. The emphasis on defence shows how the initiative had passed to the Germans.

19 Masada, seen from the north. The store-rooms and northern palace are on the promontory, and outlines of two Roman camps are shown on the right foreground, with a third to the left of the cliff.

20　The Temple of Fortune at Palestrina (Praeneste) was rebuilt by Sulla after its destruction in the Civil War. In use of material and treatment of site it is the most sophisticated example of late Republican architecture.

21 The model of Imperial Rome depicts the city as it was in the age
of Constantine. The Circus Maximus is in the foreground, with the
Imperial Palaces on the Palatine Hill beyond. To the right of these, the
Septizonium, built by Septimius Severus, and the arches of the Aquae
Claudiae. (Museo della Civiltà Romana.)

22 The Imperial Fora, the most impressive piece of urban planning in ancient Rome, spread over 150 years, from Julius Caesar to Trajan. The model shows (*left to right*) the Forum Pacis (A.D. 75), Forum of Nerva (*c.* A.D. 97), Forum of Augustus (37 B.C.–2 B.C.), Forum of Trajan and Mercatus Trajani (A.D. 113). Beyond, buildings in the Forum Romanum, the Forum of Caesar (begun in 46 B.C.), and (*top right*) the Temple of Jupiter Optimus Maximus on the Capitol.

23 The Campus Martius, showing (*left to right*) the Mausoleum of Augustus, (*bottom right*) the Stadium and Odeon of Domitian, with the Thermae of Nero above the Stadium, and the Pantheon to their right.

24 The heart of ancient Rome. In the centre, the staircase of the Cordonata leads to the Capitol, as redesigned by Michelangelo; beyond, the ruins of the Forum Romanum and Imperial Fora. The open area was retained as the Piazza di Campidoglio in which (*centre of the star*) the equestrian statue of Marcus Aurelius was placed as the symbol of world empire.

25 The layout of Ostia, as seen from the air looking E. The Sullan colony and the Capitolium are immediately above the Y junction. Later development took place along the *decumanus* to the east and west. To the east, the Theatre is conspicuous, with the Temple of Ceres and the offices of the Corporations above it. To the west the left-hand fork led to the quays by the Tiber: the right, to the coast.

26 Reconstruction of Ostian houses. Four-storey blocks of flats look inward to a courtyard, laid out as (presumably) a common garden. The flats have private balconies, and there is a penthouse.

27 Street façade of other Ostian houses. That on the right has shops and a snack-bar on the ground floor. Note the common staircase, also the balcony for tenants on the first floor—the *piano nobile*.

28 The street façade of an Ostian warehouse, the Horrea Epagathiana.
Shops occupy the ground floor: a large door gives access to the central
courtyard and a common stairway to the upper storeys, perhaps let out
to persons employed in the warehouse.

29 Air view of Arles. The Roman Amphitheatre and Theatre dominate the centre of the modern city. Between them, the church of St Trophime. Roman Arelate, a great commercial centre and, later, Imperial residence, was much more important than its modern successor.

30 Trier (Augusta Treverorum) was the capital of Gallia Belgica,
and an Imperial capital in the fourth century A.D. The building shown
is the Basilica or *aula* of the Emperor: it is now used as a Lutheran
church.

31 Reconstruction of Roman London (Londinium) in the third century A.D. The chief city and port of Britannia, Londinium may have had 25,000 inhabitants. The bridge crosses the river to what is now Southwark. The Forum (*centre*) stands where Ludgate Hill leads to St Paul's: the Tower of London is at the corner junction of the walls (*bottom centre*).

32 The Hadrianic Baths at Lepcis (A.D. 126–7) are among the more elaborate known. They were adorned with fine copies of classical Greek sculpture, as well as choice examples (Antinous, etc.) of the Hadrianic School.

33 Timgad (Colonia Ulpia Thamugadi) was built in the reign of Trajan as a 'showpiece' of Roman architecture in the Aurès Mountains of Algeria. Excavations have revealed it perhaps more completely than any other city of the Roman world. The air view shows the grid-pattern of the streets, finely paved and lined with colonnades. A triumphal arch stands in the centre: in the background the Forum and Theatre.

client king Cogidubnus or to the Roman provincial governor.

Here, too, the natural resources of the province were vigorously exploited. There is not much gold in Britain but the Romans worked it in at least one of its two Welsh sites. Lead, silver and copper were produced in quantity; so later was tin. The damp climate of Britain rules out the vine and the olive, but it produces wonderful grass and British sheep, cattle and horses became famous. The best building stones were discovered and used— among them Purbeck, Portland and Cotswold stone. Even exotics such as Whitby jet and the Blue John of the Peak District were exploited for ornament. The Fens were drained and the dykes used as waterways, so that in the late Empire Britain was able to export corn to Gaul.

Latin was taught in the schools and was the language of the peasantry, although the Celtic language and its derivatives had a long life ahead of them, which still continues in Welsh. The brilliant aristocratic art of the La Tène period, of which Britain was one of the chief centres, succumbed to the mass-produced art of the Roman provinces; but in sculpture the native tradition had enough vitality to blend with classical motifs. In religion there was give and take. The cults of Mithras, Cybele, Isis and Serapis found their way to Britain besides the official Roman gods, but the Celtic divinities (notably the mother goddesses and the horse goddess Epona) flourished, and the divinities of mountain, river, or spring held their local territory.

The Alpine provinces of Raetia and Noricum disclose a similar picture. Romanisation is promoted by colonies, as at Augsburg (Augusta Vindelicorum) and towns develop from military bases, as at Regensberg (Castra Regina). The native population, Celtic or Illyrian, is organised into *civitates*, whose capitals (Virunum, Celeia) grow into sizable cities. But since they were closer to Italy these provinces attracted more Italian settlers and were brought into the economic orbit of Italy by the merchants of Aquileia. The iron ores of Styria were extensively worked and 'Noricum steel' was famous as early as Augustus.

It is less easy to find a coherent pattern in Illyricum and the Danube lands. The cities along the Adriatic coast of Dalmatia— Salonae, Narona, Iader—did not differ much from those of Italy. A recent study has shown how they were at first dominated by Italian settlers after the conquests of Octavian had opened up the area and how later, in the second and third centuries, men of

T.R.—R

native origin came to the fore. In the highlands of Bosnia the tribal communities remained. Roman interest in the area was mainly directed to working its minerals and recruiting for the auxiliaries. Along the Save and Drave valleys cities grew from the old military bases. Emona (Ljubljana), Siscia (Sisak) and Sirmium (Srimska Mitrovica) were all Roman colonies. Poetovio (Pettau) and Mursa (Osijek) controlled the Drave. The Illyrians and Pannonians were now eagerly joining the Roman army which they had so nearly defeated in the great rising of A.D. 6–9 and which they were to redeem from disaster in the next century.

An account of the Latin West should conclude with the story of Rome's last effort at colonisation in Dacia, where for more than a century the Roman world reached almost to the Carpathians. The kingdom of Decebalus had been the most advanced of any of the northern peoples, and the wars of conquest the hardest fought. Trajan's victory had been followed by the withdrawal—voluntary or forced—of thousands of Dacians from their native lands and by the influx of new settlers from within the Empire. After only 160 years as a Roman province Dacia was to be abandoned by the Emperor Aurelian, and yet this brief period has stamped Romania as an island of Latin culture in the Slavonic world. The meagre sources mean that the historical story cannot really be told, though the work of Romanian archaeologists is throwing light on its material side. As one might expect, one of the first aims of Roman policy was to bring the gold and silver mines into production and a group of experienced miners from the Pirustae of Dalmatia was brought in to the gold mines of Veretspatak. We hear of *conductores* holding leases to exploit salt mines, forests and pasture lands, probably from the royal estates of Decebalus. Towns and colonies were founded, the most notable being Apulum and Sarmizigethusa on the site of Decebalus' old capital. In the latter Syrian merchants had an office and some of the new settlers came from Galatia, so that contact with the Eastern provinces was strong. But the bulk of the settlers came from Latin speaking lands, especially Illyricum. We do not know what happened to the native Dacians within the province, except for hints of a rebellion in the time of Marcus Aurelius. Certainly the free Dacians, descendants of those poor wretches pictured on Trajan's Column as going away to exile, remained irreconcilable enemies of Rome. To them, it seems, the final victory was to belong.

CHAPTER 39

The Eastern lands

DESPITE THE IMPRESSIVE development of the Western
provinces and of Africa the East remained the richest part of
the Empire. Here the Roman contribution is often underrated.
The Hellenistic world was the work of Alexander and his successors in lands of an older civilisation. But although Rome appeared
in the East as the champion of Hellenism she had something of
her own to convey. Roman roads opened up the great Anatolian
plateau and fostered the growth of cities in Phrygia, Pisidia and
Cilicia. In Galatia Rome was in contact with a Celtic society,
much as in Noricum or Tres Galliae. The Celtic language in
Galatia did not die out before the late Empire, and the growth of
Ancyra from the tribal centre of the Tectosages to the capital of
the Roman province of Galatia had many a parallel in Gaul. Asia,
after its dismal experiences in the late Republic, revived and
flourished under the Empire. The famous Ionian cities—Ephesus,
Smyrna, Miletus, Pergamum—were rich and prosperous and
went in for splendid new amenities. New cities rose to prosperity,
such as Alexandria Troas, Tralles and Tarsus in Cilicia.

But the great feature of this period was the growth of Syria.
The Roman peace, the new markets in the West and the energy
and commercial instincts of Syrian merchants and shipowners
added a new dimension to Syrian prosperity. It is best seen in the
growth of Antioch and of the metropolitan district surrounding
it, in which the wealthy Syrian merchants had their villas. The
population of this area of northern Syria was very much larger
than it is today. It is said that when a party of Chinese merchants
reached Antioch in the reign of Antoninus Pius they thought it
was the capital of the Roman Empire rather than its third largest
city. The cities of Syria were Hellenised, with a Roman overlay,

235

the latter marked at Berytus (Beirut) which was a Roman colony. In the countryside the Aramaic language and Semitic culture held sway. Syrian textiles, glass and metalware reached a wide market, as did its cereals, wines and oils. The ancient purple-dye industry of Tyre was reorganised and expanded. Among Syrian exports we must not fail to mention religion, for the province served as a centre of diffusion for Eastern cults. Judaism and Christianity came out of Palestine; Mithraism, which came from Persia, was spread through the Roman world by soldiers and Syrian traders. Dea Syria, the Syrian goddess, had a great vogue in the third century and later when a number of solar cults, such as that of Elagabalus, also travelled west.

For the caravan traffic on which so much of the Eastern trade depended, the best evidence is in a passage of Pliny's *Natural History*. He is describing the route from Alexandria to Berenice on the Red Sea. For the first 309 miles the merchants use the Nile, taking 12 days with favourable winds to reach the river port of Coptos. Then they join the caravan-trains for a further journey of 12 days, covering the 257 miles to Berenice. Because of the heat most of the travelling was done at night and the days were spent at a series of watering stations. One of these had a *caravan-serai* for 2,000 travellers and their camels. The tariff of Coptos, dated 90, preserves a list of the toll fees charged at that crucial stage. They relate to the personnel and draught animals of the party and tax luxury in the interests of utility. Thus 1 obol is chargeable for a camel permit, 5 drachmae for a sailor, 8 for a ship's captain, 20 for 'sailors' women', but 108 for a prostitute. The tariff of Palmyra is in greater detail and prescribes the tolls on camel loads of myrrh (according to its container), olive oil, etc. Clothing merchants, leather sellers and butchers also pay tolls to the tax farmer. For the use of the two wells, which made possible the use of Palmyra as a staging post, there is an annual charge of 800 denarii (about $240 or £100). No doubt similar conditions applied for the caravans that crossed the Saharan and Libyan deserts to the southern oases. The evidence of papyri, from Oxyrhynchus and elsewhere, has preserved the life of Roman Egypt in remarkable detail. The arrangements of Augustus continued. Egypt was the granary of Rome—its control indispensable for whoever ruled the Empire. In A.D. 69 Vespasian thought it more important to seize Egypt than to lead his armies West in person. The natural resources of the country were geared to earning a profit for the Imperial treasury. The Nile and its waterways were carefully maintained for agriculture and for transport by a system of *corvée* or forced labour imposed on all male adults among the *fellaheen*. The Nilometers at Memphis and Elephantine predicted as well as recorded the annual rises of the river, and their advance warning was used as the basis for the quotas set for every taxable crop. A Roman flotilla patrolled the river as far as the First Cataract at Syene (Asswan); the 17,000 Roman troops (later reduced) had little fighting to do and were employed to enforce the demands of the administration. They earned themselves a bad name as oppressors, to judge from the papyri. We hear of sporadic attempts to discover the source of the Nile, the most interesting being that of two centurions who in the reign of Nero got as far as the vast marshes of the southern Sudan. There was a considerable tourist traffic on the river, made up largely of merchants trading with Alexandria and officers and men of the Roman army of occupation. One of its attractions was a visit to Thebes and to the singing statue of Memnon: those who heard it saluting the dawn had some virtue conferred upon them. Hundreds of graffiti on the statue record successful visits, among them those of Hadrian and his wife Sabina.

Alexandria remained the greatest port and the second city in the world. The trade routes from India, the Red Sea and the Mediterranean met in the city and the Nile brought down the products of inland Egypt and of Nubia. The city mob of Alexandria was noted for its turbulence and its pogroms and its large Jewish community made frequent appeals for help to the Emperor. This same community was the wealthiest and intellectually the most advanced of all Jewish colonies in the Roman world. Alexandria no longer dominated the cultural life of the Hellenistic world but she was still an important centre for medicine and science. Only one new urban foundation is known in this period, that of Antinoopolis, set up by Hadrian to commemorate his favourite, drowned in the Nile. We know little of its history. But the old market towns acquired some of the physical amenities of Romanisation, though they were never thought suitable to be given municipal rights. Egypt was under the rule of a bureaucracy and there was no place for free citizens even at a local level. Alexandria itself never attained self-government as understood elsewhere in the Roman world. And there were psychological barriers between the native Egyptians and the Greco-Roman settlers. Though the cult of Isis spread through the world and other Egyptian divinities acquired Roman or Greek features, the animal gods of Egypt were profoundly antipathetic. So too were the fickleness, violence and fanaticism of the *fellaheen*, whom Juvenal and other Roman authors described as the most degenerate of mankind.

Greece proper, her natural poverty exposed by the development of other parts of the Eastern provinces, had little share in the general prosperity of the Roman world. Athens lived on historic memories, education and the tourist trade. Sparta profited from the demand for marbles. Corinth was a pleasure resort and commercial centre. In agriculture conditions favoured the growth of large estates, which in turn produced some men of wealth who acted as patrons to shrines and cities. From the writings of Plutarch one gets the impression that he and his neighbours around Delphi lived in a quiet but cultured backwater. The economic life of Macedonia and Thrace was more vigorous since they lay on the great roads between Italy and Asia, and had the stimulus of the demands of the colonies founded by Augustus and also of the Roman army on the Danube, especially in the second century. Thessalonica and Hadrianopolis became important cities and others such as Beroea and Stobi were of local importance.

Goods circulated throughout the Empire on an impressive and unprecedented scale. With the *pax Romana* firmly established and an improved system of communications in most parts of the world, the conditions existed for the greatest economic boom the ancient world was ever to know. The commerce and foreign trade of the first two centuries A.D. is known to us in some detail and from a wide range of sources. The geographer Strabo is invaluable for the period immediately after Augustus, and Pliny's *Natural History* deals with such varied topics as mining in north-western Spain and the caravan routes from the Nile Valley to the Red Sea. The Red Sea traffic itself is well known because of the survival of a mariner's guide of the first century A.D. The Greek Sophists Dion of Prusa and Aelius Aristides give vivid pictures of some of the Greek cities—Smyrna, Rhodes, Tarsus, Ephesus, Alexandria—as they were in the second century. Archaeological evidence is rich and is accumulating. It is especially valuable for the light it has thrown on the 'caravan cities' of Syria, Mesopotamia and Arabia—Edessa, Nisibis and Hatra on the route across the north Syrian Desert to Persia; Palmyra and

Dura Europos further south; Petra, Gerasa (Gerash) and Bostra in what is now the Kingdom of Jordan. The foreign trade of the Empire is attested by finds throughout northern Europe from Scotland to the Baltic lands and also in the Ukraine and the Crimea. Roman traffic with the East is illustrated by recent discoveries near Pondicherry in India, Peshawar in Pakistan and Kabul in Afghanistan. The new and growing science of marine archaeology will yield more evidence about ships and cargoes in the Mediterranean.

The establishment of peace, the suppression of piracy and brigandage and the building of roads and harbours would have been in themselves a powerful stimulus in the already highly developed parts of the Empire. The opening up of new lands in the West—in Spain, Britain, Gaul, the Rhineland and the Danube countries—provided new sources of minerals and other raw materials; their development and urbanisation was a tonic to the whole economic life of the Roman world. A common market was thus established which extended beyond the bounds of the *orbis Romanus* proper to the hinterland of the Black Sea, the Red Sea and the Persian Gulf, Nubia and Ethiopia. Beyond these limits there was the trade with free Germany and Scandinavia and with India, Ceylon and China. But, as with the United States, the home market was far more important than foreign trade—i.e. between the provinces themselves, and internally where, as in Gaul, there was a sizable regional market.

CHAPTER 40

Trade and commerce

THE POLICY OF THE EMPERORS, during the first century at
least, was to provide the conditions in which trade could flourish
and to leave its development to private enterprise. Harbour dues
and other customs charges were kept low. Money maintained its
value over long periods, though Nero's debasement of both the
gold and silver currencies was tantamount to a devaluation of
about 14 per cent. After this gold remained stable until the early
third century, although silver continued to decline. Privileges
were freely accorded to *collegia*, the trade associations which
manufacturers and traders formed to foster their special interests.
Occasionally, a military expedition or trade mission would be
sponsored for economic reasons. Possibly the campaigns of
Aelius Gallus in Arabia under Augustus, certainly the mission.
sent by Marcus Aurelius to China in A.D. 166, come under this
category. There were occasional interventions to protect the
economy of Italy. Otherwise market forces were allowed free
sway: indeed, it could hardly have been otherwise, for they were
very imperfectly understood.

Modern observers point to two contrary tendencies. In the
first century A.D. opportunities for expansion were such that
certain manufacturers were able to win a world market for their
products. Italian wine growers, for example, are estimated to
have supplied two-thirds of the demand for fine wines, sending
them to all parts of the Roman world and also to northern Europe
and to India. Egypt met the world demand for papyrus and the
growers well understood how to maintain prices by controlling
production. Campanian metal-ware and, for a time, the glazed
pottery (*terra sigillata*) of Arretium commanded a world market.
So did another Italian speciality—the terracotta lamps made by

the firm of Fortis of Mutina (Modena, in north Italy). Woollen garments from Miletus and silk from Cos were bought by all who could afford luxury clothing.

In contrast there was a tendency to decentralisation which seems to have become dominant by the second century—due mainly to the high cost of transport especially by land. As new markets opened in the developing provinces it became cheaper to offer local competition or to open new branches of the main company. Thus Fortis was faced in the second century with the competition of local imitators who did not shrink from copying his trademark. The best-known example, of course, is that of mass produced pottery. By the reign of Claudius the Italian products had lost their Western markets to new suppliers in central Gaul, especially those of La Graufesenque and Lezoux near Clermont Ferrand. These built up a big export trade, largely because they met the heavy consumer demands from the Roman armies along the Rhine and the Danube. By the second century A.D. they in their turn were being ousted by fresh centres closer to the market, of which the best known are Rheinzabern and Heiligenberg. In Britain, where pottery has been intensively studied, the picture is clear. 'Samian ware' from Gaul was imported on a very large scale in the first and second centuries. By the end of the second century Rhenish ware began to appear, though not in the same quantity. Good British pottery was now on the market, such as that from Caistor in Northamptonshire and by the third century Britain was meeting almost all her own needs, mostly from local potteries with a very limited distribution.

The story of glass is even more striking. At first it was a luxury product made in Syria and Alexandria. Then new methods of manufacture brought it into mass production and south Italy became an important centre. Like that of pottery, the industry moved to Gaul and Germany, where Trier and Cologne became famous for their glassware by the second century. The best of their products, displayed in the museums of those cities, will stand comparison with the fine glass of modern times.

But industry and mass production never developed in the Roman world on the scale to which we have been accustomed since the Industrial Revolution. The potteries of La Graufesenque must in their heyday have employed a large labour force though we do not know its number: some 6,000 potters' names have been identified from the stamps on their wares, twice as many as for the potters of Lezoux. Mining and quarrying also demanded comparatively large numbers of workers. Polybius says that in the second century B.C. 40,000 men were at work in the silver mines around New Carthage, but the mining district itself was within a perimeter of more than 100 miles in circuit. Pliny's accounts of the gold and copper mines of Cantabria and Asturia dwell rather on the technical ingenuity of their working (drainage, tunnelling, extraction of the ore) than on the size of the labour force. By his time Spanish mines were owned by the State, though their working was often sub-let to private contractors. Elaborate regulations were framed for their exploitation, for the division of profits between the State and the lessee, and for the social welfare of the miners. They appear to be derived from a model mining code laid down in Rome, but adjusted to suit local conditions and operated on the ground by Imperial procuration or Supervisors of Mines. The best-known example is the *Lex Metalli Vipascensis*, probably of the second century A.D. prescribing regulations for the silver and copper mines of Vipasca (Aljustrel, in Portugal). These mines are leased to a contractor who shares half (?) the profits with the State. He has to observe a code of practice for the working of the mines and the upkeep of galleries and shafts. Conditions are laid down for the sifting of dumps and spoil heaps. The mining contractors sublet the right to operate baths, dry cleaning establishments and barbers' shops on defined conditions. Schools are provided and the schoolmasters are exempt from taxation by the *procurator*. Working conditions were brutal and dangerous for the miner throughout ancient times, but at least these regulations—perhaps first codified in the time of Vespasian—made an attempt to improve his lot.

By far the largest labour force was in the service of the Roman Emperor himself. The Imperial possessions were enormous and constantly grew by bequest or confiscation. They were highly diversified—agricultural estates, pastures, forests, mines, quarries, brick and tile factories—and reached into almost every province. The agricultural estates or *praedia Caesaris* are the best known, notably the huge areas administered for the Emperor in the Bagradas Valley in Africa—lands first acquired by Nero's confiscation of senatorial estates. The estate offices were in Carthage and something is known of their policy from a series of inscriptions of the second century. The Emperors were concerned to bring as much land as possible into cultivation and easy terms were offered to tenants who would take over uncultivated tracts. Such *coloni* had security of tenure and exemption from rent for the first five or 10 years. The best lands were leased out to large operators with freedom to sublet on fixed conditions. This system was open to abuse and we hear of complaints to the Emperor Commodus from the small peasants that the chief lessee and the Imperial procurators are working together against them and demanding more than the periods of work laid down by the decree of Hadrian and observed by all their neigbours since his time. A brief reply from Commodus orders the procurators to conform to established practice. However benevolent, the Emperor was an absentee landlord and his agents had the chance to feather their nests.

Such was the case, also, with the agent of that rumbustious literary parody of a *nouveau riche*, the Trimalchio of Petronius. He finds it hard to keep track of all the estates bought in his name and is forced to enunciate the rule that 'if any estate is not notified to me within six months, I refuse to have it entered on the books'. Scholars have shown how the *Cena Trimalchionis* can be used for economic evidence. Trimalchio had come as a slave from Asia at the age of 14 as a fancy boy in the house of a Roman senator. He ended up as his master's steward and received half the estate on his master's death. He now set out on a business career, buying five ships, filling them with Campanian wines and sending them to Rome. All were shipwrecked—a loss of £1,000,000. Nothing daunted, he built more ships, bigger and better. His wife Fortunata sold all her jewelry and clothes and put 10,000 gold coins in his hand. After that his luck turned: he cleared £300,000 on a single voyage. Then he bought back all his patron's estates near Cumae and began to breed slaves. His luck held, but after a time he got bored with business and retired, lending out money through his freedmen. The profits were put into buying fresh estates. Already they stretch from Campania into Apulia: he hopes one day to be able to travel through Sicily to Africa on his own lands, which when he dies will be worth about £1,000,000. The house where the dinner is given has 20 bedrooms, four dining rooms, two colonnades, a fine lodge for the porter and a guest house for 100 guests. (It has been suggested that Trimalchio stands for Nero and that this is the Golden House, but it is not very likely.) Around his table are men who have lost a million and own nothing and others worth £800,000. They get rich quickly through trade and put their money into land. Land is king even in a fantasy.

There were, of course, other sources of wealth. Sextus Marius, executed under Tiberius, had built up a great fortune from silver and copper mines in Spain. The baker Vergilius Eurysaces, whose ostentatious funeral monument stands just outside the Porta Maggiore in Rome, was surely not the only man to grow rich in that essential occupation. The great merchants trading from the ports of Asia and from Syria, Gades, Narbo, Alexandria, Aquileia and the other major emporia were famous for their wealth. So were the big woollen and textile magnates of Asia, Patavium and the Moselle Valley. The Secundinii—land owners, woollen merchants and (perhaps) bankers—whose activities are known through their funeral monument at Igel near Trier, are good examples of these provincial magnates. Others are the Barbii of Aquileia, export merchants, with branches in Noricum, Histria and Dalmatia. In the Eastern provinces especially Asia, Bithynia and Syria, there were many such wealthy men known to us chiefly through their benefactions to their native city. Such was the second century plutocrat Opramoas of Rhodiapolis in Lycia, whose monetary benefactions to 28 cities of his native province exceeded 500,000 denarii, apart from his endowment of temples and festivals. Some of the Greek sophists or travelling lecturers of the second century A.D. were said to have been very wealthy, though whether as a result of their profession is uncertain. But land was the safest and most permanent form of investment and money made in other fields was commonly used to buy estates. The municipal aristocracy, in the Eastern and Western provinces alike, was basically one of well-to-do landowners, able to devote time to local politics because they had good overseers and an ample rent roll.

Natural limits were thus set to the growth of trade and industry, unless new lands could be opened up or unless the trade with Parthia and the East developed on a much greater scale. The course of Roman history was such that neither of these things came about. Trajan's conquest of Dacia was the last enduring conquest of the Empire. His wars with Parthia were unsuccessful and, in the long run, harmful to the true interests of Rome.

Although the economic prosperity of the Roman world continued for 50 years after his death its foundations were insecure. But, besides goods, ideas and religious beliefs were diffused along the trade routes of the *orbis Romanus* and some of them were to prove more durable.

CHAPTER 41

Universal religions

A UNIVERSAL STATE ENCOURAGES a universal religion. Where a tolerant polytheism prevails it may find room for several such, more especially if they serve deep and genuine human needs. Wherever the Roman armies went or Roman colonies were founded they took with them Jupiter Optimus Maximus, bringer of victory to Rome and guarantor of the permanence of her Empire. But soldiers and citizens are also individuals and as such need more than victory. Neither Jupiter nor any other divinities of the official Roman pantheon could offer the pageantry of religious ceremonial, nor the means of spiritual progress, nor the hope of immortality as a reward for the just. The Greek and Oriental cults that spread so rapidly in the late Republic and early Empire did so because they met these basic human demands. Though they might be adopted as public cults they attracted their worshippers as individuals: among the most successful were mystery cults confined to initiates.

Some of these cults are described in literary sources or are known through the survival of sacred texts: for others the only evidence is from archaeology. One such was the unknown cult whose votaries met in the underground basilica by the Porta Maggiore in Rome, which was discovered in 1917 when ballast from the Rome–Naples railway line was found to be falling into it. The roofs of the nave and side-aisles of this tiny basilica are covered with stucco reliefs of very high quality depicting mythological scenes. Analysis has shown that these constitute two programmes. One is that of redemption achieved through love, of which the supreme example is Sappho's leap over the Leucadian cliff, the other, of punishment for sin. Scholars have suggested that the cult was a form of neo-Pythagoreanism: if they are correct in associating it with Statilius Taurus who was condemned in A.D. 53 for practising 'magic arts', then such cults might have penetrated the higher circles of Roman society. The Dionysiac mysteries which the Senate had tried in vain to stamp out in southern Italy in the second century B.C. numbered rich and poor, slave and free among their adherents. Their rites are shown in the famous frescoes from the Villa of the Mysteries at Pompeii. Under the Empire the cult spread from Italy to the Western provinces, especially Gaul.

The most striking advances, however, were made by the Oriental religions, especially those of the Great Mother, Cybele, from Asia; of Isis and Osiris from Egypt and of Mithras from Persia. Augustus and Tiberius were hostile to foreign cults, but from Gaius onwards they were no longer discouraged and sometimes even received the support of the State. The 'Oriental' sympathies of Gaius were fortunate for Isis and Osiris, a cult which already had won many adherents in Rome, especially among women, freedmen and slaves. Thereafter it spread rapidly and later devotees such as the novelist Apuleius saw the cults of all goddesses subsumed under that Queen Isis. It had a rich ceremonial including daily worship and the great feasts of spring and autumn (the opening and closing of the navigation season) were spectacular public occasions. Apuleius in a famous passage describes the Release of the Ship or *navigium Isidis* on March 5 as a magnificent pageant, at the climax of which the priests of Isis offered prayers for the safety and well being of the Emperor and the entire Roman people, as well as for all ships and seafarers.

The interest in the Trojan origins of Rome, fostered by Augustus and dignified by Virgil in the *Aeneid*, encouraged the cult of Cybele. Since the end of the Second Punic War Magna Mater had had a temple on the Palatine, but under the Republic she and her mendicant priests had been confined under a kind of temple arrest save for the annual festival of the Megalesia in April. Under Claudius the temple was restored, the post of *archigallus* or chief priest thrown open to Roman citizens and restrictions on the cult removed. As 'mother of cities' Cybele received recognition from municipalities, especially in Gaul. There are striking parallels between her cult and that of Isis: each of the goddesses stands for fertility in nature; in each cult is a son or youthful adherent, Attis and Osiris, who dies annually and is revived, who functions as a redeemer to the faithful. But the Isis cult offered a more varied pantheon which included ancient Egyptian divinities such as Anubis and Horus, together with Serapis, whose cult seems to have been introduced in the Egypt of the Ptolemies.

Archaeology is the main source for our knowledge of the Persian divinity Mithras. The underground Mithraic chapels or 'caves' were deliberately destroyed and sealed after the triumph of Christianity, but in many cases this has preserved their contents for the modern excavator. At Carrawburgh on Hadrian's Wall it has been possible to recover the little basilica with its sculptured reliefs of Mithras slaying the sacred bull, his two attendants Cautes and Cautopates, the mosaic floor with the marks indicating the positions for the seven grades of initiates, and the ordeal pits in which these latter endured heat or cold to qualify for advance in the order. Originating in Persia not later than 500 B.C., Mithras reached the Roman world in the first century B.C. and his cult was spread by Roman soldiers and Syrian traders, reaching its peak in the second and third centuries A.D. A distribution map of known *Mithraea* shows them as spread along the army camps on the frontiers—especially along the Danube—and in the great seaports. In Persian belief, Mithras was subordinate to the supreme god Ahura-Mazda, and functioned as a saviour god for the good of the human race. In the Roman world he is closely associated with the solar cult and astrological motifs play a large part in the iconography. Mithraic congregations appear to have been limited to 100 initiates, worshipping without a professional priesthood or any formal 'church' organisation. So far as we know the cult never received formal recognition from the State.

It was natural that the Roman Emperor with his claim of universal rule should seek association with the Sun god, the visible ruler of the cosmos. The obelisk which Augustus brought from Heliopolis to Rome, the colossal status of Nero with the radiate crown designed for the entrance to the Golden House, perhaps also the Pantheon of Hadrian, all symbolise this relationship. But it was Septimius Severus and his Syrian Empress Julia Domna who brought the solar cults to the fore: they attained supremacy in the time of Aurelian.

The last of these world religions was one whose historic roots and expansion are known with uncommon precision. On an April day in the last years of Tiberius—most probably Friday,

April 3rd, A.D. 33—Pontius Pilatus, Roman procurator of Judaea, ordained the degrading punishment of death on the cross upon an obscure religious teacher in that province. He took this course with reluctance for at an investigation the evidence against the accused seemed far from convincing and his personality was impressive. But the Sanhedrin, as leaders of orthodox Judaism, were anxious to press the case for reasons of their own and used the argument most likely to impress a Roman official—that if the man were allowed to go free social disorder would follow. So Pontius Pilatus yielded to expediency and the man, Jesus of Nazareth, was crucified between two common thieves on the hill of Calvary outside Jerusalem. According to Roman custom the body was handed over to the relatives for burial. That should have been the end of the matter but it was not. On the third day the tomb was found to be empty and subsequently Jesus was seen by many persons as if He were still alive. His earthly ministry had been marked by miracles; now it seemed that He had achieved the supreme miracle and had risen from the dead. His disciples and followers who had given him little support at the time of His trial and passion took heart again at the Resurrection, and took it upon themselves to spread the news to all peoples. Within 50 days of Jesus' death the missionary work of the Apostles began and with it the history of the Christian Church. It is not for the historian of Rome to set the teachings of Jesus in the context of Hebrew religious tradition, nor to trace the details of His earthly ministry (which lasted for only two or three years) in Judaea and Galilee. But it should be said that there was a persistent belief among the Jews about the coming of a Messiah, a deliverer who would be born of the House of David and who would establish a kingdom to deliver the people of Israel from their oppressors. This last was interpreted literally as an independent and enduring Jewish state. Jesus disappointed these messianic hopes—His kingdom was not of this world and it was only in mockery that He ever bore the title of King of the Jews. But in the pagan world there were other, vaguer, hopes and aspirations, chief among them for a code of conduct by which all men could live and for assurance of life after death. These hopes Jesus fulfilled, when He had been proclaimed as the risen Christ to the peoples of the world. Without the widespread order of the *pax Romana* that good news could never have spread. Paul spoke of Jesus' mission as something that came into being 'in the fullness of time'. Writing in the second century A.D., Origen recognised the crucial factor of the *pax Romana*. 'A peace was prevalent which began at the birth of Christ. For God prepared the nations for His teaching so that they should be under one prince, the King of the Romans, and that it might not, because of lack of unity between nations due to the existence of many kingdoms, be more difficult for the Apostles to carry out the task laid on them by their Master when He said "Go and teach all nations." Thus it was made possible that within a generation of the death of Jesus, Christian communities were firmly established in Palestine, Syria (where the church at Antioch was prominent), Asia Minor, Corinth, Thessalonica and in Rome itself.

Christianity found most of its adherents among the urban poor. The Christian life was concerned with the sacraments of baptism, the eucharist, the *agape* or love feast and with the practical support of needy members of the communities. Its doctrines were little known to the outside world where it was regarded with suspicion as a fanatical sect of Judaism. Thanks to the Pauline writings and to the Acts of the Apostles, the Christianity of this period is best known through the missionary work of Paul of Tarsus. Paul himself exemplifies the unity and diversity of the Roman world. He grew up as an orthodox Jew in the Greek city of Tarsus, but through his father he was a Roman citizen, and in his conflicts with the authorities he could stand on the privileges thus conferred. He was sent to complete his education in Jerusalem and for some time acted as an agent of orthodox Judaism to harrass the infant Christian Church in Palestine. His conversion by a vision seen on the road to Damascus was typical of many such experiences in the religious life of the times. On his journeys he had access to the synagogues of Jewish communities—until they discovered that he taught a rival doctrine. He could quote the Greek poets to an audience in Athens. He had an ecumenical view of the Roman world: if they called him to come over into Macedonia, he would go, and his ambition (unfulfilled) was to conduct a mission in Spain where he would perhaps have had to preach the Gospel in Latin. He was martyred in Rome in the early 60's, as was Peter, traditionally the apostle and first bishop of the Roman community. Upon this community fell the first persecution as scapegoats for the Great Fire of A.D. 64.

The Neronian persecution did not halt the spread of Christianity but left it exposed to the suspicion of the Imperial authorities and no longer protected by the official tolerance accorded to Judaism. The Christians turned inward away from the world, whose concerns seemed of little import because of their belief that the second coming of Christ was imminent. In an ironic way, they suffered from the very tolerance of Roman polytheism, to which it was incredible that Christians could not go through the motions of a formal token of respect to the Imperial cult and to the gods of the Roman state. The dilemma is well brought out in the famous exchange of letters between Pliny and Trajan (A.D. 111–112). Pliny finds Christianity in Bithynia widespread in town and country alike affecting all ages and classes. It is a 'contagious superstition', but still possible to bring under control if Christians are given an opportunity to recant. The situation calls for guidance because he is receiving large numbers of anonymous denunciations of Christians. Trajan's rescript lays down working rules. There is to be no inquisition: at the same time, anyone denounced and convicted must be punished unless he gives practical proof that he is not a Christian by invoking the Roman gods. No attention should be paid to anonymous documents, 'which form a very bad precedent and are quite unworthy of the age in which we live'. These are sensible and well intentioned guide-lines, though they shrink from formulating any general principles. A later rescript of Trajan to Fundanus, governor of Asia, was rather more favourable to the Christians in that it required him to check the charges brought against them and to punish mere calumniators according to their deserts. But they left the Christians exposed to sporadic and local persecutions such as those which brought about the deaths of Ignatius and Polycarp in Asia, of Justin in Rome and of the Gallic martyrs under Marcus Aurelius. Christianity is sometimes called 'the Religion of the Book', but this it only became in the last part of the first century.

With the passing away of men who had known Jesus at first hand, it became essential that their accounts of His life and teachings should be set down in a permanent record. This is the purpose of the four Gospels, which were written between A.D. 70 and 100. They were not meant as biographies of Jesus, but rather as 'proclamations' of His Passion and Resurrection, with as much introductory material as was needed to make their significance clear. The Pauline writings and other 'Catholic' epistles were added to the Gospels to make the collection of 27 'books' that constitute the New Testament.

For Christianity the second century A.D. was a period of incubation. It continued to spread slowly through the Roman Empire, and beyond it to certain cities of the Persian Empire. It looks as though the churches of Africa and Egypt were established in this period though we have no details. In the West it certainly reached Gaul, perhaps also Britain and Spain. A vague kind of primacy was accorded to the Church in Rome. Christian apologists appeared who took up the task of explaining Christianity to the outside world. In the Christian School at Alexandria a start was made by thinkers such as Clement in equipping Christianity to meet the intellectual challenge of classical culture. But nothing happened in this period to foreshadow the spectacular trials and gains that awaited Christianity in the third century.

CHAPTER 42

The universal Empire

THERE IS NO CONTEMPORARY survey of the Empire as a whole
in the days of its Antonine prosperity. No Roman who travelled
in Hadrian's suite thought it worth while to give an account of
his provincial journeys. There is only (and we must be grateful
for it) the speech *On Rome* by the Greek sophist Aelius Aristides,
delivered perhaps in the Athenaeum, the lecture hall attached to
the newly dedicated Temple of Venus and Rome, on April 21st
A.D. 143 (?). It can be useful if it is kept in mind that the duty of an
ancient panegyrist was to praise and that one must not look to
find the reverse of the coin. Among the orator's topics are Rome's
generosity in extending her citizenship: the discipline and valour
of the armies on the frontiers: the grandeur of Rome herself: the
variety and richness of the commerce in the great harbours: the
benefits of the *pax Romana* throughout the world. Of Rome he
says that it is impossible to exclaim as with other cities, 'There
she stands! . . . No one can survey her whole extent—placed end
to end, her buildings would reach to the Straits of Otranto!' As
for the *pax Romana*, 'wars have ceased throughout the world, so
that people wonder whether they ever existed: if there are wars
on the distant frontiers they pass and are forgotten, like the
gossip of a day. . . . The only strife that is left is a contest in
beauty and splendour between the cities. . . . The Greek cities of
Ionia (Aristides' native land) are a model of elegance to the world.
Indeed, the whole world is adorned like a pleasure-garden
(*paradisus*). . . . Rome has surveyed the world, bridged mighty
rivers, driven roads through the mountains and across the deserts;
a traveller is safe everywhere, so long as he is a citizen of Rome.'
Exaggerated, but not more so than those prospects held out by

the devotees of modern technology of a world environment wholly favourable to man.

In sober fact, the longest east-west axis of the Empire was from the Caucasus to Cape Finisterre in north-west Spain, about 2,800 miles. North-south, the longest distance was from Hadrian's Wall to the fringes of the Sahara, about 1,600 miles, which is almost exactly that of the longest north-south axis across the United States from Canada to the Mexican border at the mouth of the Rio Grande. Its population, not less than 70 million, was about half that of the United States today. It contained two universal languages: Latin, the language of administration, and Greek, the common language of the eastern half and understood by most educated men in the West. (Many educated Romans like Hadrian or Marcus Aurelius were virtually bi-lingual—which could be said of very few Greek *savants*.) There were innumerable local languages and some, like Celtic in northern Europe, Punic in Africa, Aramaic in Syria, had very large numbers of native speakers. Tariff barriers were low within the Empire; there was a common currency and many local ones; a common code of laws, to which local codes tended to be assimilated. An education which gave pride of place to rhetoric, philosophy and literature was universal: the classical authors of Greek and Roman literature provided the models for a common culture. For all its deficiencies, this Roman universal state was the supreme achievement of ancient civilisation in the West. Its success in enlisting the loyalties of peoples of different race and culture, and its balance (in this period at least) between central and local government, should make it an essential object of study to the modern world. Perhaps in the history of the world the Chinese Empire is its only parallel; when there are scholars who can make comparative studies of these two great societies they may advance the achievement of a new world order.

CHAPTER 43

The Severi

IT SEEMS HARD TO INTRODUCE the story of this confused and ill-documented period without recourse to a famous sentence of Dio Cassius. According to that historian, after the death of Marcus Aurelius 'the history of Rome fell headlong from a reign of gold to one of rust and iron'. It should be borne in mind that the narrative of Dio Cassius ends in the year 229; his comment refers to the reigns of Commodus and the Severi. If this was indeed a period of rust and iron, one wonders how he would have described the military anarchy of the mid third century, say 235 to 270. In those desperate years the army seemed effective only in bringing off a series of *coups d'état* which unseated a succession of short lived Emperors. The Northern frontiers were broken and across them poured huge bands of barbarians in search of plunder. In East and West alike breakaway Empires established their independence. The Emperor Decius died in battle against the Goths; the Emperor Valerian was taken prisoner by the Persians. The State was bankrupt. Piracy and brigandage had virtually brought trade to a stop over wide areas. Somewhere about the year 260 it would not have been surprising if the entire Imperial system had collapsed and the Empire itself had disintegrated into small fragments. Certainly all surviving traces of the Augustan Principate and the Augustan army vanished during those years. But, mainly through the efforts of the Danube armies and a succession of Emperors whom they

placed on the throne, the unity of the Empire was restored by
force. At this fearful juncture, Rome reaped a rich harvest from
the work of civilisation she had accomplished in the Danube
lands. The accession in 284 of Diocletian marked the beginning
of more than 50 years of reforms which reached into every sphere
of the State's activities. Under him and his successor Constantine
the Roman Empire was transformed. It emerged with a new
concept of monarchy, a new capital in the East at Constantinople,
a new army, and a new official religion—Christianity. This
metamorphosis enabled the Empire to continue united until the
death of Theodosius in 395. After this, it split into two halves
and the Western provinces, in the course of the fifth century, were
more or less completely taken over by kings of German descent.
This last is the phenomenon commonly known as the Fall of the
Roman Empire. But in the East the Roman Empire did not fall.
Ruled from Constantinople, its existence was prolonged until the
disasters of the Latin conquest in 1204; even then independence
was regained and a tenuous East Roman Empire continued to
exist until 1453. Here I must limit myself to the reforms carried
out by Diocletian and Constantine and the price paid for them
by their contemporaries.

The death of Commodus was followed by a series of civil wars
as cruel and as devastating as those of the year 69. It was the
candidate of the Danube armies, Septimius Severus, who emerged
as victor. Septimius Severus was an Afro-Roman born at Lepcis
Magna. There was probably Punic blood in his veins and he is
said to have spoken Latin with a Punic accent. He had served
with Marcus Aurelius on the Danube, regarded that Emperor as
his model and took the name Antoninus as a mark of devotion.
But in personal character he could scarcely have been more
different from his exemplar. Ambitious, grasping and vindictive, the chief political aims for which he worked were to enrich
himself, pay the army and secure the succession for his sons
Caracalla and Geta. His wife, Julia Domna, was a Syrian lady of
great wealth, at once an intellectual and a *religieuse*, qualities never
before united in a Roman Empress. Greeks, Africans and
Orientals followed the Imperial pair to Rome to win high office
at court or in the Imperial service. Italy and her traditions were
made to suffer. Senators were put to death and their estates
confiscated. The Praetorian Guard was thrown open to soldiers
of all nations. In defiance of precedent a legion was stationed on

Italian soil (at Albano, where substantial traces of its barracks remain). It was an age in which the first qualification of a Roman Emperor was to be a good general; this requirement Septimius Severus could meet. He fought successful wars against Parthia and Arabia, commemorated in the Triumphal Arch in the Forum Romanum. His last arduous campaigns were fought in Britain which had been denuded of troops for the civil wars of 196 as a result of which the northern defences had been swamped, the invading Caledonians penetrating far south into the province. Septimius Severus led a punitive campaign into the Highlands and restored the Wall of Hadrian so thoroughly that even in modern times it was mistaken for his work. In 211 he died at York, the first but not the last Roman Emperor to die in Britain.

His sons Caracalla and Geta hated each other and disregarded his deathbed injunction that they were to live in harmony. Within a year, Caracalla had murdered Geta with his own hand—it was said, in his mother's presence. Caracalla's 5 years of sole reign (212–217) are ill-recorded. The chief feature was the famous Edict, issued in 212, which conferred Roman citizenship on virtually every inhabitant of the Empire, with only a single category of exception—that of the *dediticii* or 'formally surrendered persons', whose numbers and precise status at this time are uncertain. This might be taken for the logical and creditable climax of generosity in extending citizenship—a long if intermittent process which can be traced back through the centuries to Rome's first dealings with her Latin allies. Unfortunately in the Roman world of Caracalla's day the first duty of a citizen was to pay his taxes. There seems little doubt that the measure was intended to increase the number of taxpayers, even though the wording of the *Constitutio Antoniniana* in which it is recorded speaks of an increase in the number of those who worship the gods of Rome. Caracalla died on the eve of mounting a new expedition against Parthia in which he seems to have seen himself as the new Alexander. But soon there would be no easy victories won in that quarter, by a new Alexander or anyone else.

The dynasty founded by the grim soldier Septimius Severus ended with two youthful Emperors whose reigns are very hard to assess. That of Elagabalus (218–222) is presented in our sources as a farce, an unbroken scandal of four years' duration. By contrast his cousin Alexander Severus (222–235) appears as almost another Antoninus Pius. Mild and virtuous, he tried to rule as a constitutional Emperor, cultivating good relationships with the Senate and husbanding the resources of the State. But he could not win his wars and in the end he was murdered by the exasperated troops of the German army. Much of this information derives from Dio Cassius who voices the senatorial tradition. Behind Alexander Severus stood the powerful figure of the Empress-Mother, Julia Mammaea. Throughout the Severan dynasty the influence of these powerful Syrian princesses forms one of the most remarkable features in the history of the Empire.

CHAPTER 44

Disintegration

WITH THE DEATH OF Alexander Severus the Empire took
another headlong fall into the turbulent rapids which were to
surround it for the next 35 years. There would be little point in
trying to set out the details of this period even if the sources were
more reliable than they are. It is better to try to elucidate the
causes which had brought the Roman world to such a pass and
with which the reforming Emperors would have to grapple.
Some of these causes arose from weaknesses inherent in the
system. It was most damaging to stability that there was no
established method of succession to the throne. Each Emperor
appeared as the candidate of one or other of the army groups;
it would be necessary to kill his predecessor, often in the course
of civil war. A victorious candidate was expected to give lavish
rewards to the troops and perhaps to the Roman People as well.
The effects of such useless expenditure, repeated at frequent
intervals need hardly be stressed. In any case, expenditure on the
army was at a fantastically high level. Septimius Severus had
increased the number of troops to something over 400,000 and
had raised their pay by 50 per cent. When Maximinus Thrax,
who was the first Emperor to rise from the ranks, came to the
throne, he immediately doubled the soldiers' pay. This money had
to be found by an Empire whose resources and population were
gravely diminished. It has been maintained that some 15 per cent
of the agricultural land of the Empire was out of cultivation in the
mid third century; this does not necessarily represent a 15 per
cent drop in agricultural production, but none the less it is a
substantial one. The serious epidemics which affected the Roman
world in this period had undoubtedly brought the population
down well below the level of the previous century, though by

how much we do not know. Even if the value of the currency
had remained stable the burden of supporting the new level of
taxes would have been a heavy one. Septimius Severus left the
Treasury in a healthy state. Caracalla adulterated the coinage
and thereafter a galloping inflation took hold. By the middle of
the third century some bankers and traders were refusing to
accept the official Roman coinage at all.

With its internal resistance thus drastically reduced, the
Empire was forced to sustain shocks of unprecedented severity
from outside. The most acute of these dangers was on the
Eastern frontiers where a new and aggressive dynasty had won
the throne of Parthia. These were the Sassanids, founded by
Ardashir in A.D. 226. They represent a resurgence of the old
Persian stock and outlook, and their State may best be called
the New Persian Empire. Under the Sassanids Persia became once
again a strong centralised monarchy. A revival of the ancient
cult of Zoroastrianism provided it with a powerful state church,
at once missionary and persecuting. The stability of Sassanid
Persia was in marked contrast with the anarchy of third century
Rome. Indeed, between 226 and 379 only nine kings ruled
Persia; during the same period there were some 35 Emperors of
Rome (the uncertainty is significant in itself). And the greatest of
the Sassanid Monarchs, Shapur I (A.D. 241–272) was a conqueror
worthy to rank with Darius or Cyrus.

Roman and Persian sources are at variance about the wars
fought by Shapur against Rome throughout his reign. We know
that he invaded the provinces of Cappadocia and Syria on several
occasions and that he captured Antioch at least twice. His greatest
triumph was in the year 260, when he defeated a Roman army of
70,000 men and took the Emperor Valerian prisoner. At Naqsh-i-
Rustam the great rock sculptures and their inscriptions preserve
the memory of this Roman humiliation. Valerian, in the full
military uniform of a Roman Emperor, is seen kneeling in
supplication at the feet of the Persian king. It seems also that many
captives were taken back to Persia, both from the defeated army
and from the plundered Roman provinces, and settled in the new
city of Gundeshapur.

Fortunately for Rome Shapur was no diplomat. He rejected
advances from the great caravan city of Palmyra, which had been
a Roman colony since the time of Septimius Severus but which
now asserted its independence. It is possible that the Palmyrene

prince Odenathus would have been ready to carve up the Roman provinces in the East with Shapur. Rejected, Palmyra became the champion of Rome for a while. She was well equipped to do so. Apart from her great wealth, her troops had long been among the best elements of the Roman army in the East; her heavy cavalry could hold their own with those of Persia. So for 12 years there was the curious episode of an independent Palmyrene Empire, first under Odenathus, and after his death under his widow, the famous Zenobia and her young son Vaballath. The Palmyrene court, with its blend of Greek, Aramaic and Semitic cultures, and the Roman titles of its dignitaries, was a polyglot mixture. Its ambitious queen consciously modelled herself on Cleopatra. Rome tolerated the situation for a while; she could not do otherwise. The Palmyrene Empire extended at one moment from Egypt to Asia Minor and bade fair to become residuary legatee of the whole Roman position in the East. It was due to the Emperor Aurelian that this did not happen. In a series of hard fought campaigns he defeated the Palmyrene forces, captured the city and took Zenobia and Vaballath prisoner. They were well treated and taken to Italy to appear as the star attractions in Aurelian's great triumph of 274. Palmyra itself, following a rebellion, was destroyed; it is today one of the most fascinating archaeological sites in the East. It remained to reassert Roman prestige against Persia, but before this could be done both Aurelian and Shapur were dead. In 283 the Emperor Carus led a Roman expedition to Ctesiphon, then, honour satisfied, made peace with King Vahram II. The real settlement however came under the Emperor Diocletian after some further Roman victories had been won by Galerius. In 296 Diocletian and Narses made a concordat which ended more than half a century's hostility between the two great Powers. Once again trade was resumed, though on a diminished scale and the caravans started to pass between East and West, but the profits that had once gone to Palmyra now went to Nisibis and Hatra.

During this period there was almost continuous pressure along the Rhine and the Danube. No longer could Roman diplomacy play off tribe against tribe as in the days of Augustus and Tiberius. Now great confederacies of barbarian peoples were formed with the express purpose of raiding and looting within the Roman Empire. One such were the Franks ('free men'), a syndicate of north German tribes whose special field of operations was the

Rhine frontier. Another, the Alemanni ('all men') operated along the upper Danube opposite Raetia and Noricum. The Marcomanni remained inveterate enemies. But the greatest menace was along the lower Danube and came from a new enemy, the Goths. In the *Germania* of Tacitus these people appear among the Baltic tribes under the name of the Gottones and they have left their name on the modern map in Gothland and Goteborg. During the second century A.D. they made their way across central Europe to the shores of the Black Sea, taking with them ethnic elements of many other peoples. Here they were well placed for marauding—westwards up the Danube, southwards into Thrace and Greece, across the Black Sea to the coast of Asia Minor. They were formidable warriors and destructive enemies—as the Vikings were to Europe in the Dark Ages They had excellent cavalry and some of their leaders were generals of high ability— notably Kniva, who defeated the Emperor Decius at the Battle of the Abrittus in 251 After this their incursions grew steadily more formidable They mounted sea-borne expeditions against Asia in 256 and again in 267. In 268 they plundered Thrace and Greece. But eventually the Emperors Gallienus and Claudius Gothicus won victories against them in the neighbourhood of Naissus (the modern Nish) in the year 269 and stemmed the Gothic menace for many years to come.

CHAPTER 45

Restoration and reform

THESE NORTHERN WARS HAD far reaching effects for the Roman Empire At the time of its greatest weakness in 259 an independent Empire was formed in Gaul under Postumus, whose object was to defend the Western provinces against the peoples from beyond the Rhine This it did with a fair measure of success, but in 274 it was forcibly reunited with the Empire by Aurelian. Undoubtedly it was the Danube army (an army of Balkan peasants) which was the hard core of Roman resistance during those years. The real bastions of the Empire were the great military bases—Carnuntum, Aquincum, Lauriacum, Viminacium. Sirmium (Srimska Mitrovica), from its association with so many fighting Emperors, was effectively the capital of the Roman world. From this command Aurelian and Probus, Diocletian and Maximian, rose to the purple. They and their troops were closely bound together, conscious that their valour (*virtus Illyricorum*) was saving the Roman world. East and West we have seen the work of Aurelian; in his short reign (270–275) he earned the title of *restitutor orbis* (the restorer of the Roman world). But he did not restore to it its full complement of provinces. He saw that under the conditions of the third century Dacia, with its open frontiers on the north, was no longer tenable. In 271 he abandoned that province, resettling those Roman colonists who could be persuaded to go south of the Danube.

The name of the lost province was preserved in the two new provinces he organised between the Lower Danube and the sea— Dacia Ripensis and Dacia Mediterranea, with their capital at Serdica, the modern Sofia. The abandonment of Dacia and its mineral wealth was a serious economic loss, although the strengthening of the Lower Danube was worth while. Above all

263

it was a sign of the times. For the Augustan system of frontier defence had finally and irretrievably broken down. It had been based on the belief that Rome would not have to fight two major wars simultaneously along the frontiers. This in its turn meant that no strategic reserve was needed. But in the third century, Rome might have to face simultaneous attacks along the entire line of the Northern and Eastern frontiers, from the mouth of the Rhine to the Euphrates—with perhaps Britain and North Africa involved as well. No longer could she rely as before on the superiority of the legions; battles were now won by heavy cavalry and by archers. In organisation and tactics, as in drill and equipment, the Roman army at this time stood in need of complete overhaul.

The beginnings of army reform were almost certainly the work of the much maligned Emperor Gallienus, though the process was not completed until Constantine. But Gallienus promoted in several ways a new concept of defence in depth which was demanded by the situation on the Northern frontier. A revised posting of legions guarded strategic points on the invasion routes into Italy. Milan, Verona and Aquileia became fortified supply bases, anticipating the 'Fortified Quadrilateral' by which nineteenth century Austria once maintained her grip on north Italy. A new cavalry force was created based on Milan, together with detachments (*vexillationes*) from the legions; this brought into being a mobile field army. Aurelian's victories in their turn were due to this reorganisation.

But the central problem was that of the monarchy itself. Gallienus, Aurelian, Probus—for all their achievements—had been killed by their own troops. How could these endless military *coups d'état* be avoided and an orderly succession secured? This was the chief of the many issues tackled by Diocletian who reached the throne as the army's choice in 284. His solution was the famous Tetrarchy or College of Four Emperors. First he appointed Maximian, an old friend and an Illyrian like himself, to take charge of the West while he looked after the East in person. In 286 he rewarded Maximian with the title of Augustus, and in 293 each of the *Augusti* chose and adopted a 'junior Emperor' or Caesar to be his successor—Maximian taking Constantius Chlorus and Diocletian Galerius. All four Emperors were Illyrians of humble origin who had risen from the ranks to high command and had proved themselves in the field. They divided the Empire between them, each having a capital, a court, a field army and an administrative machine. Constantius Chlorus ruled from Trier, Maximian from Milan, Galerius from Sirmium and Diocletian from Nicomedia. It was a splendid team and it worked brilliantly. Britain—where a certain Carausius had established a break-away Empire in 287—was reunited with the Empire and its northern defences repaired. The Rhine and Danube frontiers were swept clear of invaders. A peace with Persia was concluded on terms favourable to Rome. After the disasters of the mid century, this military recovery was one of the most remarkable achievements in the history of Rome.

The Tetrarchs themselves—and especially Diocletian—ascribed their successes to the favour of the gods. This went further than the belief, common to the early Principate, that the official cults must be supported in the interests of the State. Ever since the second century, certain Emperors had affirmed a special relationship with a particular divinity—as did Commodus with Heracles, the Severi with Serapis, Aurelian with Sol Invictus, the Unconquerable Sun-god whom he proclaimed in 274 as 'Lord of the Roman Empire'. Diocletian and Maximian also made such a choice, and with peculiar intensity, placing themselves under the protection of Jupiter and Hercules respectively and taking the names of Jovius and Herculius to show that they (and their dynasties) acted as the gods' representatives on earth. It was a reaffirmation by men with the simple pieties of the frontier lands from which they came of faith in the old Roman gods. That faith had been justified by happenings. It could not be a matter of indifference that there was in the Empire a large and growing body of people whose Christian religion forbade them to offer sacrifice to the gods of Rome, even to pray for the success of Roman arms. There had of course been sporadic persecutions of Christians earlier, notably under Marcus Aurelius and in the third century under Decius (251) and Valerian (257). But in 303 Diocletian, incited by the fanatical paganism of Galerius, began the last and greatest persecution of the Christian Church. It aroused no enthusiasm among the Emperors of the West. But it made relations between Christianity and the Roman state the dominant political issue, reinforcing the personal rivalries that came to a head as soon as Diocletian and Maximian retired from the Tetrarchy in 305.

The Church which bore the brunt of the great persecutions

was very different from early Christianity. It had extended its range and strengthened its organisation. By A.D. 300 there were Christians in almost every province and in most important cities. In Egypt and North Africa the faith had been carried to the countryside. The work of the Church was sustained by the bishops who were assisted by the minor orders of clergy. Since Christian communities had grown up in the cities, it was natural that the bishops should make these their centres: natural, also, that a bishop's standing should in some measure depend on that of the city from which he came. Hence the notion of a Primacy for the Bishop of Rome, and the reluctance of those of Antioch, Alexandria and Carthage to concede it. The Church was also attracting wealthy converts, including senators and knights and benefiting from the bequests of the faithful, so that it now posessed considerable wealth. It was intellectually respectable and writers such as Origen in Greek and Arnobius and Lactantius in Latin gave it a standing in literature. In the 40 years peace that preceded the persecution of Galerius and Diocletian many churches had been built so that Christianity was visibly present almost everywhere. Martyrdom, when it was inflicted, took place with a publicity that helped the Christian cause. By the time of Constantine it is reckoned that the Christian community included perhaps a tenth of all the people of the Empire; certainly it was the most closely knit and best organised. No government could neglect a minority of that calibre.

Diocletian fostered a new concept of royalty. Everything was done to emphasise the sacrosanct, superhuman character of the Emperors. Court ritual became more elaborate, the Imperial vestments and insignia more gorgeous than ever before. Many features were adopted from the Persian court whose Oriental etiquette had been scorned by Romans of the first century. The process which led to the hieratic formalism of Byzantium began here.

Divinity may hedge a king and yet not protect against rivals or assassins. To make it harder for rivals to emerge was probably the main reason for Diocletian's massive reorganisation of the provinces, which, though more numerous, were still substantially as they had been set up by Augustus. The provinces were now subdivided into smaller units and in each there was a separation of military and civil powers. The 100 or so 'mini-provinces' were then regrouped into 12 '*dioceses*', each presided over by a '*vicarius*', an official of equestrian rank who was directly responsible to the Praetorian Prefect of one of the four Emperors. This last office, incidentally, had lost all military function: it now dealt with administration and finance. There were no senatorial or Imperial provinces any more; Italy was brought into the provincial system and sheared out into 16 (?) provinces. Clearly this new system led to closer control by the central governments; no less clearly it must have enlarged the bureaucracy—as did Diocletian's other reforms—and so added to the economic problems of the times.

These economic problems Diocletian tackled with his customary energy but with rather less expertise. Historians are divided as to the success of his currency reforms, which comprised new issues in all three metals. It is likely, however, that the gold *solidus* which provided the hard currency of international exchange for more than a thousand years was that issued by Constantine rather than Diocletian. It is certain that his new silver and copper issues did nothing to halt the spiral of inflation, which became so vicious that in 301 he issued the famous Edict on Maximum Prices, a desperate attempt to fix a ceiling on wages, freight charges and the prices of more than 1,000 articles of consumer goods. It is prefaced with a tirade against the wickedness of profiteers and speculators whose operations 'rob a soldier of his bounty and pay in a single retail sale. The uncurbed passion for profiteering goes on regardless of good supplies and bounteous years. . . . So the time for restraint is gone. . . . It is now our pleasure that the prices listed in the attached schedules should be observed throughout the Empire. . . . Anyone who resists these measures will face a capital charge. Let no one complain that this is a harsh statute: danger can easily be avoided by the use of moderation. . . . The prices for the sales of specific items which no one may exceed are listed below:

'Wheat	1 modius:	100 denarii
Barley	ditto:	60 denarii
Rye	ditto:	60 denarii'

etc., etc., through the whole schedule of what has rightly been called the most comprehensive economic document from antiquity. It further appears that the guilds of craftsmen (and perhaps also shopkeepers) had to file an affidavit that they did not exceed the ceilings imposed. It did no good of course. Any modern trader in the market could tell Diocletian what would happen. First, all goods retailed at ceiling prices—the maximum became a minimum. Later, all goods disappeared on to the black market. Loud protests from the business community caused the edict to be revoked, probably by Constantine.

Diocletian's tax reforms were more sophisticated. Unfortunately the evidence for them is hard to interpret and not abundant so that we cannot be sure whether they were uniformly applied. The most interesting are those which provided for the tax in kind (*annona militaris*) of basic supplies for the army which was levied on all agricultural land throughout the Empire after a census taken in the year 297. As applied in Syria it was based on first the *jugum*, a notional agricultural or production unit equivalent to, for example, 5 *jugera* of vineyard or 20 *jugera* of grainland or 60 *jugera* of poor class mountain land. It will be seen how this unit is a variable which can be weighted according to the nature of the soil or crop. A second unit was the *caput*, a notional labour unit, also variable comprising the labour available of men, women and work animals on each property to be taxed. Exactly how the tax assessment was reached we do not know. Some think the *iuga* were equated with the *capita*: others, that they were added together. Others again think that the *capita* were introduced by Constantine. Whatever the system each property bore its tax assessment, or as we should say, its Tax Code Number. These were revised at first every 5, later every 15 years. Taxes however were paid annually, according to estimates prepared in advance by each Praetorian Prefect of what supplies he would want from each of his dioceses for the next tax year. Cities and districts received their schedule and were responsible for notifying the taxpayers individually and collecting the amount due. ('Provincials should pay their taxes', declares in effect an officious Prefect of Egypt, 'with all speed and without waiting for the final demand note from the tax collector.')

The advantages of this system were that the government could plan its budgets annually and with accuracy, that it had a good picture of what resources were available and that the taxpayer knew what was expected of him. The disadvantages were that assessments might not be equitable and could bear more heavily on the poor than on the rich. (It should of course be kept in mind that this system was for taxes in kind; there were still money taxes levied on trade and customs.) In the course of time further disadvantages appeared. Since each piece of land had to produce its quota it had to keep up its labour force: hence *coloni* or tenants were increasingly tied to the soil. And since the municipalities, or more accurately, their leading citizens or *curiales* had to collect the taxes or make up arrears from their own pockets, they might be faced with a choice between personal bankruptcy and extortionate collection. None the less, it was an improvement on the arbitrary requisitions which were one of the harshest features of the previous century, and it paved the way for the modest economic revival that marked the next.

Diocletian's true greatness was shown by his decision to retire after completing 20 years as Emperor. How far this was meant to be standard practice we do not know. Maximian, forced to follow his example, did so with a bad grace. Galerius and Constantius Chlorus now became Augusti and there were two new Caesars, but it was soon clear that the Tetrarchy would not function without its captain. Before long, there were more than four Augusti: no one wanted to be a Caesar. Diocletian built himself a great palace in Dalmatia for his retirement, which is still there today, enclosing the old town of Split, and there he went to grow his cabbages.

CHAPTER 46

Constantine

THE ROMAN WORLD WAS FORTUNATE to have had 20 years of Diocletian and it was to be fortunate (on the whole) in having the still longer reign of Constantine, who established himself as sole Emperor of the West by defeating Maxentius in 312. Constantine was born at Naissus about 280, son of Constantius Chlorus by his first wife (or concubine) Helena. (That lady had a career possible only in a time of troubles. Starting as a barmaid in a Balkan inn, she ended as the most pious of Empress Mothers, the traditional finder of the True Cross in Jerusalem.) The career of Constantine himself has rightly been described as an outstanding example of the way in which individual characters can sway the course of history. It began with his frantic dash from Galerius' clutches to join his father in Britain—never knowing whether he would be recalled or murdered on the way, but riding to death each horse that carried him. Later there were many battles won against hopeless odds, and many portents to himself and to his enemies which Constantine read right and they wrong. The classic instance of course was the Battle of the Milvian Bridge. Maxentius, with a large army, was firmly entrenched behind the strengthened Walls of Aurelian—why should he come out? Because he consulted the Sibylline books and was told 'that on that day the enemy of Rome should perish'. Constantine, sleeping before the battle, dreamed he was told to mark his men's shields with the *Chi-Rho* monogram (the sign of Christ) and attack the enemy. Constantine won. (The vision of the Cross in the sky—IN HOC SIGNO VINCE—is quite distinct from this.) Again, Galerius savagely persecuted the Christians and was smitten with a loathsome disease; shortly before his death he ˙ssued an Edict of Toleration. No wonder that one of the first public acts of Constantine was to join with Licinius, Emperor of the East, in a declaration of religious tolerance: 'When I, Constantine Augustus, and I, Licinius Augustus', declares the Edict, 'met under good auspices in Milan, we discussed everything bearing on public advantage and security. First, we considered regulations should be framed to secure respect for divinity on these lines: that the Christians and all other men should be allowed full freedom to subscribe to whatever form of worship they desire, so that *whatsoever divinity may be on the heavenly throne* may be well disposed and propitious to us, and to all placed under us.' 'Whatsoever divinity may be on the heavenly throne . . .': there spoke men who had grown up under the Tetrarchy, uncertain where power might lie. But Constantine became more and more convinced that power lay with the God of the Christians and that God favoured him. He was in his own phrase 'the Man of God'. As such, it was his business to see that the Christian Church preserved unity and kept the true faith. During the dispute about the Donatist heresy he wrote: 'I think it contrary to the divine law to overlook these controversies and quarrels, for they may rouse the Highest Divinity to anger, not only against the human race, but against myself also, to whose care He has by His Heavenly Will given the government over all earthly things.' In the same spirit Constantine summoned and presided at the Council of Nicaea in 325 to suppress Arianism and formulate a creed for all men. And again, when he was tracing the ritual furrow for the foundation of Constantinople and they were astonished that he took it so wide. 'I shall go on', he said, 'wherever He who goes before me bids me follow.' It is necessary to insist on this visionary exalted aspect, this consciousness of a mission, as the clue to the understanding of Constantine. It accords well of course with the temper of the age. The alternative is to see in him no more than the master propagandist—which accords so well with the temper of our own age. But the visionary and the statesman are surely indissoluble, in the Edict of Milan as at the Council of Nicaea.

In secular politics Constantine was very much the pupil of Diocletian, at whose court he grew up. Although after the defeat of Licinius he was supreme ruler for thirteen years (324–337), he was sole ruler for only three years, while for the rest his sons ruled various parts with the title of Caesar. The principle of a College of Emperors was thus maintained in another form. He completed the army reforms which had gone on since Gallienus, establishing mobile field armies (*palatini* and *comitatenses*) of élite troops in both East and West and leaving the frontiers defended by second rate armies of *limitanei*. As a personal bodyguard there were units of *scholae palatinae*. In all the armies cavalry had become the senior arm of service and there was heavy recruitment of Germans and other barbarians, even in the higher commands. This army, about 500,000 strong, was the army of the Late Empire and with its heavy cavalry, mounted archers and largely barbarian personnel, it was wholly unlike the armies of Augustus or Trajan.

In the field of economics, it was probably Constantine who established the gold *solidus* on its lasting value of 72 to the pound. He continued Diocletian's tax structure and added to it, taking the logical but drastic step of binding the *coloni* to the soil. In the same compulsive spirit he established an Eastern capital and did so on a scale previously unknown. There were several candidates. Nicomedia was one, but it had an undesirable rivalry with Nicaea and its choice would hardly bear the personal stamp of Constantine. Sirmium was another and Constantine himself had spoken warmly of his regard for Serdica. Then there was Troy . . . but the time had gone by for the revival of the Trojan legend. Strategy and the site of his naval victory over Licinius meant that there was really only one choice—Byzantium. Here, then, in November 324—a few weeks only after the final defeat of Licinius —there was a solemn act of foundation of the city of Constantinople or New Rome: its formal dedication was on May 11th 330. In vision and foresight the founding of Constantinople may be compared with that of St. Petersburg by Peter the Great. Indeed, it was to prove (so far) more lasting and more beneficial. For Constantinople stands at one of the great nodes of the world. The narrows of the Bosphorus command the sea route from the Black Sea to the Mediterranean—and, for good measure, Nature has thrown in the landlocked harbour of the Golden Horn. Here is the intersection of major land routes: from Europe to Asia via the Danube Valley and across Turkey, and from Egypt, Syria and Asia to south Russia. Constantinople was a base from which the Danube and Euphrates fronts could be reached and it was a fortress that was almost impregnable. Here Constantine planned to establish a fusion of the three great civilising potencies in the world. First the Hellenic tradition, for Constantinople was to be the first city of the Greek East, drawing its inhabitants from all the great historic cities and culling their artistic treasures. Second the Roman tradition of administration, civic as well as Imperial; the New Rome should have its Imperial Palace, its Senate, its *plebs,* its corn dole, its circus; its factions, to match those of the old. Third and most important it was to be a Christian city, the first such in the world, whose symbolisation lay in its great churches of the Holy Peace (St Eirene) and the Holy Wisdom (Hagia Sophia). And it was fitting that when he died in 337, the first Christian Emperor—'man of God' and 'Equal of the Apostles'—should be buried in the Church of the Twelve Apostles in Constantinople.

CHAPTER 47

Culture and religion

IT MIGHT BE THOUGHT that such a protracted time of troubles would be fatal to intellectual and cultural life and indeed it is common enough to find the third century A.D. dismissed as a barren period. Such a verdict derives from the habit of regarding literature as the criterion of vitality. On this basis the verdict does not lack force. The *Metamorphoses* of Apuleius, the last major work of creative writing in Latin for more than a century, belongs to the age of the Antonines. The Greek novelists of the third century wrote for what might be termed the unintelligent general reader, who found in them entertainment, excitement and insulation from the real world. If we seek concern with real issues we must look to the Christian writers—notably Tertullian, Origen, and Lactantius. For these men the work of Christian apologetics was no mere *kulturkampf*: they lived in the world of persecutions and some of them became martyrs. But if we agree to regard the age as barren for classical literature, we must insist on the vitality it showed in other fields.

First, then, the period from Marcus Aurelius to the end of the Severan dynasty is marked by a succession of great names in Roman jurisprudence. Cervidius Scaevola, Paulus and, above all, Papinian and Ulpian continued the work of interpreting and codifying the vast corpus of Roman Law, which became a more urgent task after the Edict of Caracalla brought almost all inhabitants of the Empire directly under its scope. The contrast between the growing humanity of written law and the growing harshness of its application in the courts is often pointed out as another of the painful aspects of the Late Empire. But the work of Papinian and Ulpian came into its own when it became a major source for the final codification of Roman Law in the time of Justinian.

A feature of the growing humanity of the law was its attitude to slavery. Many tendencies converged to improve the position of slaves in the Late Empire. They became rarer for one thing, and more expensive to buy: hence they qualified for the good treatment accorded to valuable property. Then again, slavery was increasingly condemned as inhumane: pagan philosophy took this view and it was heavily endorsed by the Christian Church. In agriculture free tenants or *coloni* were more and more replacing slaves so that the field hands who had once borne the worst brutalities were thinner on the ground. There were few victorious wars to bring in barbarian slaves: the stock was kept up by breeding and the *verna* or house born slave had always been better treated. The Emperor's estates and those of a few great land-owners were the only substantial users of slave labour; even on these estates there were openings for skilled work and the prospect of manumission. But the emancipated slave would have to make his way in the class of *humiliores* whose standing was permanently depressed. In the Late Empire there could be no career like that of Trimalchio, from slave to multi-millionaire.

Philosophy, now shrunken to ethics and metaphysics, had moved closer to religion. Within these limits there was much activity and one great new formulation, that of Plotinus (202–270). A native of Alexandria, where he once worked as a docker, Plotinus was a pupil of Ammonius Saccas. He came to Rome in 244 and opened a school which attracted the best minds of the day, winning him the patronage of the Emperor Gallienus. There was talk of an Imperial benefaction for the founding of a philo-sophic community in Campania, but it came to nothing. But the neo-Platonic school which Plotinus established spread to the intellectual centres of the Eastern provinces and lasted until the early sixth century. Plotinus' teachings are known to us through his pupil Porphyry who published a collection of his works—the *Enneads*—in or about 301. What Plotinus offers is a brilliant synthesis of the work of Plato and Aristotle, together with his own spiritual experience as one of the greatest contemplative mystics ever to appear in the West. The supreme object of Plotinus' philosophy is to attain unity with the One in a moment of beatific vision, which is possible only to those who have undergone a long and painful training as spiritual athletes. Such moments of illumination may be apprehended but not described, save in such inadequate words as derive from the ecstasy of lovers. They embody the deepest wish of the soul—to know the Good from which derive life, thought and being. Here Plotinus is very close to Christian thought and to the words of Augustine: *'fecisti enim nos ad te et inquietum est cor nostrum donec requiescat in te'* ('Thou hast made us for Thyself and our hearts are troubled until they have found rest in Thee'.)

Seeking the same ends of access to divine revelation, but on a much lower intellectual level, were the Gnostics and the followers of the great Persian heresiarch, Mani. Gnosticism is a complex phenomenon which is not yet well understood, but the name is used to describe a number of mystic and esoteric cults which sought by magic and ritual to reach knowledge (*gnosis*) of the truth and which promised initiates life after death. Marcion and Valentinus in the second century A.D. were the most important of the Gnostics. A new collection of Gnostic tracts recently found in Upper Egypt may put their teaching in a clearer light when they have been studied. Mani began to preach his dualistic creed in Persia about A.D. 240 but he was expelled by the Magi as a heretic. Later he travelled widely in Asia and India and his missionary journeys won so many adherents that for a while the Manichees were serious rivals of the Christian Church. Readers of the *Confessions* will recall the dangerous attraction they had for the young Augustine.

In art, the Severi were building Emperors. Septimius Severus adorned his birthplace of Lepcis Magna and left his mark on Rome; Caracalla founded the huge baths in Rome called Thermae Antoninianae. During the anarchy of the mid third century there was neither the money nor the scope for architecture and town planning. The minor arts such as sculpture continued vigorously and a recent study has brought out the high interest of the Imperial busts and sarcophagi of this period. Aurelian built a Temple of the Sun in Rome and the Walls that bear his name—the latter required forced labour to meet the emergency New forms of architecture came into being for the great projects of Diocletian, Maximian and Constantine. This Late Roman architecture passes without a break to Byzantium, and it can thus be said that the highest achievement of classical architecture is Justinian's great church of Hagia Sophia in Constantinople.

CHAPTER 48

The Late Roman Empire

FROM THE ACCESSION OF Diocletian to the death of Constantine was a period of 53 years. In that time were far reaching reforms applied to every aspect of the Roman state, changing it as thoroughly and irrevocably as did those of Augustus. The Late Roman Empire is a world of which Rome is no longer the real capital. Its alliance with Christianity brings a new dimension into politics, for the conflict between orthodoxy and heresy in its many guises becomes paramount. These issues must be treated on their own terms and on the proper scale. So, although the Empire remained united until the death of Theodosius in 395 and although there was a Western Emperor until 476, historians of classical Rome commonly feel the right to stop at the death of Constantine. Nevertheless, since the Late Roman Empire came into being because it was essential to solve the problems of the third century crisis, a sketch of its main features must be attempted in conclusion.

These are best understood in the light of the absolute priority accorded to the demands of the State. To save itself the Roman Empire had to become totalitarian. A crippling taxation in money and goods had been imposed to meet the expenses of the army, the bureaucracy and the Imperial court. Where there was once a healthy balance between central and local government there was now none, the central government having now taken over completely, and local officials were tied to its service as unpaid hereditary agents and tax-collectors. The results were fatal to the freedom and civic patriotism that made the cities the matrices of classical culture. As and when they could the urban gentry slipped away to their country estates, which they ran so far as possible as self-sufficient economic units. The great landlord exercising a more or less benevolent despotism over hereditary tenants tied to the soil is a characteristic figure of the Late Empire, especially in the Western provinces. In the shrunken towns trade and commerce did not disappear, but they were confined to guilds or *collegia* which had been turned into closed corporations. No one in fact had any scope for personal initiative or free enterprise—except in the Imperial service with its opportunity to grow rich through corrupt practices. Although the Edict of Caracalla made almost everyone equal as Roman citizens a new division had been imposed on a world divided into the *honestiores* (officers, landowners, bureaucrats) who enjoyed a privileged standing in the eyes of the law, and the *humiliores* or unprivileged, to which class the great majority belonged. Nations of the modern world have learned to their cost the dangers of having large numbers of second class citizens. The apathy displayed by ordinary people of the Roman world in the face of barbarian invasions in the fourth and fifth centuries has recently been stressed. From a state that made incessant and brutal demands on its citizens, the common people had (understandably) withdrawn their loyalty and hopes.

The Emperors who clamped down these bonds on Roman citizens did not do so from any dogmatic totalitarianism, but as an inescapable part of their duty as they saw it. Modern scholars trying to find out whether any other options might have been open to them are struck by the failure of the Roman world to advance in its technology. This failure needs to be looked at. In the first place it was not absolute. In the art of warfare, for example, there were improvements in methods of fortification and in the design of war machines such as the catapult or *ballista*. But their effects were marginal. They made it harder for barbarians to capture fortified cities, but did not prevent them from ravaging the countryside by which those cities were fed. They did not give Roman armies anything like the measure of superiority that gunpowder gave to the Spaniards in the conquest of Mexico and Peru. Again, the Roman knowledge of hydraulics brought into use some powerful machines, such as water pumps for draining mines and water mills for grinding corn. Of these latter, the best example is the flour mill at Barbegal, near Arles, where 16 mill wheels are set in pairs down a steep slope with a drop of about 80 feet. Powered by water from a specially constructed aqueduct, this machine had a productive capacity of 240–320 kilos of flour a day. It is dated to the second or third century A.D. and must be connected with the *annona*, the corn supply of Arles, where the remarkable *cryptoporticus* or store galleries under the Forum provided storage capacity in dry conditions and at a constant temperature. This labour-saving flour mill is the most sophisticated piece of machinery from Roman times. But in general the Romans gave little thought to labour-saving devices. It is surprising that with their knowledge of dye stamps and moulds they did not go a little further and invent printing, which would have reduced the very large number of scribes employed in copying documents and manuscripts. (They had strong enough paper: all that was needed was a viable printer's ink.)

Although ships increased in size—and in the second century A.D. there were freighters of 3,000 tons—very little was done to improve their primitive rigging. Knowledge of winds, stars and the coastline were the only navigational aids; the instruments that made possible the ocean voyages of the Portuguese, Spanish and English explorers were unknown. These latter voyages led to continuous improvements over three centuries in hull construction and design, in the rigging of sails and masts, and in navigational aids. By the early nineteenth century the European wooden sailing ship had reached ultimate perfection. It was commonly smaller than the biggest freighters of Roman times and not yet power-driven, but the difference between them in seaworthiness and navigability was immense.

Reliance on human and animal labour conditioned Roman technology to operate within narrow limits. To increase production it had recourse to two means. One was to regularise and improve labour operations—a kind of rudimentary system of Organisation and Method. The second was to improve the design of implements. This latter was fundamental and is well illustrated by a recent study of the agricultural instruments of the Roman world by K. D. White. Agriculture was the basic ancient economic activity and had at its disposal an admirably designed range of manual implements—spades, shovels, knives, sickles, hooks, scythes, forks, saws, shears—to name the main types studied in detail by White. The multi-purpose vine dresser's knife (*falx vinitoria*) shows Roman design at its best: it is, to quote White, 'a beautifully designed implement, developed from the simple billhook, which has remained virtually unchanged to the present day'. The range of agricultural machines—ploughs, reaping machines, threshing machines—was more restricted. White stresses three major inventions—the wheeled plough, the wheeled threshing machine with spiked axles known as *plostellum poenicum* and the two types of reaping machine, light and heavy, used in the corn lands of northern Gaul and apparently confined to that area. Some very large scythe blades, found in Gaul and Britain, may indicate a fourth invention but their use is not understood. It is not a long list for so many centuries.

The modern world, of course, cannot be unduly critical of this Roman failure to invent machines to replace human labour. In the nineteenth century the great railway lines of Britain and North America were built by gangs of navvies who were mostly Irish. The Irish navvy is today at work on the motorways, but in smaller numbers; the heaviest work is done by powerful earth shifting machines. The railway engineers of the last century could have designed earth-shifting machinery if they had wanted to. But Irish labour was cheap and abundant and they turned their energies to improving the steam locomotive.

There remains a more fundamental question which we can raise but scarcely answer. How far is it inevitable that universal Empires—or societies that think of themselves as such—should sooner or later fall into stagnation? The arts and sciences seem to grow and flourish best under the stimulus of contacts between a group of communities on the same cultural level. Such were the conditions that obtained between the city states of classical Greece, of Renaissance Italy, or between the nations of modern Europe. By contrast, the 'advanced' cultures of Central and South America showed their deficiencies when faced with the challenge of invaders from Europe. China provides a still more striking example. Over many centuries Chinese culture was far in advance of that of the West, but she was fatally impeded by her own concept of herself as the only truly advanced civilisation of the world, surrounded by barbarian societies beneath the interest of the 'Middle Kingdom'. The impact of the West in the eighteenth and nineteenth centuries shattered these illusions and the whole fabric of Chinese society with them. As for Rome, when she had built up the One World of the *orbis Romanus*, she too lacked the stimulus of a rival. Parthia could not play that part. There were borrowings from Parthia, certainly, in religion and in military techniques, but the two societies were basically uncongenial and the contact between them too limited. So while Rome was learning little and advancing slowly, the Northern peoples were learning from her and their advance was fast. But at the death of Constantine it was still possible to believe that the eternity of Rome had been reasserted, and that the statue of Victory in the Senate House retained its powers.

CHAPTER 49

The loss of the West

IT WAS POSSIBLE TO SUSTAIN that hope for a full generation after the death of Constantine. The Germans were still a danger and the Rhine frontier was breached, but the situation in Gaul was restored by Julian. However in the reign of Valentinian the First and Valens (364–378) things took a sharp turn for the worse. It so happens that we have a good narrative account of the years 353–378 in the last of the great Roman historians, Ammianus Marcellinus, and his later books are filled with the sense of impending catastrophe. Two events are landmarks. First about 370 there was the appearance of the Huns, a nomadic Mongol people driving west from the steppes of south Russia towards the Danube frontiers. Ammianus' description of this most formidable of all barbarian peoples shows the fear and loathing they inspired in the Roman world, which looked on them as scarcely human. Even the Goths could not withstand them. A large section of the Gothic nation crossed into the Empire under arms. Wisely handled these Ostrogoths might have brought an accession of strength, but they were not. In 378 a Gothic army met and defeated the Roman army of the East and killed the Emperor Valens at the Battle of Adrianople, which Ammianus termed an irremediable disaster. Even so the Empire had powers of recovery. Theodosius the Great (379–395) kept the Goths in check, bribed or diverted the Huns and lost no vital ground. On his death (395), there was a disastrous division of the Empire between his two feeble sons, Arcadius ruling the East and Honorius the West.

From this point the collapse of the West was rapid. In only 81 years all the Western provinces were lost, to be parcelled out among a number of Germanic kingdoms. Franks, Burgundians and Goths were in control of Gaul—except for Armorica in the west. Eastern Britain was in the hands of Angles, Saxons and Jutes, and was confronted in the west by British kingdoms which looked on themselves as the heirs of Rome. Arthur of Britain—if he belongs to history—fits into this context. Visigoths ruled in Spain and Vandals in Africa. In Italy itself there was a barbarian King—Odoacer, ruler of the minor people of the Heruli. Having deposed the last Western Emperor, Romulus 'Augustulus', himself a usurper, Odoacer ruled from Rome, his position recognised by the Emperor Zeno at Constantinople. In theory the Empire was one and the Western provinces were expected to be recovered in due course. The time seemed to have come in the reign of Justinian I (527–565), whose determined efforts did for a while recover Africa, Italy and a small part of Spain. In fact the centrifugal tendencies in the West were too strong to be reversed. Already in the sixth century it is possible to discern those patterns of life which would mould Western Europe in the early Middle Ages.

Such, in bald outline, was the collapse of the Empire in the West—commonly but loosely called the fall of Rome. To account for it has been for centuries a major problem of historical scholarship, and in the last resort it may well be insoluble. But thanks largely to the advance of Byzantine scholarship in modern times it is possible to bring the phenomenon into sharper focus and to see that its quintessence is to account for the different reactions of the two parts of the Empire to the events of 395–476. The West collapsed: the East resisted and survived for another thousand years. Why? This approach rules out almost all the explanations of what may be called the monist school. Epidemics, soil erosion, climatic change, racial degeneration, immorality (a favourite view over the centuries!), class warfare, a fall in the birth-rate, the institution of slavery—all these factors can be shown to have been at work in both parts of the Empire and none by itself was so rampant as to cause the collapse of the West. The pluralists remain, headed by Gibbon, who saw the answer as 'the triumph of barbarism and Christianity'. His explanation involves an internal and an external cause, and it would seem—though Gibbon does not actually say so—that he gave them equal weight. In this, few modern scholars have followed him. The majority have preferred internal causes in several combinations, of which the best known is undoubtedly the synthesis which Michael Rostovtzeff put together from his encyclopaedic knowledge of the ancient world and from his experience of the Russian Revolution. Briefly, Rostovtzeff pointed first to the virtual elimination of the city bourgeoisie, the chief agents of classical civilisation, in the economic collapse of the third century; then to the increasing barbarisation of the army and finally to the alienation of soldiers and peasants from the governing classes and their aims. More recently, A. H. M. Jones and other scholars have returned to the concept of barbarian pressure as the chief factor and have shown how it fell on the Western Empire with such severity as to be insupportable.

The military weaknesses of the Late Empire are plain to see. It was disastrous that there was such reliance on barbarian mercenaries of doubtful loyalty. In the late fourth and early fifth centuries the highest commands were often in the hands of Germans: even when, as with Stilicho, their services were outstanding, it was hard to give them full confidence. The Imperial armies suffered fearful casualties, sometimes unnecessarily, as in the civil wars of 351 and 394. In the crucial years the East was in a far better position for strategy and for recruitment. It had the provinces of Illyricum and Asia Minor, still reserves of manpower. Constantinople, its natural strengths reinforced by the Walls of Theodosius, was a fortress impregnable to the barbarians. The capture of Rome by the Goths in 410 and by the Vandals in 455 had no parallel in the Eastern capital. Moreover, the East retained the wealthy provinces of Asia, Syria and Egypt whose taxes were enough to keep its armies in the field—or to subsidise the barbarians and make them go away, all too often to turn West. But the more exposed Western Empire constantly lost provinces, and with them their taxes and man power.

Among social causes the crippling effects of high taxation and the unparalleled harshness with which the demands of the State bore down on the individual must have been paramount. The evidence of this is voluminous and comes from all parts of the Empire. It is seen most vividly in a fragment of the historian Priscus, which J. B. Bury quotes to great effect in his *History of the Later Roman Empire*. In 448 Priscus went on a diplomatic mission from Constantinople to the court of Attila, king of the Huns. There he met a Greek who, formerly a rich merchant of Viminacium, had been captured by the Huns and who had now adapted himself completely to barbarian life, thinking it far better

than that of the Romans. The barbarians, he maintained, lived
after war in the enjoyment of what they had and were very little
disturbed. The Romans on the other hand were very likely to
perish in war, either because they had to rely on others to defend
them, or if they served in the army through the cowardice of their
generals. In peace their lot was worse still—severe taxes, one law
for the rich and another for the poor, the need to buy justice—
'even to get a hearing a man must pay the judge and the judge's
clerks'. Besides this formidable indictment Priscus' apology
seems rather feeble, based as it is on the proposition that 'the
Emperor of the Romans treats his slaves better than the King
of the Huns treats his subjects'. Even so the renegade was
moved to tears and confessed that 'the laws and constitutions
of the Romans were fair, but the governors, who lacked the
spirit of former times, were ruining the State'. This anonymous
witness must represent many thousands who were alienated
from the Empire and who could not care less in its time of
troubles.

Of other factors, the failure to advance technology has already
been discussed. That Christianity was a source of weakness can
scarcely be denied, but not in the way often supposed—as tending
to pacifism or quietism. Pacificism is a charge not easily sustained
against the Christianity of the fourth and fifth centuries. It was
rather unduly quarrelsome, pursuing heresies with an untimely
zeal that brought serious dissension. The strength of Arianism,
the faith adopted by so many of the barbarian rulers, was especially
divisive. Constantine's insistence on orthodoxy had been politically farsighted, but it was his fears that were realised.

Perhaps none of the weaknesses need have been fatal to the
West but for contingent circumstances, for which Bury, almost
alone of modern historians, makes due allowance. If even one of
Theodosius' sons had been a strong personality; if Attila had not
been a nomadic leader of the calibre of Genghis Khan; if there
had been an Emperor of the West of the vigour of Theodosius II
or Anastasius in the East; if the great attack on the Vandals in
466 had been successful . . . then the West might have recovered.
The prosperity enjoyed by Italy under Theoderic the Ostrogoth
shows that recuperation was not impossible. But these are ifs
which history does not care for. Finally perhaps we should turn
to an apposite passage of Lucretius. Speaking of diseases of the
mind, he said:

'at quaecumque queunt conturbari inque pediri,
significant, paulo si durior insinuarit
causa, fore ut pereant aevo privata futuro'.

'but whenever things can be so confounded and entangled, they testify that, if a cause a little stronger shall have made its way within, they must needs perish, robbed of any further life'. In both East and West things were confounded and entangled— the *durior causa* was the barbarian menace, which fell upon the West and thus 'robbed it of further life'.

Bibliography

The literature on all aspects of Rome and the Roman world is enormous, and is added to each year. I can only attempt to cite some of the standard works (especially those which I have used in writing this book). Since most of my readers will be from English-speaking countries, I have quoted books in that language wherever possible as the most accessible to them, but one cannot get far in this field without the help of French, German and Italian scholarship. I have further tried to choose up-to-date books with good bibliographies, and have included a few articles in learned journals.

GENERAL WORKS

Rome is the main theme of Vols. VII–XII of the *Cambridge Ancient History*, from the earliest times to A.D. 324. This great work of cooperative scholarship is more than thirty years old, but nothing on a comparable scale has been attempted since. It is now under revision.

There are numerous one-volume histories and surveys of which I cite the following, with terminal dates: A. E. R. Boak, *A History of Rome to 565 A.D.* 4th ed., New York, 1955; D. R. Dudley, *The Civilisation of Rome* (to A.D. 476), 2nd ed. New York, 1962 (paperback); M. I. Rostovtzeff and E. Bickerman, *A History of the Ancient World, Rome* (to A.D. 337), New York, 1961; F. M. Heichelheim and C. A. Yeo, *A History of the Roman People to 337 A.D.*, New York, 1962. The economic sources are collected in Jenney Frank, *An Economic History of Rome*, 2nd ed., Baltimore, 1927; see also O. Davies, *Roman Mines in Europe*, Oxford, 1935. The major collections of inscriptions, and the abbreviations used for them, are:

CIL　=*Corpus Inscriptionum Latinarum,* 16 vols., Berlin, 1862–.
ILS　=H. Dessau, *Inscriptiones Latinae Selectae,* 3 vols., Berlin, 1892–1916. Reprint 1960.
IGRR=*Inscriptiones Graecae ad Res Romanas Pertinentes,* 3 vols., Paris, 1906–.
OGIS=W. Dittenberger, *Orientis Graecae Inscriptiones Selectae,* 2 vols., Leipzig, 1904–5.

Documentary sources are collected in N. Lewis and M. Reinhold, *Roman Civilisation*, 2 vols. (Harper Torchbook ed., New York, 1966), here quoted as LR. I have not been able to use the most recent source book—A. H. M. Jones, *A History of Rome through the Fifth Century*, 2 vols., Vol. 1, London, 1968, Vol. II 1970-.

COINS H. Mattingly, *Roman Coins from the Earliest Times to the fall of the Western Empire*, 2nd ed., London, 1960; H. Mattingly and others, *The Roman Imperial Coinage*, 9 vols., London, 1923; M. Grant, *Roman History from Coins*, Cambridge, 1958.

GEOGRAPHY A. A. M. Van der Heyden and H. H. Scullard, *An Atlas of the Classical World*, London, 1959; M. Cary, *The Geographic Background of Greek and Roman History*, Oxford, 1949; J. O. Thomson, *History of Ancient Geography*, Cambridge, 1948

REFERENCE WORKS *Oxford Classical Dictionary*, Oxford, 1949 (under revision); Pauly-Wissowa-Kroll, *Real Enkyklopädie der Altertum-wissenschaft*, Stuttgart, 1894–1960; *Lexikon der Alten Welt*, Stuttgart and Zürich (the most modern one-volume encyclopaedia).

LITERATURE A. Lesky, *A History of Greek Literature*, London, 1966; J. W. and A. M. Duff, *A Literary History of Rome: Golden Age.*, 3rd ed., London, 1953; *Silver Age*, 3rd ed., London, 1964; G. W. Williams, *Tradition and Originality in Roman Poetry*, Oxford, 1968. Brief biographies of classical authors are given in *The Penguin Companion to Literature*, Vol. I, *Classical and Byzantine*, ed. D. R. Dudley, London, 1969.

ART AND ARCHITECTURE J. M. C. Toynbee, *The Art of the Romans*, London, 1965; G. M. A. Hanfmann, *Roman Art*, Greenwich, 1964; R. E. M. Wheeler, *Roman Art and Architecture*, London, 1965.

THE CITY OF ROME The basic work is S. B. Platner and T. Ashby, *A Topographical Dictionary of Ancient Rome*, 2 vols., 1929 (out of print: new and revised edition under preparation.) Ernest Nash, *A Pictorial Dictionary of Ancient Rome*, 2 vols., London, 1961 is authoritative and finely illustrated. D. R. Dudley, *Urbs Roma*, London, 1967, collects the chief literary and other sources. The best guide to the antiquities of Rome is G. Lugli, *Roma antica, il centro monumentale*, Rome, 1946. Their history since ancient times is dealt with by M. Scherer, *Marvels of Ancient Rome*, London, 1955.

LAW AND RELIGION H. F. Jolowicz, *Historical Introduction to the Study of Roman Law*, 2nd ed., Cambridge, 1961; *Roman Foundations of Modern Law*, Oxford, 1957; F. Altheim, *A History of Roman Religion*,

New York, 1938; W. Warde Fowler, *The Religious Experience of the Roman People*, New York, 1911.

EDUCATION S. F. Bonner, *Roman Declamation,* Liverpool, 1949; M. L. Clarke, *Rhetoric at Rome*, London, 1953; H. I. Marrou, *A History of Education in Antiquity*, Toronto, 1964.

ABBREVIATIONS
JRS   = Journal of the Society for Roman Studies.
MAAR = Memoirs of the American Academy at Rome.
PBSR = Papers of the British School in Rome.

PARTS I *Early Rome and Italy: c. 850–c. 500 B.C.*
       II *The Roman Republic and the Conquest of Italy: c. 500–264* B.C.

GENERAL

Vols. VII and VIII of the *Cambridge Ancient History* cover the period. R. M. Ogilvie, *A Commentary on Livy Books 1–5*, Oxford, 1965, deals with the early historical tradition. A. N. Sherwin-White, *The Roman Citizenship*, Oxford, 1939, is basic for Rome's relations with her allies. Roman colonisation and the Roman Confederacy are studied in detail in Arnold J. Toynbee, *Hannibal's Legacy, The Hannibalic Wars' effects on Roman Life*, 2 vols., Oxford, 1965. Much of the archaeological material is discussed in chapters 1–4 of P. MacKendrick, *The Mute Stones Speak, The Story of Archaeology in Italy*, London, 1962. For a modern historical narrative see H. H. Scullard, *A History of the Roman World, 753–146* B.C., London, 1951.

ITALY, Geography and Peoples.

J. Bradford, *Ancient Landscapes in Europe and Asia,* London, 1957; V. Gordon Childe, *What Happened in History*, London, 1954; Graham Clark and Stuart Piggott, *Prehistoric Societies*, London, 1965; T. G. E. Powell, *The Celts,* London, 1958; J. Whatmough, *The Foundations of Roman Italy*, London, 1937.

EARLY ROME, Latins and Etruscans.

A. Alföldi, *Early Rome and the Latins*, Ann Arbor, 1963; R. Bloch, *The Origins of Rome*, London, 1960; E. Gjerstad, *Early Rome*, 2 vols., Lund, 1953, 1956., and *Legends and Facts of Early Roman History*, Lund, 1962; A. Momigliano, *An Interim Report on the Origins of Rome*, JRS, LIII,

(1963) 95–121; M. Pallottino, *The Etruscans*, London, 1955; P. Roman-elli, *Etruscan Painting*, Geneva, 1952, and *Tarquinia, The Necropolis and Museum*, 4th ed., Rome, 1959; H. H. Scullard, *The Etruscan Cities and Rome*, London, 1967.

CONQUEST OF ITALY

E. Badian, *Foreign Clientelae* (264–70 B.C.), Oxford, 1958; F. E. Brown, *Cosa I. History and Topography*, MAAR 21 (1951) 7–113; L. Homo, *Primitive Italy and the beginnings of Roman Imperialism*, New York, 1926; A. H. McDonald, *The Rise of Roman Imperialism*, Sydney, 1940, and *Republican Rome*, London, 1966; E. T. Salmon, *The Coloniae Maritimae*, Athenaeum, XLI (1963), 3–38, and *Samnium and the Samnites*, Cambridge, 1967; J. B. Ward-Perkins, *Early Roman Towns in Italy*, Town-Planning Review 26 (1955), 127–54.; A. G. Woodhead, *The Greeks in the West*, London, 1962.

ROMAN REPUBLIC, Politics and Society.

F. Altheim, *A History of Roman Religion*, New York, 1938; T. R. S. Broughton, *Magistrates of the Roman Republic*, 2 vols., New York, 1951, 1952; D. C. Earl, *The Moral and Political Tradition of Rome*, London, 1967; Tenney Frank, *The Scipionic Inscriptions, Classical Quarterly*, 15, 1921; M. Gelzer, *Die Nobilitat der Römischen Republik*, Berlin, 1912; K. von. Fritz, *The Theory of the Mixed Constitution in Antiquity*, New York, 1954; Inscription at Pyrgi: J. Heurgon in JRS, LVI 1966, 1 f; The Regolini-Galassi Tomb: L. Pareti, *La Tomba Regolini—Galassi*, Rome, 1947; VI, 95, 1–3, LR 85 f.; *Foedus Cassianum*: Dionysius of Halicarnassus Settlement with Latins: LR 86 ff.; Scipionic Epitaphs: CIL VI, 1284–94; Speech on L. Caecilius Metellus: Pliny, *Natural History*, VII, 139; Origins of Latin literature: H. Bardon, *La Littérature Latine Inconnue*, ch. 1, Paris, 1952.

PART III *Rome and the Conquest of the Mediterranean World* (*264–133* B.C.)

GENERAL

From 220 B.C. the historical sources are fairly good, Polybius and Livy being the most important. We have Polybius' two introductory books and the narrative for 220–216 B.C. in full, and parts of the narrative to his closing date of 146 B.C. F. W. Walbank, *A Historical Commentary on Polybius*, Oxford, Vol. I, 1957, vol. II, 1967, is indispensable. The period 218–167 B.C. is covered in Livy, books 21–45. Plutarch wrote biographies of Aemilius Paullus, Cato, Flamininus, and Marcellus. Appian deals with the wars in Spain, Illyria, and Syria, besides the Punic Wars. Cato, *de Agricultura*, is a contemporary source for economic conditions in Italy. The evidence of inscriptions begins to be important, though not on the same scale as for the Empire.

Of modern works, Vol. VIII of the Cambridge Ancient History covers 218–133 B.C. For the Hellenistic world, see M. I. Rostovtzeff, *Social and Economic History of the Hellenistic World*, 3 vols., Oxford, 1941; W. W. Tarn and G. T. Griffith, *Hellenistic Civilisation*, 3rd ed., London 1952.

Arnold Toynbee, *Hannibal's Legacy* (cited above) is good for the social and economic consequences of the Punic Wars. A. E. Astin, *Scipio Aemilianus*, Oxford, 1967, is a modern study of one of the leading Roman politicians of the period. Struggle with Carthage: F. E. Adcock, *Delenda Est Carthago*, Cambridge Historical Journal, VIII (1946), 117–28; G. P. Baker, *Hannibal*, New York, 1936; F. M. Haywood, *Studies on Scipio Africanus*, Baltimore, 1933; G. C. and L. C. Picard, *The Life and Death of Carthage*, 1968; H. H. Scullard, *Scipio Africanus in the Second Punic War*, Cambridge, 1930; B. H. Warmington, *Carthage*, Baltimore, 1965.

PROVINCES IN THE WEST E. Badian, *Foreign Clientelae* (cited above); U. Ewins, *The Early Colonisation of Cisalpine Gaul*, PBSR XXff, 1952), 54–71; A. H. McDonald, *Republican Rome* (cited above); C. H. V. Sutherland, *The Romans in Spain*, 217 B.C.–A.D. 117, London, 1939.

ROME AND THE HELLENISTIC WORLD E. Badian, *Rome and Antiochus the Great, A Study in Cold War*, Classical Philology, LIV (1959) 81–99; M. Cary, *A History of the Greek World*, from 323 to 146 B.C., London, 1951; Tenney Frank, *Roman Imperialism*, New York, 1914; M. Holleaux, *Rome, la Grèce, et les monarchies hellénistiques au III siècle av. J. C.*, Paris, 1921; D. Magie, *Roman Rule in Asia Minor*, 2 vols., Princeton, 1950; F. W. Walbank, *Philip V of Macedon*, Cambridge, 1940; *Polybius and Rome's Eastern Policy*, JRS, LIII (1963), 1–13. G. Colin, *Rome et la Grèce de 200 à 146*, Paris, 1905.

ROME AND ITALY, SOCIAL, ECONOMIC, CULTURAL W. Beare, *The Roman Stage*, rev. ed., London, 1965; D. Keinast, *Cato der Zensor*, Heidelberg, 1954; F. Münzer, *Romische Adelsparteien und Adelsfamilien*, Stuttgart, 1920; H. H. Scullard, *Roman Politics, 220–150 B.C.*, London 1951.

SPURIUS LIGUSTINUS Livy, 42, 34, LR, 452 ff.

DELOS W. A. Laidlaw, *A History of Delos*, Oxford, 1933.

PERGAMUM E. V. Hansen, *The Attalids of Pergamum*, Ithaca, 1947.

PANAETIUS M. Van Straaten, Panetius, sa vie, ses écrits, etc., Amsterdam, 1946.

PART IV *The Decline of the Imperial Republic (133–31 B.C.)*

For the period from the Gracchi to Sulla the historical sources are patchy, at best. The contemporary historians who wrote on the agrarian crisis are lost, as are the annalists of the time of Sulla. We are left with Sallust's *Jugurthine War*, Plutarch's *Lives* of the Gracchi, Marius, and Sulla, and the Epitome of Livy, together with fragments of contemporary historians and orators.

By contrast, the period from the death of Sulla to the Battle of Actium is known in greater detail than any other in Roman history. Primarily, this is due to the scale on which the writings of Cicero have survived, 57 speeches, more than 800 letters, besides his works on philosophy and oratory. But there are other major sources. Caesar wrote on the *Gallic Wars* in seven and the *Civil Wars* in three books: the wars in Egypt, Africa, and Spain were written up by his lieutenants. Sallust wrote a monograph on the Conspiracy of Catiline: Plutarch's *Lives* deal with Mark Antony, Brutus, Julius Caesar, Cato the Younger, Cicero, Crassus, Lucullus, Pompey, and Sertorius. Suetonius' *Divus Julius* is a biography of Julius Caesar, and his *Divus Augustus* has useful material on Octavian—Appian deals with the Wars with Mithridates and the Civil Wars. Varro *De Re Rustica* is informative on Italian agriculture. Epigraphic and numismatic evidence is by now substantial.

GENERAL

Of modern works, Vol. IX of the Cambridge Ancient History goes from 133 to 44 B.C.; Vol. X, from 44 B.C. to A.D. 70. H. H. Scullard, *From the Gracchi to Nero* 2nd ed. London, 1963, provides a succinct and up-to-date account, with invaluable notes. R. Syme, *The Roman Revolution,* Oxford, 1939; *Sallust,* Cambridge, 1964, are basic. I also mention here D. C. Earl, *The Moral and Political Tradition of Rome* (cited above); R. E. Smith, *The Failure of the Roman Republic,* Cambridge, 1955; L. R. Taylor, *Party Politics in the Age of Caesar,* Berkeley, 1949; C. Wirszubski, *Libertas as a Political Idea at Rome in the Late Republic and Early Principate,* Cambridge, 1950.

THE GRACCHI J. Carcopino, *Autour des Gracques,* Paris, 1928; D. C. Earl, *Tiberius Gracchus, A Study in Politics,* Brussels, 1963.

ON HISTORIOGRAPHY *Latin Historians,* ed. T. A. Dorey, London, 1966.

MARIUS TO SULLA T. F. A. Carney, *A Biography of Gaius Marius.* Proceedings of the African Classical Association, Supplement, Vol. I; R. E. Smith, *Service in the Post-Marian Roman Army,* Manchester, 1958; C. Jullian, *Histoire de la Gaule,* Vol. 3 (for the Roman conquest and the Cimbri), ed. 2, Paris, 1920; J. Carcopino, *Sylla, ou la monarchie manquée,* Paris, 1931.

POMPEY, CRASSUS, CAESAR M. Gelzer, *Pompeius,* 2nd ed., Munich, 1959; *Caesar ae a politician and statesman* (P. Needham), Oxford, 1968; T. Rice Holmes, *Caesars Conquest of Gaul,* Oxford, 1911; J. Dickinson, *Death of a Republic, Politics and Political Thought of Rome 59–44 B.C.,* New York, 1963.

MITHRIDATES T. Reinach, *Mithridate Eupator,* Paris, 1890; D. Magie, *Roman Rule in Asia Minor* (cited above).

SERTORIUS A. Schulten, *Sertorius,* Leipzig, 1926.

CICERO K. Büchner, *Cicero,* Heidelberg, 1964; F. R. Cowell, *Cicero and the Roman Republic,* 3rd ed., London, 1963; T. A. Dorey (ed.), *Cicero,* London, 1965.

ANTONY J. Weigall, *The Life and Times of Mark Antony,* London, 1931;

ACTIUM W. W. Tarn, *The Battle of Actium,* JRS XXI (1931), 173–99.

SOCIAL AND ECONOMIC M. I. Finley (ed.), *Slavery in Classical Antiquity,* Cambridge, 1960; J. A. Crook, *Law and Life of Rome,* London, 1967; T. Frank, *Life and Literature in the Roman Republic,* Berkeley, 1930; H. Hill, *The Roman Middle Class in the Republican Period,* Oxford, 1952; U. E. Paoli, *Rome: Its People, Life, and Customs,* New York, 1964.

POSIDONIUS K. Reinhardt, *Kosmos und Sympathie;* H. Strasburger, *Posidonius on the Problems of the Roman Empire,* JRS, LV, 1965.

CATULLUS Kenneth Quinn, *The Catullan Revolution,* London, 1959; C. J. Fordyce (edition), Oxford, 1961.

LUCRETIUS C. Bailey (edition), 3 vols., Oxford, 1947; D. R. Dudley (ed.), *Lucretius,* London, 1965; A. D. Winspear, *Lucretius and Scientific Thought,* Montreal, 1963.

SALLUST D. C. Earl, *The Political Thought of Sallust,* Cambridge, 1961.

PART V *Augustus (31 B.C.–A.D. 14)*

GENERAL

One document is unique—the *Res Gestae Divi Augusti*, Augustus'
account of his own achievements, drawn up in the last year of his life
for display on bronze tablets in Rome and the chief cities of the
Empire. Parts of three copies survive, the most important at Ancyra
(Ankara) in Turkey. It is edited, with commentary, by P. A. Brunt
and J. M. More, Oxford, 1967. Together with the most important
epigraphic material, it is included in V. Ehrenburg and A. H. M. Jones,
Documents Illustrating the Reigns of Augustus and Tiberius, 2nd ed.,
Cambridge, 1955. The ancient literary sources are poor, the most
important being the *Life* by Suetonius.

The period is covered in Vol. X of the Cambridge Ancient History.
R. Syme, *The Roman Revolution*, Oxford, 1939, is indispensable. Other
important modern works are G. W. Bowersock, *Augustus and the
Greek World*, Oxford, 1965; M. Hammond, *The Augustan Principate*,
Harvard, 1933; D. Earl, *The Age of Augustus*, London, 1968, an up-to-
date survey with fine illustrations. On Agrippa: M. Reinhold, *Marcus
Agrippa: A Biography*, Geneva, N.Y., 1933. On the constitutional
settlement: articles by P. A. Brunt, JRS, 51, 1961, 236 ff.; A. H. M.
Jones, *The Imperium of Augustus*, JRS 41 (1951), 112–19.

THE FORUM OF AUGUSTUS Attilio DeGrassi, *Inscriptiones Italicae*,
XIII, Rome, 1937, 3.

THE ARA PACIS G. Moretti, *Ara Pacis Augustae*, 2 vols., Rome, 1948;
J. M. C. Toynbee, *Proceedings of the British Academy*, XXIX, 1953,
67–95. The passage from Strabo is V.3.8. Augustan building in Rome,
see D. R. Dudley, *Urbs Roma*, 14–16. On the provinces, E. Badian,
Roman Imperialism in the Late Republic, 1968.

EDICTS OF CYRENE LR, II, 36–42.

ARMINIUS Tacitus, *Annals*, II, 88.

NORTHERN FRONTIERS article by J. Wilkes, *University of Birmingham
Historical Journal*, 1965, 1 ff.; E. Nordern, *Die Germanische Urgeschichte
und Tacitus*; J. J. Hatt, *Histoire de la Gaule romaine*, Paris, 1959; Armed
forces: G. L. Cheesman, *The Auxilia of the Roman Imperial Army*,
Oxford, 1914; H. M. D. Parker, *The Roman Legions*, rev. ed., Cambridge, 1958; C. G. Starr, *The Roman Imperial Navy*, 2nd ed., Cambridge,
1960; Graham Webster, *The Roman Imperial Army*, London, 1969.

PALATINE LIBRARIANS AND CLERKS D. R. Dudley, *Urbs Roma*, 157 ff.

IMPERIAL CULT L. R. Taylor, *The Divinity of the Roman Emperor*, Middletown, 1931.

SECULAR GAMES LR II, 57–61.

AUGUSTAN LITERATURE from the vast number of modern books on the great Augustans I confine myself to: Virgil—Brooks Otis, *Virgil, A Study in Civilised Poetry*, Oxford, 1963; Kenneth Quinn, *Virgil's Aeneid, A Critical Description*, London, 1968; Horace—E. Fraenkel, *Horace*, Oxford, 1957; L. P. Wilkinson, *Horace and His Lyric Poetry*, Cambridge, 1945; Livy—P. G. Walsh, *Livy, His Historical Aims and Methods*, Cambridge, 1961; Ovid—L. P. Wilkinson, *Ovid Surveyed*, Cambridge, 1962; Brooks Otis, *Ovid as an Epic Poet*, Cambridge, 1966; The Elegists—G. Luck, *The Latin Love Elegy*, London, 1955.

PART VI *Orbis Romanus (14–192 A.D.)*

GENERAL

The fundamental works are: The Cambridge Ancient History, Vols. X, *The Augustan Empire*, 44 B.C.–A.D. 70; XI, *The Imperial Peace*, A.D. 71–192; M. I. Rostovtzeff, *The Social and Economic History of the Roman Empire*, 2nd ed., revised by P. M. Fraser, 2 vols., Oxford, 1957; R. Syme, *Tacitus*, 2 vols., Oxford, 1958.

See also, M. P. Charlesworth, *The Roman Empire*, Toronto, 1951; M. Hammond, *The Augustan Principate in Theory and Practice*, Harvard, 1933; M. Hammond, *The Antonine Monarchy*, Rome, 1959; F. Millar and others, *The Roman Empire and Its Neighbours*, London, 1967; E. T. Salmon, *A History of the Roman World from 30 B.C. to A.D. 138* 3rd ed., London, 1957; C. G. Starr, *Civilisation and the Caesars*, Ithaca, N.Y. 1954.

STUDIES OF INDIVIDUAL EMPERORS F. B. Marsh, *The Reign of Tiberius*, London, 1931; J. P. V. D. Balsdon, *The Emperor Gaius*, Oxford, 1934; A. Momigliano, *Claudius, the Emperor and His Achievement*, Oxford, 1934; V. Scramuzza, *The Emperor Claudius*, Harvard, 1940; B. W. Henderson, *Five Roman Emperors*: Vespasian, Titus, Domitian, Nerva, Trajan, Cambridge, 1927; B. W. Henderson, *The Life and Principate of the Emperor Hadrian*, London, 1923; R. Paribeni, *Optimus Princeps, Saggio sulla storia e sui tempi dell' Imperatore Trajano*, Messina, 1926–7; A. Birley, *Marcus Aurelius*, London, 1966.

THE PROVINCES Th. Mommsen, *The Provinces of the Roman Empire*, 2 vols., 2nd ed. by F. Haverfield, London, 1909, remains basic. A more modern study is G. H. Stevenson, *Roman Provincial Administration*, 2nd ed., Oxford, 1949. A new series on the history and archaeology of the provinces of the Roman Empire is being published by Routledge and Kegan Paul. Volumes so far published are: *Britannia*, by Sheppard Frere, London, 1967; *Dalmatia*, by J. Wilkes, London, 1969. Others are in preparation.

STUDIES OF INDIVIDUAL PROVINCES H. I. Bell. *Egypt from Alexander the Great to the Arab Conquest*, Oxford, 1948; O. K. Brogan, *Roman Gaul*, London, 1953; T. R. S. Broughton, *The Romanisation of African Proconsularis*, Baltimore, 1929; G. E. F. Chilver, *Cisalpine Gaul*, Oxford, 1941; D. Magie, *Roman Rule in Asia Minor*, 2 vols., Princeton, 1950; I. A. Richmond, *Roman Britain*, London, 1955; A. L. F. Rivet, *Town and Country in Roman Britain*, London, 1964; C. H. V. Sutherland, *The Romans in Spain, 217 B.C.–A.D. 117*, London, 1939.

PARTHIA N. Debevoise, *A Political History of Parthia*, Chicago, 1938; R. N. Frye, *The Heritage of Persia*, London, 1963.

DACIA V. Parvan, *Dacia, An Outline of the Early Civilisation of the Carpatho-Danubian Countries*, London, 1928; H. Daicoviciu, *Dacii* (The Dacians), Bucarest, 1965.; F. A Lepper, *Trajan's Parthian War*, Oxford, 1948.

MASADA Y. Yadin, *Masada*, London, 1966; I. A. Richmond, *The Roman Siege Works of Masada, Israel*, JRS LII, 1962, 142–155.

The invasion and conquest of Britain, see G. Webster and D. R. Dudley, *The Roman Conquest of Britain*, A.D. 43–57, London, 1965; *The Rebellion of Boudicca*, London, 1962. The new edition of Tacitus *Agricola*, by R. M. Ogilvie and I. A. Richmond, Oxford, 1967, supersedes earlier editions and gives a full account of recent archaeological work on Agricola's campaigns. For the lower Rhine frontier see H. von Petrikovitz, *Die römische Streitkräfte am Niederrhein*, Düsseldorf, 1967.

AFRICA J. Baradez, *Fossatum Africae*, Paris, 1949.

FRONTIERS IN BRITAIN See J. Collingwood Bruce, *Handbook to the Roman Wall*, 11th ed., I. A. Richmond, Newcastle, 1957; H.M. Ordnance Survey, *Map of Hadrian's Wall*, Chessington, 1964; A. S. Robertson, *The Antonine Wall*, Glasgow, 1960; also D. R. Wilson. *Roman Frontiers in Britain*, London, 1967 (a school book).

CITIES F. F. Abbott and A. C. Johnson, *Municipal Administration in the Roman Empire*, Princeton, 1926; A. H. M. Jones, *The Cities of the Eastern Roman Provinces*, Oxford, 1937.

URBANISM IN GAUL A. Grenier, *Manuel d'Archéologie Gallo-Romaine*, Vol. III, *L'Urbanisme, Les Monuments*, Paris, 1958; Vol. IV, *Les Monuments des Eaux*, Paris, 1960.

ROMANISATION F. Haverfield, *The Romanisation of Roman Britain*, 3rd ed., Oxford, 1915 (a pioneer study); L. Harmand, *L'Occident Romain*, Paris, 1960. L. Homo, *Rome impériale et l'urbanisme dans l'antiquité*, Paris, 1951.

ROME AND ITALY T. Ashby, *Aqueducts of Ancient Rome*, Oxford, 1935; A. Boethius, *The Golden House of Nero*, Ann Arbor, 1960; William A. MacDonald, *The Architecture of the Roman Empire*, I, New Haven (1965). On the visit of Constantius II, see D. R. Dudley, *Urbs Roma*, London, 1967, p. 29 f. On Pompeii and Herculaneum: M. Brion *Pompeii and Herculaneum: The Glory and the Grief*, London, 1960; A. Maiuri, *Pompeii*, 8th ed., Rome, 1956; On Ostia, R. Meiggs, *Roman Ostia*, Oxford 1960; on the *alimenta*: R. P. Duncan-Jones, *The Purpose and Organisation of the Alimenta in Rome and the Empire* BSR XXXII, 1964, p. 123 f. On racial tensions, etc.: R. MacMullen, *Enemies of the Roman Order*, Cambridge, Mass., 1963; A. N. Sherwin White, *Racial Prejudice in Imperial Rome*, Cambridge, 1967.

PLINY A. N. Sherwin-White, *The Letters of Pliny: an historical and Social Commentary*, Oxford, 1966.

THE HADRIANIC RELIEFS OF THE PROVINCES J. M. C. Toynbee, *The Hadrianic School,* Cambridge, 1934, pp. 152 f.

DEMETRIUS OF TARSUS R. H. Barrow, *Plutarch and His Times*, London, 1967, pp. 24 f.

TRADE AND COMMERCE M. P. Charlesworth, *The Trade-Routes and Commerce of the Roman Empire*, 2nd ed., Cambridge, 1926; R. E. M. Wheeler, *Rome beyond the Imperial Frontiers*, London, 1954; M. I. Rostovtzeff, *Caravan Cities*, Oxford, 1932; E. H. Warmington, *The Commerce between the Roman Empire and India,* Cambridge, 1928.

CARAVAN-TRAINS Pliny NH, vi. XXVI, 100–6=LR 205–6. On the Tariff of Coptos OGIS 674=LR 147–8. For the Tariff of Palmyra OGIS 629=LR, pp. 330–2. On Africa: G-C Picard, *La Civilisation de l'Afrique Romaine*, Paris, 1959. On Syria: G. Downey, *A History of Antioch in Syria from Seleucus to the Arab Conquest*, Princeton, 1961.

FOR THE ROMAN ORATION OF AELIUS ARISTIDES Proc. of the American Philosophical Society, XLIII (1953), pt. 4.

PLAUTIUS SILVANUS AELIANUS ILS 986.

INSCRIPTIONS T. Caesernius Statius: ILS 1069=Smallwood 195; L. Burbuleius Optatus Ligarianus: ILS 1066=Smallwood, 206; M. Maenius Agrippa: ILS 2735=Smallwood, 265; C. Minicius Italus: ILS 1374=Smallwood, 268.

PART VII *Military Autocracy: Totalitarian State (A.D. 193–337)*

GENERAL

Vol. XII of the *Cambridge Ancient History* (*The Imperial Crisis and Recovery*) covers A.D. 193–324 The most important recent work is A. H. M. Jones, *The Later Roman Empire*, 3 vols., Oxford, 1964; available in a shorter version as *The Decline of the Ancient World*, London, 1966. M. Grant, *The Climax of Rome*, London, 1968, presents the period 161–337 on the final achievement of the Ancient World. Some of the finest parts of Edward Gibbon's, *Decline and Fall of the Roman Empire*, deal with this period (ed. J. B. Bury, 1897–1900). To this list add the books of M. I. Rostovtzeff and C. G. Starr already cited, and H. M. D. Parker, *A History of the Roman World from A.D. 138–337*, 2nd ed., London, 1958.

INDIVIDUAL EMPERORS M. Platnauer, *The Life and Reign of the Emperor Septimius Severus*, Oxford, 1918; *The Age of Diocletian, A Symposium*, Metropolitan Museum, New York, 1953; A. Alföldi, *The Conversion of Constantine and Pagan Rome*, New York, 1948; J. Burckardt, *The Age of Constantine the Great*, New York, 1949.

CHRISTIANITY AND THE EARLY CHURCH From the enormous literature I select: P. Carrington, *The Early Christian Church*, 2 vols., Cambridge, 1957; C. N. Cochrane, *Christianity and Classical Culture*, Oxford, 1940; J. G. Davies, *The Early Christian Church*, London, 1965; W. H. C. Frend, *Martyrdom and Persecution in the Early Church*, London, 1965; A. D. Nock, *Conversion: The Old and New in Religion from Alexander the Great to Augustine of Hippo*, Oxford, 1933; J. M. C. Toynbee and J. B. Ward-Perkins, *The Shrine of St Peter and the Vatican Excavations*, London, 1956; F. Van der Meer and C. Mohrmann,

Atlas of the Early Christian World (tr. M. F. Hedlund and H. H. Rowley), London, 1958. The legal documents on Christianity are collected in P. R. Coleman-Norton', Roman State and Christian Church, 2 vols., London, 1966.

ORIENTAL RELIGIONS F. Cumont, Lux Perpetua, Brussels, 1949; M. J. Vermaseren, Mithras, the Secret God, 1963; L. Patterson, Mithraism and Christianity: A Study in Comparative Religion, Cambridge, 1921. On Plotinus: A. H. Armstrong, Plotinus, London, 1953. Gnostics: J. Doresse, The Secret Books of the Egyptian Gnostics, 1960. Mani: F. C. Burkitt, The Religion of the Manichees, Cambridge, 1925.

IMPERIAL EDICTS Edict of Caracalla, LR, 427–8; C. Sasse, Constitutio Antoniniana, Wiesbaden, 1958; Edict of Maximum Prices, LR 464 ff. (excerpts). The various fragments are contained in CIL, Vol. III; Edict of Milan LR 602, cf. Eusebius, Ecclesiastical History, X. V., 2–14.

TAXATION see articles by A. H. M. Jones, Capitatio and Jugatio JRS XLIII (1957), 88–94; Over-Taxation and the Decline of the Roman Empire, Antiquity, XXXIII (1959), 39–49.

SASSANID PERSIA Cambridge History of Iran, Vol. III, 1968; J. Gagé, La Montée des Sassanides et l'heure de Palmyre, Paris, 1964.

CONSTANTINOPLE N. H. Baynes and H. Moss, Byzantium: An Introduction to East Roman Civilisation, London, 1948; S. Runciman, Byzantine Civilisation, London, 1958.

BARBEGAL MILL L. Eydoux, Trésors de la Gaule, Vol. I, 203 ff., Paris, 1958.

TECHNOLOGY M. I. Finley, Technical innovation and economic progress in the ancient world, Economic History Review, 2nd ser., XVIII, I (1965), 29–45; K. D. White, Agricultural Implements of the Roman World, Cambridge, 1967.

Index